Library of
Davidson College

THE INDIANS OF GREATER NEW YORK AND THE LOWER HUDSON.

EDITED BY

CLARK WISSLER.

AMS PRESS
NEW YORK

ANTHROPOLOGICAL PAPERS

OF THE

American Museum of Natural History.

Vol. III.

HUDSON-FULTON PUBLICATION.

THE INDIANS OF GREATER NEW YORK AND THE LOWER HUDSON.

EDITED BY

CLARK WISSLER.

NEW YORK:
Published by Order of the Trustees.
September, 1909.

Library of Congress Cataloging in Publication Data

Wissler, Clark, 1870-1947, ed.
 The Indians of Greater New York and the Lower Hudson.

 Reprint of the 1909 ed. published by the Trustees of the American Museum of Natural History, New York, which was issued as v. 3 of Anthropological papers of the American Museum of Natural History, and which was a Hudson-Fulton publication.
 Includes index.
 CONTENTS: Skinner, A. The Lenapé Indians of Staten Island.—Finch, J. K. Aboriginal remains on Manhattan Island.—Bolton, R. P. The Indians of Washington Heights.—Skinner, A. Archaeology of Manhattan Island. [etc.]
 1. Indians of North America—New York (State). 2. New York (State)—Antiquities. 3. Indians of North America—New Jersey. 4. New Jersey—Antiquities. I. Title. II. Series: American Museum of Natural History, New York. Anthropological papers; v. 3.
 E78.N7W8   1975   974.7'004'97   74-9017
 ISBN 0-404-11914-X

Reprinted from the edition of 1909, New York
First AMS edition published in 1975
Manufactured in the United States of America

AMS PRESS INC.
NEW YORK, N. Y. 10003

CONTRIBUTORS.

Alanson Skinner.
James K. Finch.
Reginald Pelham Bolton.
M. Raymond Harrington.
Max Schrabisch.
Frank G. Speck.

CONTENTS.

	PAGE
Introduction	xiii

The Lenapé Indians of Staten Island (Plates I–XII). By Alanson Skinner.

Introduction	3
Archaeological Sites	4
1. West New Brighton, Upper or Pelton's Cove	4
2. West New Brighton, Ascension Church	5
3. Mariners' Harbor, Arlington	5
4. Mariners' Harbor, Bowman's Brook	6
5. Mariners' Harbor, Old Place	8
6. Bloomfield (Watchogue)	9
7. Chelsea	9
8. Long Neck (Linoleumville), north side	9
9. Long Neck (Linoleumville), south side	9
10. New Springville, Corson's Brook	10
11. Green Ridge, near Richmond Plank Road	10
12. Green Ridge, Lake's Island	10
13. Woodrow	10
14. Rossville	11
15. Tottenville, "Burial Ridge"	11
16. Huguenot	16
17. Arrochar	16
18. New Brighton, Harbor Hill Golf-Links	16
19. New Brighton, Silver Lake, etc.	16
20. New Brighton, Harbor Hill	16
21. New Brighton, Nannyberry Hill	16
22. Richmond	16
23. Oakwood	17
24. Tompkinsville	17
Collections of Specimens	17
Descriptions of Specimens	18
Stone Implements	18
Hammerstones	19
Rubbing or Polishing Stones	19
Knives, Drills and Scrapers	19
Banner Stones	20
Plummets	20
A Stone Mask	21
Bone and Antler Tools	21
Pottery	23
Pipes	26
Copper	28
Trade Articles	28
History and Ethnography of Staten Island	29
Cultural Reconstruction	38
Personal Appearance and Costume	39

	PAGE
Vegetable Resources	42
Hunting	43
Fishing	44
Food Materials	45
Habitations	46
Transportation	48
Mortuary Customs	49
Social and Religious Organization	51
Mythology	53
Art as Shown in Pottery	53
Résumé	58
Bibliography	62

Aboriginal Remains on Manhattan Island. By James K. Finch.

Introduction	65
Location of Archaeological Sites	66
Fort Washington Point	68
The Knoll	68
Cold Spring	68
Inwood Station Site	69
Harlem Ship Canal	70
Harlem River Deposit	70
Isham's Garden	70
Academy Street Garden	70
Dog Burials found in 1895	70
Shell Pockets at 211th Street	71
Historical References	72

The Indians of Washington Heights (Plates XIII–XVII). By Reginald Pelham Bolton.

Introduction	77
Aboriginal Remains on Washington Heights	85
Relations with the First Settlers	94
The Town of New Haerlem and the Passing of the Red Man	102

Archaeology of Manhattan Island. By Alanson Skinner . . . 113

The Rock-shelters of Armonk, New York (Plates XVIII–XX). By M. R. Harrington.

Introduction	125
Finch's Rock House	125
Nebo Rocks	132
Helicker's Cave	132
Leather Man's Shelter	134
Little Helicker's	134
Mahoney Shelter	134
Quartz Quarry Rock-shelter	135
Riverville Shelter	136

Indian Rock-shelters in Northern New Jersey and Southern New York. By Max Schrabisch.

Passaic County, New Jersey	141
Upper Preakness	141
Pompton Junction	143

	PAGE
Morris County, New Jersey	145
Pompton Plains	145
Bear Rock	149
Towakhow	150
Rockland County, New York	154
Torne Brook	154
Torne Mountain	156
Ramapo River	157
Pound Hill	158
Mine Hill	159
Orange County, New York	159
Tuxedo	159
Horsestable Rock	160
Goshen Mountain	163
Ancient Shell Heaps near New York City. By M. R. Harrington	169
Notes on the Mohegan and Niantic Indians (Plates XXI–XXIV). By F. G. Speck.	
Introduction	183
The Mohegan Indians	184
Local Traditions	185
Material Life	187
Clothing and Ornaments	191
Customs and Miscellaneous Notes	193
Shamanism	195
Beliefs and Folk-lore	200
Myths	203
The Scaticook Indians	205
The Western Niantic Indians	206
Archaeology of the New York Coastal Algonkin. By Alanson Skinner.	
Introduction	213
Chipped Articles	213
Arrow Points	213
Spear Points and Knives	214
Scrapers	214
Drills	214
Rough Stone Articles	214
Hammerstones	214
Net-sinkers	215
Hoes	215
Hand Choppers	215
Grooved Axes	215
Celts	216
Adzes	217
Gouges	218
Pestles	219
Mullers, Grinders, and Polishing Stones	219
Sinew Stones	219
Stone Mortars	219
Pigments, Paint-cups, etc.	219

Stone Plummets	220
Stone Masks	220
Semilunar Knives	220
Stone Beads	220
Polished Stone Articles	220
Gorgets	220
Amulets	220
Banner Stones	221
Pipes	221
Steatite Vessels	222
Articles of Clay	222
Pottery Pipes	222
Pottery Vessels	222
Articles of Metal	227
Beads	227
Articles of Shell	228
Wampum	228
Pendants	228
Scrapers	228
Pottery Tempering	228
Pottery Stamps	228
Fossils	228
Articles of Bone and Antler	229
Bone Awls	229
Bone Needles	229
Bone Arrow Points	229
Harpoons	229
Bone Beads and Tubes	230
Draw Shaves or Beaming Tools	230
Worked Teeth	230
Turtle Shell Cups	230
Turtle Shell Rattles	230
Antler Implements	230
Cylinders	231
Pottery Stamps	231
Trade Articles	231
Conclusion	231
Index	237

ILLUSTRATIONS.

Plates.

I. Bowman's Brook Site.
II. Grave of a Child — Tottenville.
    Grave of Adults — Tottenville.
III. Position of Points in Bones, Tottenville. Fig. 1 (Museum No. 20–3198), Human clavicle showing puncture; Fig. 2 (20–3194–5), Stone arrow point found between fourth and eighth rib of skeleton; Fig. 3 (20–3156–

7), Bone arrow point found near vertebrae of skeleton; Fig. 4 (20–3155–6), Antler arrow point found near lumbar vertebrae of skeleton, as indicated by its position; Fig. 5 (20–3182), Left femur of skeleton showing puncture; Fig. 6 (20–3160–1), Fibula of skeleton fractured by stone arrow point, found in position; Fig. 7 (20–3192–3), Rib of skeleton perforated by antler arrow point, found in place; Fig. 8 (20–3162–3), Argillite arrow point found among ribs of skeleton in one of which it made an incision; Fig. 9 (20–3158–9), Tip of antler arrow point as found among vertebrae; Fig. 10 (20–3164–5), Bone arrow point found with point resting against scapula; Fig. 11 (20–3196), Flint arrow point found under sternum.

IV. Stone Implements. Fig. 1. Grooved ax, type 1, class A; Mariners' Harbor; Fig. 2. Grooved ax, type 2, class A, Chelsea; Fig. 3. Grooved ax, type 3, class A, New Brighton; Fig. 4. Grooved ax, type 4, class A, Mariners' Harbor; Fig. 5. Grooved ax, type 4, class A, Mariners' Harbor; Fig. 6. Grooved ax, type 4, class A, Kriescherville; Fig. 7. Grooved ax, type 5, class A; Fig. 8. Celt, Moravian Cemetery; Fig. 9. Incipient grooved ax, class A, Mariners' Harbor; Fig. 10. Grooved ax, class B, Chelsea; Fig. 11. Grooved ax, class B, Chelsea; Fig. 12. Hand chopper, Tottenville; Fig. 13 (Museum No. T–24118), length 8 cm., Grooved ax, class B, Tottenville; Fig. 14. Grooved ax, class B, Mariners' Harbor; Fig. 15. Grooved adze, Elm Park; Fig. 16. Notched ax, Tottenville; Fig. 17. Celt, Tottenville; Fig. 18. (Museum No. 20–8113), length 22 cm., Celt, Watchogue. Figs. 1–6, 8–12, 14–17 from the Staten Island Association of Arts and Sciences: Fig. 7 from the William T. Davis Collection.

V. Stone Implements. Fig. 1. Grooved maul, Richmond; Fig. 2. Grooved maul or club, Mariners' Harbor; Fig. 3. Pitless hammerstone; Fig. 4 (Museum No. T–23005), length 12 cm., Double pitted hammerstone, Tottenville; Fig. 5. Muller or grinder, Mariners' Harbor; Fig. 6. Muller or grinder, Arrochar; Fig. 7 (Museum No. T–24117), length 8 cm., Net sinker made of broken grooved ax, Tottenville; Fig. 8. Grooved net sinker, Tottenville; Fig. 9. Grooved net sinker, Mariners' Harbor; Fig. 10 (Museum No. T–23012), length 7 cm., Notched net sinker, Tottenville; Fig. 11 (Museum No. T–24107), length 9 cm., Notched net sinker, Tottenville; Fig. 12. Polishing or rubbing stone, Tottenville; Fig. 13. Gouge, Mariners' Harbor; Fig. 14. Notched hoe (?), Kriescherville; Fig. 15. Notched hoe (?), Tottenville; Fig. 16. Plain hoe, Old Place; Fig. 17 (Museum No. 20–3304), length 16 cm., Pottery smoothing stone (?) or polisher, Tottenville; Fig. 18. Pestle, Arrochar. Figs. 1–7, 9, 12–16, 18 from the Staten Island Association of Arts and Sciences; Fig. 8 from the William T. Davis Collection.

VI. Drills, Scrapers and other Objects. Fig. 1. Round flint scraper, Fig. 2. Flint scraper; Fig. 3. Flint scraper made from broken arrow point, Rossville; Fig. 4. Stemmed flint scraper; Fig. 5. Stemmed scraper, unusually large, Mariners' Harbor; Fig. 6. Scraper, very large, Tottenville; Fig. 7 (Museum No. 20–3296), length 5 cm.; Fig. 8. Scraper, serrated, Rossville; Fig. 9 (Museum No. 20–6613), length 4 cm., Mariner's Harbor; Fig. 10. Scraper, stemmed, made from broken arrow point, Mariners' Harbor; Fig. 11. Drill, Krieschervil!e; Fig. 12. Drill, very small, double pointed, Mariners' Harbor; Fig. 13. Drill, very small, double pointed, Linoleumville; Fig. 14. Drill, rough-based, Mariner's Harbor; Fig. 15. Drill, argillite, Mariners' Harbor; Fig. 16. Drill, argillite, very large base, Mariners' Harbor; Fig. 17. Drill, Old Place; Fig. 18. Drill, Mariners' Harbor; Fig. 19 (Museum No. 20–6607), length 5 cm., Drill, red jasper, Old Place; Fig. 20 (Museum No. T–24061), length 5.5 cm., Drill, argillite, Tottenville; Fig. 21 (Museum No. T–24055), length 5 cm., Drill, Tottenville; Fig. 22 (Museum No. T–2406), length 3.3 cm., Drill, rare type, Tottenville; Fig. 23. Drill, Mariners' Harbor; Fig. 24. Drill, Mariners' Harbor; Fig. 25. Drill; Fig. 26. Museum No. 20–3105), length 5.4 cm., Broken pottery, showing drilling to facilitate mending, Tottenville; Fig. 27. "Sinew Stone," so-called, Tottenville; Fig. 28. "Plummet stone," so-called, Watchogue; Fig. 29. Brass arrow point, "trade" article (perforated), Watchogue; Fig. 30. Brass arrow point, "trade" article (non-perforated), Old Place; Fig. 31. Pewter ring, "trade" (?), Old Place; Fig. 32. Perforated fragment of brass or copper, Old Place; Fig. 23. Brass thimble, "trade" object, Rossville; Fig. 34. Fossil shark's tooth, Watchogue. Figs. 1–6, 8, 10–13, 15–18, 23–25, 28–34 from the Staten Island Association of Arts and Sciences, Figs. 14, 27 from the William T. Davis Collection.

VII. Knives and Scrapers. Fig. 1. Large flint knife, New Brighton; Fig. 2. Large flint knife or spear head, Lake's Island; Fig. 3. Argillite knife, Watchogue; Fig. 5. Chert knife, West New Brighton; Fig. 6. Yellow jasper knife, Watchogue; Fig. 7. Yellow jasper knife, New Brighton; Fig. 8. Flint knife covered with oyster spots, Fresh Kill; Fig. 9. Round flint knife, Tottenville; Fig. 10 (Museum No. T–24051), length 8 cm., flint knife or spear Tottenville; Fig. 11. Flint knife or spear, Watchogue; Fig. 12. Flint knife, Tottenville; Fig. 13. Flint knife, Lake's Island; Fig. 14. Flint knife, Linoleumville; Fig. 15. Flint knife, Lake's Island; Fig. 16. Fragment, semilunar knife, Mariners' Harbor; Fig. 17. Fragment, semilunar knife, Old Place; Fig. 18 (Museum No. 20–3286), length 9 cm., Cache blade, Tottenville; Fig. 19 (Museum No. 20–3231), length 7 cm., Cache blade, Tottenville; Fig. 20. Unfinished semilunar knife, Mariner's Harbor; Fig. 21. Cache blade, Old Place; Fig. 22. Cache blade, Old Place. Figs. 1–4, 6–8, 11–17, 20–22 from the Staten Island Association of Arts and Sciences, Figs. 5, 9 from the William T. Davis Collection.

VIII. Banner Stones. Fig. 1. Double holed gorget, Old Place; Fig. 2 (Museum No. 50–7189), Double holed gorget, Canadian Lenapé; Fig. 3 (Museum No. 20–3302), length 8.5 cm., Single holed gorget, two previous perforations broken out, Tottenville; Fig. 4. Single holed gorget, broken, Tottenville; Fig. 5 (Museum No. 20–3280), length 10 cm., Irregularly shaped mica object, perforation started, Tottenville; Fig. 6. Unfinished gorget or banner stone, Tottenville; Fig. 7. Fragment grooved banner stone, Mariners' Harbor; Fig. 8. Fragment perforated banner stone, Tottenville; Fig. 9. Broken perforated banner stone, Mariners' Harbor; Fig. 10. Broken perforated banner stone, Mariners' Harbor; Fig. 11. Broken perforated banner stone, Mariners'

Harbor. Figs. 1, 6–11 from the Staten Island Association of Arts and Sciences, Fig. 4 from the William T. Davis Collection.

IX. A Stone Head — Grasmere.
Tobacco Pipes: Fig. 1. Rude straight clay pipe (fragment), Rossville; Fig. 2. Flat sided angular clay pipe (fragment), Mariners' Harbor; Fig. 3. Decorated fragment clay pipe bowl, Watchogue; Fig. 4. Decorated fragment clay pipe bowl, Watchogue; Fig. 5. Decorated fragment clay pipe bowl, Watchogue; Fig. 6 (Museum No. 20–3270), length 6 cm., Steatite pipe, monitor type, Tottenville; Fig. 7. Straight clay pipe, plain partially restored; Mariners' Harbor; Fig. 8. Bent clay pipe, plain (fragment), Mariners' Harbor; Fig. 9. Decorated clay pipe stem reworked into bead, Watchogue; Fig. 11. Decorated clay pipe stem, Tottenville; Fig. 12. Decorated clay pipe bowl (fragment), Mariner's Harbor; Fig. 13. Decorated clay pipe, broken, bent stem, Tottenville; Fig. 14. Decorated clay pipe stem, Mariners' Harbor; Fig. 15. Decorated clay pipe stem, Mariners' Harbor; Fig. 16. Decorated clay pipe stem, flat type, Watchogue; Fig. 17. Plain clay pipe stem, flat type, Richmond Valley. Figs 1, 2, 7–10, 12–17 from the Staten Island Association of Arts and Sciences; Figs. 3–5, 11 from the William T. Davis Collection.

X. Bone and Antler Tools. Fig. 1 (Museum No. 20–3306), length 12 cm.; Fig. 2 (20–3308), length 8.3 cm.; Fig. 7 (20–3191), length 7.5 cm.; Fig. 8 (20–3166), length 6.3 cm.; Fig. 9 (20–3199), length, 6.9 cm.; Fig. 10 (20–3167), length 6.1 cm.; Fig. 13 (20–3318), length 5.5 cm.; Fig. 14 (20–3315), length 20.7 cm.; Fig. 22 (20–3133); Figs. 3, 4, 5, 6, 11, 12, 15, 16, 17, 18, 19, 20, 21 (Staten Island Association of Arts and Sciences).

XI. Shell Objects. Figs. 7–14 (Museum No. 20–3278); Fig. 18 (20–4986), length 2.7 cm.; Figs. 1, 2, 3, 4, 5, 6, 15, 16, 17 (Staten Island Association of Arts and Sciences).

XII. Arrow Points. Fig. 52 (Museum No. T–44059), length 3.5 cm.; Figs. 20, 21, 27 (William T. Davis Collection); Figs. 1–20, 22–37, 38–52, 53–65 (Staten Island Association of Arts and Sciences).

XIII. A Shell-Pit on Seaman Avenue.
The Core of a Shell-Pit.

XIV. A Cut on Seaman Avenue showing relic-bearing Strata.
Uncovering an Indian Pot at 214th Street and 10th Avenue.

XV. Pottery Vessel found at 214th Street and 10th Avenue. (Bolton and Calver Collection), length 34 cm.

XVI. Inwood Rock-shelter, Manhattan.
An Indian Burial on Seaman Avenue.

XVII. Relics from Manhattan Island. Fig. 2 (Museum No. 20–3247), length 10.7 cm.; Fig. 4 (T–23272), length 9.7 cm.; Fig. 8 (20–3411), length 15 cm.; Fig. 10 (20–3437), length 14.7 cm.; Fig. 12 (1–4088), length 12 cm.; Fig. 1 (Bolton and Calver Collection), length 3.7 cm.; Fig. 3 (Bolton and Calver Collection), length 3.5 cm.; Fig. 5 (Bolton and Calver Collection), length, 3.8 cm.; Fig. 6 (Bolton and Calver Collection), length 10.4 cm.; Fig. 7 (Bolton and Calver Collection), length 7.8 cm.; Fig. 9 (Bolton and Calver Collection), length 8.4 cm.; Fig. 11 (Bolton and Calver Collection), length 33 cm.

XVIII. Finch's Rock House.
Helicker's Cave.
XIX. Leather Man's Rock-shelter.
Riverville Shelter.
XX. Mahoney Rock-shelter.
Quartz Quarry Rock-shelter.
XXI. Mohegan Specimens.
XXII. Brotherton-Mohegan in Costume.
Group of Mohegan Indians.
XXIII. Niantic Woman.
Mohegan Woman.
XXIV. A. S. Nunsuch, Niantic.

TEXT FIGURES.

		PAGE.
1.	Sites at Mariners' Harbor	6
2.	Fragments of Pottery, Staten Island Museum	54
3.	Pottery Designs and Rims, Staten Island Museum	55
4.	Fragment of Pottery, Staten Island Museum	56
5.	Pottery Designs, Staten Island Museum	59
6.	Location of Burials, Pits and Shell-Beds near Inwood	86
7.	Implements of Bone and Horn, Van Cortlandt Park	87
8.	Bottom of an Algonkin Vessel Showing a Peculiar Point. Manhattan Island	89
9.	Incised and Stamped Fragments of Algonkin Pottery, Manhattan Island	90
10.	Designs from Vessels found on Manhattan Island	93
11.	Piece of Worked Bone. Van Cortlandt Park	113
12.	Stone Implement. Van Cortlandt Park	114
13.	Incised Designs from Iroquoian Vessels. Manhattan Island	115
14.	Incised Designs from Iroquoian Vessels. Manhattan Island and Van Cortlandt Park	116
15.	Incised Designs from Iroquoian Pottery Vessels, Showing Conventional Faces. Kingsbridge and Van Cortlandt Park	116
16.	Stamped Designs from the Intermediate Type of Vessel. Van Cortlandt Park	117
17.	Stamped and Incised Designs from Intermediate and Iroquoian Types. Van Cortlandt Park	118
18.	Incised Designs from Algonkin Pottery Vessels. Manhattan Island	119
19.	Potsherds of the Intermediate Type, Showing Odd Designs	120
20.	Ground Plan of "Finch's Rock House"	126
21.	Vertical Section of Refuse in Finch's Rock House, Trench 2	128
22.	Vertical Section of Refuse in Finch's Rock House, about midway of the Cave, Fig. 21	129
23.	Rock-shelter Region of Westchester Co., N. Y. and Fairfield Co., Conn.	131
24.	Ground Plan of Helicker's Cave	133
25.	Ground Plan of Quartz Quarry Rock-shelter	135
26.	Plan of Riverville Rock-shelter	137
27.	Diagram of a Typical Shell Deposit	169
28.	Cross Section of a Shell-Pit	170

		PAGE
29.	Map Giving the Locations of Shell Deposits	178
30.	Mohegan Bow	190
31.	Cross Section of a Bow	190
32.	Heads and Feathering of Mohegan Arrows	191
33.	Basketry Design	209
34.	A hafted Celt from a Pond at Thorndale, Dutchess Co., N. Y.	218
35.	Pottery Forms of the Coastal Algonkin	223
36.	Typical Algonkin Pottery Pipe, from Port Washington, L. I., and fragment of an effigy Pipe from the same Locality	224
37.	Incised Designs from Pottery Vessels	225
38.	Incised Designs from Algonkin Vessels	226
39.	Map showing the Location of the New York Coastal Algonkin and their Neighbors	232

INTRODUCTION.

This volume was issued on the occasion of the Hudson-Fulton celebration in New York City, for which a special exhibition of anthropological material from the Lower Hudson River was made in this Museum. This exhibition not only contained representative specimens from the Museum's collection, but from those of several private collectors, thus presenting a general view of the entire locality. At the same time, it seemed advisable to bring together at least a part of the results accruing from the labors of the various students of local problems to whose interest, enthusiasm and self-sacrifice, the existing data concerning the aboriginal inhabitants of the locality is due. Naturally, these contributors view the local problems from somewhat different points of regard and are not always in agreement as to their interpretations. In the main, all have followed the same general method of reconstructing the prehistoric culture by welding together the available ethno historical and archaeological data, a method justified by the failure to find neither local evidences of great antiquity nor indications of successive or contemporaneous culture types. The work on Staten Island is more advanced than that of Manhattan and the adjacent shores, Mr. Skinner having brought together all the available data with the results of his own detailed survey. This Island presents somewhat unique conditions in that it constitutes a definite geographical unit of convenient size but without effective barriers to intrusion; that its archaeological remains seem to have belonged to one and the same culture, that of the historic Indians; and in that it appears to have been uninhabited during remote times. Its aboriginal culture has been classed with that of Manhattan and adjacent shores as of the coastal Algonkin type, and may serve as a characteristic of the whole.

In many respects, the most unique feature of this volume, is the discussion of rock-shelters of which a number have been explored and doubtless many more remain to be discovered. Interest in them is partly due to the obvious analogies to European caves, but chiefly to their apparent presentation of chronological cultural differences respecting the use of pottery. While the evidence so far presented does not warrant the assumption that the absence of pottery in the lower levels of these shelters indicates its contemporaneous absence throughout the whole area, no adequate explanation for these differences presents itself, a condition raising a problem of something more than local significance. Attention to local rock-shelters was first due to Mr. Alexander Chenoweth's discovery of a small cave among some fallen rocks at Cold Spring near the extreme northern end of Manhattan Island during the year 1894. About and in the cave itself were evidences of former Indian occupation. In 1900, Mr. M. R. Harrington, then an officer of this Museum, began a systematic investigation of Manhattan and adjacent territory, discovering a number of relic-bearing rock-shelters in Westchester County, New York, the most promising of which were carefully excavated. At about the same time, Mr. Max Schrabisch, privately and chiefly at his own initiative, began a search for rock-shelters on the opposite, or west side of the Hudson. Several other persons have reported rock-shelters from the surrounding regions but, so far, the only systematic presentation of the subject is to be found in this volume. There is every reason to believe that such shelters abound throughout the adjacent parts of New England and the Middle Atlantic States, offering an important field for further investigation.

Another peculiarity of local archaeology, concerning which the various observers have quite different opinions, is the "dog burial." While this may be of considerable ethnographic importance, its ethnological significance is little more than a puzzle.

The best known local remains are the shell deposits, a number of which have been explored for this Museum. These are scarcely to be considered unique forming as they do an integral part of the well known Atlantic coast chain of such deposits. The local deposits are not necessarily of great antiquity and so far, seem to show but one type of culture, that of the locality as a whole.

Throughout the archaeological sections of this volume, the plan was to omit the long detailed descriptions of the minute individualities of specimens so often encountered in our literature on the ground that such microscopic work reveals, in the main, what are relatively unimportant variations, rarely of value in the solution of cultural problems. In the present case, at least, it seemed best to point out what appeared to be the type characters of the various specimens and their respective distributions, referring to such minute features as seemed to be correlated with particular localities only, or such as had some bearing upon the particular problems under consideration. In the final paper of this volume special emphasis has been given to the distribution of the several specimen types and varieties as indicating the geographical limits of cultures, a kind of archaeological work now greatly needed in most parts of North America.

Unfortunately, there is now available no systematic study of surviving representatives of tribes related to those formerly residing in this locality. We have in small measure made some amends for this omission by the presentation of historical data and a paper upon the few surviving Mohegans of the Connecticut Valley. Though not strictly representatives of the extinct local bands of Indians the Mohegans were probably closely allied to the historic Mahican once holding the middle of the Hudson Valley; and, making due allowance for New England influence, may be taken as a suggestion as to the former culture of tribes occupying the Bronx, the shores of the Harlem and the Sound. That there was not available a study of the surviving Delaware and Muncey, whose ancestors were closely affiliated with tribes formerly holding the Jersey shore is to be regretted, since there are not wanting in these pages suggestions that their cultural traits were in many respects the prevailing characteristics of this locality.

The editor hopes this volume may stimulate the investigation of local problems, especially the collection of such data as may yet be obtained from the scattered remnants of local tribes now on the verge of extinction; for while the anthropology of the Hudson Valley has a peculiar local interest to this Museum, its problems have an important bearing upon the general anthropology of the Atlantic States.

The editor is under great obligations to the officers of the Staten Island Association of Arts and Sciences for illustrations of many specimens in the collections of that institution and to the several authors of the integral parts of this volume for the use of photographs and specimens. He desires to make special acknowledgment to Mr. Alanson Skinner, who arranged the local anthropological exhibition for the Hudson-Fulton Celebration, for assistance in arranging the details of the publication. He is also under obligations to Mr. William Orchard for many photographs and the arrangement of the illustrations, to Miss Ruth B. Howe for a number of drawings and to Miss Bella Weitzner for assistance in preparing the volume for the press. Finally, recognition should be given the members of the Hudson Fulton Commission for the opportunity of making the exhibit that suggested this publication and the special exhibition guide prepared at that time. In this connection the Editor wishes to acknowledge his personal obligations to Dr. George F. Kunz for many helpful suggestions in the formative stages of the work.

THE EDITOR.

THE LENAPÉ INDIANS OF STATEN ISLAND.

BY

ALANSON SKINNER.

INTRODUCTION.

Staten Island, better known as the Borough of Richmond, New York City, is geographically a part of the state of New Jersey, from which it is separated only by the narrow tidal waters of the Kill Van Kull and the Staten Island Sound. The shore bordering these bodies of water is apt to be marshy. Salt meadows and swamps, cut by innumerable tidal creeks, stretch back a distance of a few hundred yards to a mile or more, towards the generally wooded upland; but here and there long dunes or, as they are locally called, "hummocks" of red sand run out on the meadow, or rise as isolated meadow islands some distance from the upland. This is especially the case with the northern and northwestern shores of the Island. Towards the southern end, the mainland itself becomes of a sandy character, frequently overlying beds of clay and kaolin at comparatively shallow depths, as in the immediately adjoining mainland of New Jersey. Serpentine hills occur in the interior of the Island and are wooded, even to the present day. The eastern shore, bordering upon the Raritan and New York Bays, is mostly sandy beach; sometimes with a clay bluff. On the northeastern shores, salt meadows terminating in mud flats or beaches occur immediately behind. Along this coast, the continual beating of the waves has eroded and worn away the shore line many feet within the memory of living man, and consequently the shore line of aboriginal days must lie far out beneath the surface of the water. It may be said that, in its present condition, there are very few traces of aboriginal occupation along this eastern shore.

On the Sound side of the Island, beginning at West New Brighton and continuing all the way to Tottenville, wherever there are sand dunes, there lies one practically unbroken chain of sites of former Indian habitations and the like. In no instance, excepting near the southern end of the Island, at Rossville and Woodrow, where the sandy soil extends inland, and along one or two brooks and lakes in the interior, do these sites occur elsewhere than along the shores of the Island.

The aboriginal remains occurring in this region may be easily classified into villages, shell-heaps, burials and camps. By a village site, the writer means an area showing traces of prolonged occupation by several lodges, with their attendant dump holes or refuse pits.

Shell-heaps, or kitchen-middens, are of two sorts. Spots where the useless shells have been thrown away when shell fish were being dried, and refuse heaps containing the shells of bivalves consumed on or near the spot, together with animal bones, whole and broken implements, pottery and various debris. The latter differ from shell pits or refuse pits by their greater magnitude, and were probably more generally used as public dumping grounds. They are invariably found near village sites, although not every such site has its shell-heap. Heaps of shells, discarded when drying oysters for future consumption, often occur at a long distance from other traces of occupation. To these, we have given the title of "Drying Heaps;" they contain no relics. The custom of drying oysters for preservation was well remembered by the Shinnecock Indians of Long Island in 1902. They claimed to have paid tribute to the Iroquois in these.

The title "Burial Site" sufficiently explains itself. A camp or lodge site is, according to the definition here adopted, a temporary abiding place usually some distance from the nearest village. Such sites sometimes yield potsherds or a few bones, shells and implements; but never have the appearance of having been permanent abodes.

Rock-shelters, quarries, etc., for obvious geologic reasons, do not occur. Owing to the constant encroachment of householders, factories, etc., many sites have been obliterated.

ARCHÆOLOGICAL SITES.

In the following list of sites, the writer has endeavored to give a résumé of the data personally collected, or published elsewhere, mainly in the Proceedings of the Natural Science Association of Staten Island:[1]

1. *West New Brighton, Upper or Pelton's Cove.* A village site and burial ground at Upper or Pelton's Cove occur between Livingston and West New Brighton. When the Shore Road was cut through this place many years ago, numbers of skeletons, etc., were found. This site is now obliterated. During the last ten or twenty years, there has been absolutely nothing to show aboriginal occupation. Old people now living remember when a large sand dune was to be seen at this spot, and the finding of human bones and other objects washed out by rains. In Hagedorn's "Staten Islander," June 4th, 1856, the following account concerning this site occurs:

---

[1] On the map accompanying Mr. Wm. T. Davis' pamphlet on "Staten Island Names, Ye Olde Names and Nicknames," published by the Natural Science Association of Staten Island, in March, 1896, a number of sites are shown where Indian implements had been found up to that time.

"Mr. Dissosway's lecture on the Indians of Staten Island, last Friday evening, was attended by many of our most prominent citizens. The Church was filled as usual. Mr. Dissosway delighted his audience with a mass of historical facts and incidents highly instructive and interesting. At the close of his remarks, he exhibited to the audience some skulls of the Red men, found on Mr. Samuel Pelton's farm, together with their arrows and other articles used by them in peace and war. Mr. Pelton had very kindly sent them to the Society that the public might have an opportunity to see them."

2. *West New Brighton, Ascension Church.* A village site, now obliterated, has been reported at West New Brighton. This is said to have been situated, in part, between Cedar and Dongan Streets. When the foundation for the new Parish House of the Church of the Ascension was being dug in the spring of 1903, shells, skeletons and implements are said to have been found. A three-pitted hammerstone and a small fragment of pottery were found by the writer. The skeletons, or rather the human bones seen by the writer, were recent white men's bones; but we were told that, in the older part of the graveyard, skeletons were found in unmarked graves, with which implements were discovered. As these skeletons were said to have been flexed in the usual Indian fashion, possibly the succeeding Whites selected the same spot for their graveyard that the Indians had used, as has often happened. It is improbable that Indians and white settlers used the same burial ground simultaneously; although there has been a cemetery here for many years. The objects said to have been found were stone axes and the like, while Indians at the time of the settlers would undoubtedly have had the iron tomahawk and usual trade articles. It is to be regretted that no one versed in archæology was present at the discovery of these Indian graves, if such they were.

At Mariners' Harbor, beginning about half a mile south of the station and running north to Bowman's Point, in every field are traces of prolonged occupation, fire-cracked stones, flint chips, potsherds and the like (Fig. 1). Two spots, however, are deserving of especial mention.

3. *Mariners' Harbor, Arlington.* On South Avenue, just opposite the Arlington station of the Staten Island Rapid Transit Railroad, is what remains of a once much larger low sandy knoll, most of which has been dug away (Fig. 1). In May, 1902, half-a-dozen shell pits were opened, all of which averaged from four to six feet deep, with about an equal breadth. They were all bowl-shaped and contained animal bones, oyster shells, etc. Several bone and antler implements, a quantity of typical Algonkin pottery, fragments of quite a number of clay pipes, stone arrow points, scrapers, hammerstones and a flat, thin, double-sided mortar or metate were found. A portion of a pestle, a grooved axe, and a grooved adze were picked up

nearby. Several small shell-heaps averaging ten by six feet, and from four to six inches deep, containing the usual camp refuse, were also opened. In the nearby fields, portions of a couple of bannerstones, grooved axes, a couple of celts and a number of celt (?) blades were picked up. Celts are very rare on the north shore of Staten Island; the writer in ten years of collecting has never obtained a single specimen, and has not seen more than

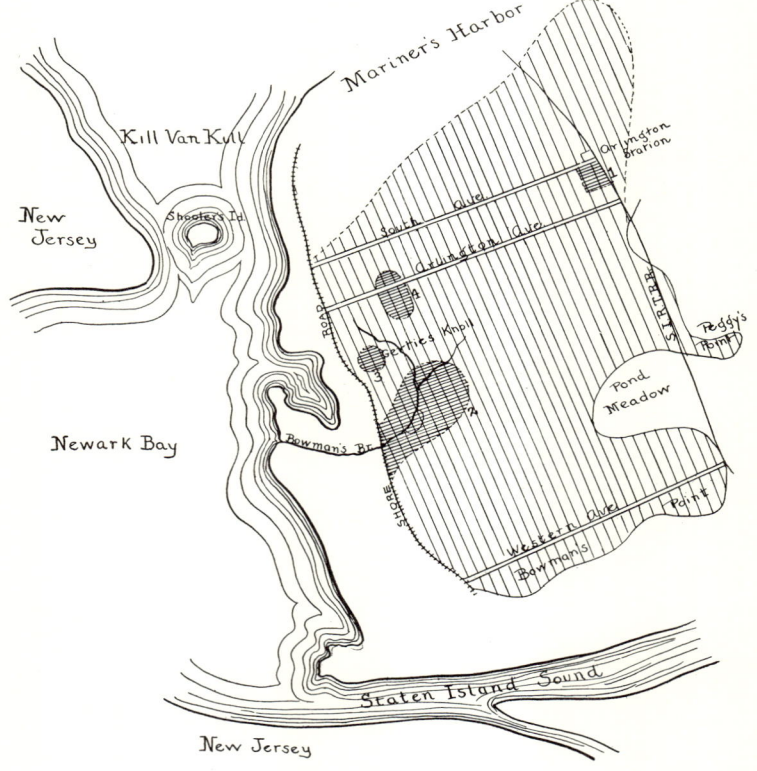

Fig. 1. Sites at Mariner's Harbor.

two or three. A stone gouge, the only one reported from Staten Island, was also found nearby.

4. *Mariners' Harbor, Bowman's Brook* site is situated on the shore of Kill van Kull, running inland for some distance along the north shore of Bowman's Brook, or, as it is often called, Newton's Creek or Deharts Brook (Fig. 1). In the early spring of 1903, the firm of Milliken Bros.

started work on a large steel plant which now covers the entire ground once occupied by this site. As the sand was dug out and carted away, the shell pits, fireplaces and refuse dump of a large village were exposed and many examined by us. Later the village cemetery also came to light. Probably from fifty to one hundred pits were exposed in all, during the years 1903–7, and the contents of most of these were lost. These pits were bowl-shaped and, like those at the site at Arlington station, averaged from four to six feet in width; the average depth was from three to six feet. In some cases, the pits had the appearance of having been used for some time, probably as garbage dumps. A layer of fresh clean sand having been thrown over them when they became offensive, a new deposit of refuse was started, a practice which now may be observed sometimes among both Whites and Indians. In one case, the complete skeleton of a dog, laid out in regular order on one side, was found. It was buried at a considerable depth, and covered with a layer of oyster shells and charcoal.

The abundance of potsherds on this site was remarkable, and the earthenware varied greatly in quality and design. The majority of the specimens were of the typical Algonkin type, but some were distinctly Iroquoian in design. The constricted neck, raised and peaked rim, notched angle, and, in one case, a crude attempt at depicting the human face,— pointed clearly to the influence of the Mohawk or other Iroquois. The fragments of the vessel just referred to, showed the pot to have been one of very large size. It was decorated by a series of incised lines in a sort of chevron pattern; at intervals, curious little knobs occurred on which the human face was represented by three incised lines,— two for the eyes and one for the mouth. As far as the writer knows, no other similar article has been obtained in this neighborhood.

Implements of bone and antler were comparatively abundant, though lacking in variety. They comprised bone awls, antler cylinders and turtle shell cups. A notable object was a fragment of an antler implement, apparently a pin, which had a carved head. Stone implements, such as arrow points and grooved axes, were fairly abundant; but no celts at all occurred.

At first no burials were discovered; but, later, widening the railroad cut disclosed many on the southerly side of the knoll on which the village was situated (Plate I). The skeletons were found beneath three or four feet of sand, as a rule; and, in the case of regular burial, always with arms and knees flexed. As many as four of these were found in one grave. No relics of any kind occurred with them except in one instance.[1] In some

---

[1] The graves explored by Mr. George H. Pepper at Tottenville, some years ago, were different in that they almost invariably contained relics.

instances "bone burials" occurred. Apparently, the flesh had been allowed to rot away from the bones; they were then buried in a hole and covered with sand.

A burial of the more regular form was thus described by the writer in the Proceedings of the Staten Island Association of Arts and Sciences, for May, 1906: —

> "On May 12th, 1906, while carrying on my investigations on the pre-historic Indian village site exposed by the building of Milliken Brothers' [steel] foundry at Mariners' Harbor, a grave was found exposed by the recent enlarging of the railroad cut which runs through the plant" (bisecting the Bowman's Brook site).
>
> "The grave was found about 10 feet south of the first one which I had opened in that vicinity. It was about 7 feet broad by $5\frac{1}{2}$ feet deep and of peculiar structure. A streak of black earth ran through the yellow sand and formed a bowl-shaped pit. This streak was about 6 inches thick, broadening into pockets at both ends, and contained relics. At the bottom of the pit were some very large sherds, which were later restored and found to be the rim and most of the sides of a pot of typical Algonkin style. The bottom only is missing. On the sherds lay several stones, which indicates that the pot was whole or nearly so when placed in the grave, and that the stones had been cast upon it with the purpose of breaking it.
>
> "About 1 foot higher than the sherds and 3 feet to the west was found the skeleton of a person above average age, flexed as usual, heading north, with the face to the east. The skull was crushed, probably by the weight of the earth. No relics were found with it, but an oyster shell lay upon the bones of the hands, which were folded before the face. Fire-cracked stones also lay upon and near the skeleton. A small pocket of blackened earth immediately surrounded the skeleton, but the other soil within the black boundary was hard, compact, yellow earth. About 8 inches above these was a deposit of oyster shells about $2\frac{1}{2}$ to 3 feet thick above the bones.
>
> "With this exception, no relics were found with any skeletons taken out personally or removed by laborers. During the summer a perfect pottery vessel is said to have been found by the workmen, but whether with a burial or not the writer was unable to ascertain. It was described as being of typical Algonkin style, without any attempt at ornamentation. The vessel has disappeared and it is alleged to have been sold to a collector in New Jersey. While still with this subject, it may be interesting to mention that a skull found by the writer, from this site, has more than 20 Inca bones or inter-parietals."

This site is now practically obliterated, as are the "Indian fields" northward to Bowman's Point.

5. *Mariners' Harbor, Old Place.* On Tuinessen's, or Old Place Neck, there is a large village site. Near the extreme point are shell pits and fireplaces, unusually far apart. Some of the refuse pits here are of considerable size and depth. Evidently this is a site the date of which can be placed at the early historic period. Pottery occurs, bearing a strong resemblance to the Iroquoian, though not so marked as that found at the Bowman's Brook

site. A brass arrow point, gun flints, leaden bullets, a pewter trade (?) ring, fragments of trade pipes, etc., have been found on the surface, and a tiny piece of a brass kettle, perforated (perhaps for suspension), came from a shell pit on this site. Trade articles are generally rare throughout Staten Island. Iron trade axes have never been found, nor has the writer ever seen any from hereabouts, although they are often mentioned in early deeds. No antler or bone implements have been found here. Graves, with relics in or near them, were reported on the property of the Rev. Jas. Kinney some years ago. Some graves opened here by the writer proved to be those of Whites.

6. *Bloomfield (Watchogue).* There is no special large village site in this region, but relics occur more or less abundantly on all of the dunes and sand-hills. A stone plummet (?), grooved axes, Iroquoian pottery, pipes, arrow points, etc., have been found here. Mr. Isaiah Merrill has a fine collection of objects said to have been collected about here, among which is a steatite bead. An inscribed clay bead, with incised figures, is also said to have been found here.

This site is peculiar on account of the scarcity of shell pits and similar remains. Relics occur almost entirely as surface finds. Celts have been found. A fine perforated brass arrow point was found by the writer some years ago at a spot where Iroquoian pottery was frequent. Objects which seem to be gun flints, but are chipped from native yellow jasper, etc., were in the collection of Mr. Merrill. These seemed to the writer to be authentic, and it is possible that the Indians did manufacture these useful objects rather than buy the English flints from the Whites. The stone bead in Mr. Merrill's collection is of pink steatite,— thick, square, and altogether remarkable. It is said that Mr. Merrill had at one time a "handful" of these beads; but when the writer viewed the collection, some years ago, only one remained. Other notable objects in his collection were a banner stone, fragments of others and several celts.

7. *Chelsea.* At the angle of Watchogue road, near its junction with Union Avenue, graves are reported to have been found. The site is well known locally as the "Burying ground." Several grooved axes have come from this site. Attempts to locate any remaining graves have been unsuccessful. Another dune with relics is between Chelsea and Travisville.

8. *Long Neck (Linoleumville), north side.* Scattered lodges and some shells are found along the north side of the Neck.

9. *Long Neck (Linoleumville), south side.* Scattered lodges are to be seen on the south side of the Neck, opposite Price's Island; also a shell-heap, with pits, which contain no relics. Relics are found all over the end of the Neck, but nowhere abundant. Excavations on the south side of the

Neck proved unsuccessful, the shell-heap there being apparently only a shell-fish drying heap. Price's Meadow Island, a sand dune rising from the salt meadows, has many indications of being an Indian site. There are no shells there, however.

10. *New Springville, Corson's Brook.* A site is said to be located at New Springville on Corson's brook. Shells and graves are reported; also an iron arrow-head. The writer has not been successful in personally locating this site, up to date. The locality differs from almost all the others on the Island, in that the soil is not sandy, and we have seen no indications of aboriginal occupation of any kind. Many people have said that they found Indian implements there, however, and at one time a skull, said to be Indian, was found in the bed of Corson's brook after a freshet had eaten away the banks.

11. *Green Ridge, near Richmond Plank Road.* A camp site is reported between Journeay Avenue and Annadale road, near Richmond Plank road, which contains early relics.

12. *Green Ridge, Lake's Island.* There is a small village site on Lake's Meadow Island, with a small shell-heap, where are found early relics of Indian origin. In a letter to his sister, Miss Helen Thoreau, dated from Staten Island, July 21, 1843, Thoreau says,— "Last Sunday I walked over to Lake Island Farm.... As I was coming away, I took my toll out of the soil in the shape of arrowheads, which may after all be the surest crop, certainly not effected by drought."

13. *Woodrow.* Following up Sandy Brook, and from there to Kreischerville, is a series of "Indian fields." Inland at Woodrow there are relics about the Sandy Brook. Relics occur at Sandy Ground, on the farm of Mr. Isaac Wort, Sr., and also near one of the clay pits in the woods, isolated from all others.

The sites from the Sandy Brook to the Wort Farm are remarkable for the number of stone mortars found there. According to Messrs. Samuel and Isaac Wort, Sr., some very peculiar burials were discovered during the leveling of a knoll on the property of Mr. Samuel Wort many years ago. When earth was being removed, a stone-walled "chamber" was discovered, and, on removing the stones, several skeletons were found, with many relics, including a great many arrow and spear points and a "stone bowl" (probably a steatite pot). None of these objects now remain; but most of the stones taken from the grave are still to be seen piled up near the original site. There are very many of these, and they appear to have been brought some distance. A number show the action of fire. Mr. Isaac Wort claims to have found other similar stone graves thereabout; but adds, they contained no relics. He also says that, in his boyhood, iron trade axes were abundant on these sites; but, unfortunately, none have survived the years. Glass beads, etc., have been found.

14. *Rossville*. Lodges, shells, etc., run from Cedar Hill to Winant's Brook. There are sites all along the shore to Kreischerville, with early relics. All the sandy fields along the shore yield relics, but here and there shell pits and heaps proclaim more specialized occupation. At Burial Point, graves are said to have been found.

One site, near Rossville Post Office, has yielded very many arrow points, of a strange archaic "double-ended" type. There is a large shell-heap in this field, containing pottery. A hill near the Rossville Road is known as "Hammerstone Hill," to local collectors, on account of the abundance of pitted hammerstones found there. Brass thimbles, etc., have been found.

15. *Tottenville*. Extensive shell mounds may still be seen near the Billop house. Burial Ridge, near by, was excavated by Mr. George H. Pepper for the Museum, in 1895. Horn and bone implements are found, bearing traces of fabrics and copper. Shells occur all over the point, and as far north as Richmond Valley. A grooved axe weighing twelve pounds was found here.

During the past few years, excavation on some sites has been prohibited, and little plowing has been done; so that surface hunting was profitless. Clandestine attempts at digging in the famous "Burial Ridge" met with no success on account of the comprehensiveness of former excavations. However, in former years much was written about this site, especially by Mr. George H. Pepper, Captain R. D. Wainwright and others.

The shell-heaps themselves have been little worked, except by Mr. Max Bedell of Pleasant Plains; but there is considerable literature extant concerning the famous "Burial Ridge."

The first record we have of human remains is in 1858, when workmen employed by Mr. Joel Cole in digging a foundation, discovered a skeleton and a number of skulls. One skeleton was flexed and near it were a number of implements, including a grooved stone axe, weighing twelve pounds, which is now in the possession of the Staten Island Association of Arts and Sciences. Five years later, while digging the foundation for an addition to his house sixteen feet square, twenty skeletons were discovered. After this, from time to time, skeletons have been unearthed by accident or design in most of the surrounding fields. One skeleton was found in a "standing position." Many of these burials were accompanied by implements, a rare occurrence in the region inhabited by the Algonkin Indians of southeastern New York and nearby New Jersey.

Beginning August 10th, 1893, Mr. George H. Pepper received permission from Mr. Richard Christopher to dig in a sandy field adjoining the Cole property, where, at a depth of four feet, he uncovered a skeleton buried in a sitting posture, the crown of the skull up, and facing northeast. At the base of the cranium, there was a stone upon which rested the inferior maxillary, and a larger stone supported the head; but they were apparently thrown carelessly into the hole and not placed there for any purpose. Two marks, perhaps from tomahawk blows, were seen upon the cranium. No implements of any kind occurred, but about fifteen split deer bones were found.

In the same field, on September 30th, 1894, Mr. Pepper discovered a cache of fish bones, circular in form and about a foot and a half in diameter and two inches thick. A mass of oyster and other shells and débris was about one foot above this. Again, on January 27th, 1894, Capt. Robert D. Wainwright unearthed ten skeletons in this vicinity. One showed evidence of having met his death by being burnt from the knees upward, perhaps in a torture fire.

In the Proceedings of the Natural Science Association of Staten Island for February 13th, 1897, we have a report that:—

"Capt. Robert D. Wainwright presented a number of bones, representing parts of two Indian skeletons, recently exhumed at Tottenville, and read the following account of the same:—

"'On January 27, having received permission from Mr. C. H. Leland, with the assistance of Mr. John Cochran, I made several excavations on the old Billop estate, on the land next adjoining that of Mr. Decker. About a half a foot down, in the last trench that we dug that day, we came to a bed of oyster shells, thickly packed, evidently the remains of an old Indian feast. There I found fragments of human bones, ribs, vertebræ, teeth, parts of a skull, etc. Many of the bones had been burnt, and all were thoroughly mixed with the shells. Continuing the main trench further, and at a much lower depth, in mixed sand, the lower bones of the leg, including feet and toes, lying parallel to each other, were found. These limbs were packed on the sides by broken clam shells. Not finding any implements, I concluded that, as the body of the Indian had been burnt from the knees upward, he had met his death by fire.

"'Again on the 30th inst., Mr. Cochran and myself found the perfect skeleton of an Indian. First, digging through a foot of sandy loam, we came to oyster shells, then through half a foot of this material, after which we came to mixed sand. About a foot down lay the skeleton, head towards the east, face facing north, lying on the side, the ribs over towards the left, knees drawn up, arms close to the body, hands before the face, middle finger of the right hand in the mouth, on which the teeth were closed tightly. In front of the hands was a ball of sand, inclosing deer bones, flanked on its eastern side by a tortoise shell. This skeleton measured 7 feet 4 inches. Several conch shells were found lying some distance away, seemingly pointing towards the skeleton. No implements were found. On taking up the skeleton, which was done most carefully, it went to pieces and became much broken, as may be seen from its present condition.'"

In the Proceedings of the same Association for April 10th, 1897, is the following account,—

"Capt. Robert D. Wainwright exhibited portions of Indian skeletons, implements and photographs of the skeletons as they appeared when first uncovered, and read the following paper:

"'Since my last report to the Association in connection with excavations at Tottenville, I have been quite successful in exhuming other remains of Indians. All these were found on the estate of Mr. Acker, which is just below that of Mr. Decker, whose property adjoins that of the Billop estate. From the entrance of Mr. Acker's property, and a little to the left, is a raised eminence, which extends to his residence on the left and to the bluff beyond. Noticing that oyster shells were very plentiful on this ridge, and in some places forming circles, I dug at one of these about the latter part of last month.

"'Passing through a thin layer of shells I came to disturbed earth, where two and a half feet down I unearthed five skeletons. These were in very bad condition, and in nearly every instance many parts were missing. Two skulls were mashed perfectly flat; the teeth of one being a long distance from the head. Judging from the teeth, the remains consisted of two adults and three young persons. The head of one of the latter was found under the pelvis of one of the adults. These bodies were evidently jammed into the hole, which was a small one, and not regularly buried. There was nothing to show the cause of death. Underneath the remains were burnt shells and charcoal, and mixed with the bodies were shells and a few small pieces of pottery. No other object was found.

"'A short distance away, on the same ridge, Mr. Acker unearthed another skeleton. This one was found the same distance down, and the same materials (shells, etc.) were encountered as in the excavation of the ones previously mentioned. This skeleton was one of very large size. It lay on its right side, face facing northwest knees drawn up, and hands in front of face. The skull had been evidently beaten in, on its left side, which no doubt was the cause of death. No implements of any kind were found and only a few chippings and some pottery were found with the body, which, though intact, was in a most fragile state. From the appearance of the teeth, which were worn down almost to the quick, I judged the remains were that of a very old man.

"'On March 30th, two or three yards to the west of the remains of the five skeletons already mentioned, I dug down two feet and a quarter through one half a foot of shells and disturbed earth, and discovered another skeleton. The remains were those of a middle aged man and were in terrible condition. The skull was intact, but the ribs of the left side were missing, as was also the left arm and the lower parts of both legs. The pelvis was very large. The fingers of both hands were piled in front of and to the left of the skull. At the fracture of the leg bones and at right angles to them, lay a neck of a large glass bottle, while across this and balanced on it, lay a piece of (as I believe) Dutch pottery. These were the only articles found, but they are of interest as indicating communication with the whites, a fact not previously noted by any one. On the 2nd of April, while clearing away the remains of the above mentioned skeleton, I found burnt shells and charcoal. Digging through this, half a foot downward, I discovered another skeleton, which, though intact, was in a very fragile state, and could not be exhumed, except in a very bad condition. The head lay on the left side, face facing north-west and downward. The upper jaw with skull had fallen, the jaw being in rear of the lower one. The left lower leg was badly out of shape, probably at one time broken and not having knitted together properly. No articles were found with these remains.

"'On the 3rd of April, I removed the remains and noticing disturbed earth to the right I continued my excavation in that direction and a half a foot further found another skeleton. The remains were in excellent condition, the skull faced west-north-west and slightly downward. One hand was under the chin and the other lay on the left leg. The lower limbs were drawn up as is usual with remains which seem to be regularly interred. No objects were found with this skeleton except shells and a little pottery, which no doubt, as in other cases, were thrown in after burial.'"

In 1895, Mr. Geo. H. Pepper again began work on this site, this time for the Museum. Several very interesting finds were made. With one skeleton, that of an old woman, were two cups made of the carapaces of box tortoises.

One of the most remarkable burials unearthed was the skeleton of a child (Plate II). At a depth of four feet, the remains were found, a block of white sandstone at the head and a similar slab of gray sandstone at the feet. Two feet away, to the north of the body, was another mass of sandstone. The skeleton lay on its back with the head to the east. Beads made of tiny *olivella* shells, with rubbed perforations, and a few small disk beads were found about the neck. Six flaked implements of clear-grained yellow jasper were packed about the base of the head. Five leaf-shaped objects of the same material were resting upon these pieces and almost covered the skull.

Another piece was lying upon the right arm. The lower part of the face had evidently been covered with a copper ornament; for copper salts had discolored the upper and lower jaws, and even the cervical vertebræ were thoroughly impregnated and had become a dull green color. Under the jaw, a slab of mica was found. It was over four inches in length and had been worked. Near the right knee there was a cache of implements. In it were three stone arrow points and twelve flakes of yellow jasper; and pieces of deer bone with which to fashion new points had also been added.

Six antler tips had been prepared. These needed but little cutting and drilling to make them into arrow points. Three sections of antler suitable for game sticks or for handles of knives or drills came next; then three beautifully chipped yellow jasper scrapers, also two leaf-shaped pieces of jasper. A large stone pendant, that had probably been worn for many years, was also in the deposit. The hole for suspension had been broken twice, and a third hole had been drilled in it. A moccasin-shaped stone was there, perhaps a last, and with it a flat stone upon which the buckskin might be cut. The topmost piece was a large crystal of smoky quartz. Beneath the mass was a large digging implement made from a shoulder blade of a deer. Beaver teeth, deer bones, and fragments of tortoise shell were also found; and lastly there was a paint receptacle made from the lower jaw of a fox.

Not far from this grave, at a depth of one and a half feet below the surface, three skeletons were found (Plate II). Two were well-developed men in the prime of manhood; the third was somewhat older. They were lying side by side with the legs flexed, and, though less than two feet below the surface, the bones were well preserved.

Among and in the bones of these skeletons were twenty-three stone, bone and antler arrow points (Plate III). In the first skeleton, it was found that two points of antler and one of bone had pierced the body and lodged near the spinal column. Another point of argillite had been driven between two ribs, forming a notch in each. A bone arrow point had struck the shoulder and was resting against the scapula. Among the bones of the right hand, an arrow point of antler was discovered, and there was a similar one near the left hand. Another antler point was lying in the sand just beneath the body and had, no doubt, dropped from it when the flesh wasted away. The most interesting wound of all was one where an antler-tipped arrow had ploughed through one side of the body and fully one-third of the point had passed through one of the ribs, making a hole, where it remained, as smoothly as if drilled.

The second body was also terribly injured. The left femur showed an elongated puncture near the lower end, probably made by an arrow point. Among the ribs was the tip of an antler point, and a yellow jasper one was among the ribs on the left side of the body. Three other points were among the bones.

The third skeleton was likewise an example of old-time bow play. There was an antler point among the ribs on the left side. The end of one of the fibulæ was shattered by a stone arrow point, and a second point had lodged between two ribs. Beneath the sternum was a flint point, and the right shoulder blade showed a fracture near the end, caused by a blow of some hand implement or an arrow. Near the base of the skull, the end of an antler arrow point was discovered, broken perhaps by its impact with the occiput. Two bone points were near the lower bones of the left leg. A second point was found upon search among the left ribs; under the vertebræ was the base of another antler point, and two broken points were found beneath the body.

The position in which several of the points were found certainly speaks well for the great force which propelled them. The long bows of the old Lenapé must indeed have been formidable weapons. Taking into consideration the number of arrows which must have been imbedded in the bodies of the warriors, it is perhaps probable that the majority of the projectiles were driven into the victims at close range after death. There are very many historic incidents of similar mutilation inflicted by Indians elsewhere in North America upon the corpses of their enemies. From the fact that the arrows were left sticking in the bodies when buried, it is perhaps possible that these skeletons were the remains, not of Staten Island Lenapé proper, but of some of their enemies. All of the stone points found in and among these bones were of the triangular so-called "war-point" type.

A site has been recorded on Bunker Hill, Huguenot, near Arbutus Lake, but this is an error. An arrow point or two have been found, but there are no traces of occupation.

16. *Huguenot.* A small shell-heap is located on the bluff overlooking the Bay, near Seguine's point. This is only a small shell-heap at a point where the Indians probably camped while fishing. A few tiny fragments of pottery and deer bones were found. A few small isolated heaps are near Prince's Bay.

17. *Arrochar.* On Richmond Avenue near Arrochar Station, there is a site apparently much older than many others; but still Lenapian in origin. There are probably more sites in this neighborhood, but none have been reported.

Grooved axes, arrow points, etc., with an occasional bit of pottery, are found and shell pits occur. From the appearance of the objects found, this is perhaps a very ancient camp site. "Oude Dorp," a Dutch town burned by the Indians during the historic period, was located near here; still no objects such as the Indians would have used at that date seem to have been discovered.

18. *New Brighton, Harbor Hill Golf-links.* A camp site and scattered relics have been reported on Harbor Hill Golf-links, a little above Castleton Avenue and near Richmond Turnpike.

19. *New Brighton, Silver Lake, etc.* There are camp sites at Silver Lake; one shell pit, with pottery, was opened by the writer. Scattered relics appeared along the Shore Road near St. George.

20. *New Brighton, Harbor Hill.* A camp site is located on Harbor Hill near Harbor Brook and Lafayette Avenue.

21. *New Brighton, Nannyberry Hill.* A camp site occurs near the junction of Bard Avenue and Clove Road, at the foot of Nannyberry Hill, just above Schoenian's pond. Most of these sites are fully described in the Proceedings of the Natural Science Association of Staten Island for January 10th, 1903.

22. *Richmond.* A large camp site is back of Richmond in a clearing in the woods near Ketchum's Mill Pond, on Simonson's Brook, where grooved axes and other relics have been found. It is near Richmond Creek and distant from all other sites. The ground is hard, with many boulders, as is the case at Silver Lake, and no shells whatever appear.

Up to date, no pottery has been found; but the writer has never had an opportunity to examine the site thoroughly, as it has never been plowed or bared of vegetation during his time. He has found a few objects, however, and formerly a number were obtained by others.

23. *Oakwood.* A shell-heap has been reported on the salt meadow near Lake's mill. A search by the writer has led to the discovery of a few shells, on the meadow towards Giffords, which are apparently aboriginal. No pottery or relics occur, but a few flint flakes are found. Apparently, this is a "clam-drying" place. We have been shown and have found a few arrow points in this vicinity, but they occurred on higher ground.

24. *Tompkinsville.* On Ward's Hill, near Cebra Avenue, many triangular so-called "war-points" have been found in a small area. Such an abundance of these war-points, so far from any known camp or village site, is remarkable.

Collections of Specimens.

The collections of Staten Island Indian remains now in existence are few in number. The largest of these, in order of importance, are given below:

1. The Skinner Collection, now in the Museum of the Staten Island Association of Arts and Sciences, illustrating almost the entire prehistoric life of the local tribes; about 1,500 specimens.

2. The Collection of the American Museum of Natural History, from the famous cemetery at Burial Ridge, Tottenville; several hundred specimens.

3. The Collection of the Staten Island Association of Arts and Sciences, made up of various donations; about 400 specimens.

4. The W. T. Davis Collection, mainly Tottenville surface material; about 200 specimens.

5. The Almar Decker Collection, from the Tottenville shell-heaps and cemetery.

6. The Wort Collection, mainly Rossville surface material.

7. The Max Bedell Collection, from surface at Richmond Valley and the Tottenville cemetery.

8. The Isaiah Merrill Collection, old surface material from Watchogue, perhaps not now in existence.

9. The Wainwright Collection, from the Tottenville Cemetery, now lost.

10. The Page Collection, from Richmond Valley, now lost.

11. There are a few Staten Island specimens in the New York State Museum at Albany.

12. The Charles Benedict Collection. Several choice objects from Rossville and Mariners' Harbor.

Most of these collections were examined in preparing the accompanying account.

Description of Specimens.

Stone Implements. Grooved axes occur on most of the sites. In almost every case, they are made of trap and other local stone. The following types occur,—

Class A, worked stone axes, pecked all over, sometimes polished, Plate IV:
 (1) groove encircling 3 sides, one side flat; Fig. 1.
 (2) ridged groove encircling 3 sides, one side flat; Fig. 2.
 (3) groove encircling 3 sides, one side flat, with longitudinal groove on flat side and on opposite side; Fig. 3.
 (4) groove encircling all sides; Figs. 4, 5, 6.
 (5) ridged groove encircling all sides; Fig. 7.

Class B, unworked stone axes, made of natural pebbles merely edged and grooved; Figs. 10, 11, 13, 14.

An axe of the first class, in the process of manufacture, blocked out, partially grooved, but discarded because of an accidental fracture which spoiled the tool is shown in Fig. 9.

The grooved adze (Fig. 15, Plate IV), a rare type hereabouts, is very like the grooved axe except that it is flat and ungrooved on one of the broad sides, favoring its hafting at right angles with the handle.

Grooved axes were hafted by the modern northern Cree near Hudson's Bay, in a handle split to receive the blade and bound above and below the head with withes, sinew or rawhide. In the case of those specimens having a flat edge, with or without a longitudinal groove, the edge was away from the user, and a wedge inserted there to hold the blade more securely.

A notched axe (Fig. 16, Plate IV) from Tottenville represents a rare type. It was doubtless hafted in the same manner as the grooved axe. The writer has seen but two specimens of this type from Staten Island. The grooved axe seems to have been the typical axe of the Algonkin of southeastern New York.

The celt (Fig. 8 and 17, Plate IV) is rare on the sites of the northern shore of the Island, but a number have been found in Tottenville and the vicinity. A specimen with a flaring blade (Fig. 18, Plate IV) comes from Watchogue and is the only specimen of this type recorded. From general information, it seems that celts were hafted in two ways: large specimens were set into and through the handle, smaller ones were set into it club fashion.

The rude hand chopper (Fig. 12, Plate IV) from Tottenville seems to have preceded or taken the place of the celt and grooved axe in some areas; but is, in this region, certainly a hastily-made makeshift for a misplaced axe. Choppers are rare throughout the Island, but a few have been found at Tottenville. They were certainly not of immense utility as cutting tools.

A single specimen of stone gouge (Fig. 13, Plate V) comes from Mariners' Harbor. It is the only one ever seen or reported to the writer. These are very common in the New England district and Long Island, but this locality seems to be out of their area. They were doubtless used with the adze in canoe, mortar and bowl making.

The grooved club or maul (Figs. 1 and 2, Plate V), from Richmond and Mariners' Harbor, seems rare. It may have served the purpose of a weapon at times; but from the battered appearance of those seen by the writer, probably drove in more tent-pegs than heads. A small, all wood, ball-headed war club seems to have been used by the historic Lenapé for the latter purpose up to modern times.

Hammerstones. A very common class of implement is the so-called pitted "hammerstone." This simple tool is abundant on most sites. It consists of a simple pebble, pitted on one or more sides, presumably for convenience in handling. The fact that about one-half the number of hammerstones found show no evidence whatever of battering, makes their use in these cases somewhat problematic. Fig. 4, Plate V, shows one, from Tottenville, of the ordinary type, pitted on two opposite sides. In some cases, only a single side is pitted; others show three or more pits. The writer has seen a seven-pitted specimen from Hackensack, New Jersey, a site probably inhabited by a people similar to those on the north shore of the Island. Larger stones of this same pitted type are popularly called anvils. Some hammerstones have no pits whatever, yet show long use and battering, as Fig. 3.

Rubbing or Polishing Stones. Two or three forms of rubbing or polishing stones, like Figs. 5 and 12, Plate V, have been found. The most simple and abundant are merely ordinary waterworn pebbles ground or granulated on one or more surfaces from friction caused by contact with other stones in grinding or polishing. Other specimens seem more specially shaped. Fig. 27, Plate VI, from Tottenville, is an example of a pebble bearing a number of grooves about its edges which have apparently been caused by rubbing. It is popularly supposed that such stones were used to reduce or rub bow strings to the proper size. Certainly the implement seems to have been used to rub cords upon. These objects are not common, and all that the writer has seen have come from the South Shore Raritan sites.

Knives, Drills and Scrapers. The semilunar knife is a very rare article.

A few fragments but no perfect specimens have been found. Fig. 20, Plate VII, from Mariners' Harbor, shows a semilunar knife in the process of manufacture. Figs. 16 and 17 show fragments of finished knives. Certainly the first specimen shows that not all such knives were objects of barter from the Eskimo as some have supposed.

The ordinary knife appears to have been flint, jasper, quartz or argillite, the usual stones possessing the proper conchoidal fracture hereabouts. They were of varied shapes, as in Figs. 1 to 15, Plate VII. Chipped crooked knives occur.

Stone drills (Figs. 11 to 25, Plate VI) are not common. Gorgets, pottery and the like were drilled with these; but banner stones usually show the marks of a drill leaving a core.

Scrapers are of two types; mere fragments of flint or other stone with an edge chipped on (Figs. 1, 2, 6 and 7, Plate VI), and stemmed scrapers (Figs. 4, 5, 9, 10). These were doubtless used, as the name implies, in scraping and fleshing skins, sharpening bone implements, etc. A very large type (Fig. 5, Plate VI), reminding one of the hafted ones used by western Indians in scraping large skins, comes from Mariners' Harbor and is the only one reported. Fig. 8, Plate VI, represents a serrated scraper, and Fig. 3 a scraper made from a broken arrowpoint.

Flint, when freshly quarried, is saturated with "quarry water," and easier to work. The aborigines realized this; and, in order to retain the requisite dampness, it was customary among them to bury blanked-out forms in the ground for future finishing. These hordes, or "caches" as they are sometimes called, are occasionally found. A horde of six large blanks was found at the Milliken site, a horde of thirty-two (?) pieces was plowed out at Watchogue years ago, and Mr. Wm. T. Davis found in the same vicinity a large cache of flint blocks not even blanked out. The writer found blank forms (perhaps once buried together, but scattered when discovered) at Old Place, and Mr. George H. Pepper found a number of yellow jasper blanks in a child's grave at Burial Ridge, Tottenville, in 1895. Figs. 18 to 22, Plate VII, are good examples of "cache blades."

Banner Stones. The class of articles, to which the highly unsatisfactory title of "Banner stones" has been applied, occur here in two types, grooved (Fig. 7, Plate VIII) and perforated (Figs. 8 to 11), the latter type being by far the more common on the Island. These seem, from the drill marks to be found within, as in Fig. 11 (Mariners' Harbor), to have been perforated by a hollow drill, making a core. Perhaps this drill was a reed used with sand.

Plummets. Fig. 28, Plate VI, from Watchogue, is an example of an implement commonly known as a "plummet," but which may equally well have been used as a sinker for a fishing line, or indeed for any one of half a dozen purposes. These implements are very common throughout the New England region but so far this example from Watchogue is the only specimen of the kind reported from Staten Island.

A Stone Mask. In the collections of the Staten Island Association of Arts and Sciences, there is a human head carved in stone (Plate IX) which was found near the Fingerboard Road, Grasmere. While this specimen is the only one of its kind from the Island, it is not unique for Lenapian territory, as there is at least one other specimen known, from Monmouth County, New Jersey (not very far from Staten Island), which is in the possession of the Smithsonian Institution, and is figured by Wilson with the Staten Island specimen.[1] C. C. Abbott[2] illustrates two gorgets of the pendant type with incised ornamentation, representing the human face, one from Hunterdon and the other from Burlington County, New Jersey. He mentions also a maskette of greenish steatite found in Monmouth County in a shell-heap. On page 394 of the same work, he illustrates and describes still another large stone "mask" found near Trenton. Mr. A. C. Parker, State Archæologist at the New York State Museum, Albany, states that carved stone heads have been found in the Mahikan territory along the Hudson.

That representations of the human face and figure have been and are of great esoteric significance to the Lenapé cannot be questioned. At the present day, wooden masks are still worn and used by Lenapé in medicinal and mystery ceremonies. These are usually painted longitudinally half red and half black, representing the warriors and women of the people respectively, and this is also true of some curious forked wooden drumsticks from the Canadian Lenapé seen by the writer. These sticks also had a head carved in bass relief upon them.

Early writers frequently mention "idol images" and posts carved with representations of the human form among the Delawares. The writer found rough raised human heads upon the rim of an otherwise typically Algonkin vessel in a shell pit on the Bowman's Brook site at Mariners' Harbor. Stone maskettes, although rare, occur among the modern Iroquois, carried as luck-charms to ward off evil, disease, etc.; but are made in exact imitation of the larger wooden dance masks.

Bone and Antler Tools. Considering the proximity and influence of the Mohawk Iroquois, who were such skilled workers in bone and antler, it is remarkable that so few objects of these materials have come to light. At Tottenville, in the famous "Burial Ridge," Mr. George H. Pepper found

---

[1] Wilson, Prehistoric Art, Plate 52, opposite page 481, Annual Report, Smithsonian Institution, 1896.

[2] Primitive Industry, pp. 390–391.

twenty-three arrow points in and among the bones of three skeletons. C. C. Willoughby, in his article on "Antler Pointed Arrows of the Southeastern Indians,"[1] gives figures of three of these. They are of three types: the first being merely an antler tip cut off, pointed and hollowed at the base for the reception of the shaft (Fig. 10, Plate x); whereas the second is identical with the first save for a single barb (Fig. 9). The third type (Fig. 8) has several barbs.

Antler prongs, a number of which were found together, broken off, perhaps for the purpose of being made into arrow points, were obtained at Mariners' Harbor in 1901. Fig. 6, Plate x, shows a fragment of an antler prong from which the tip has been cut by grooving and breaking, the common method hereabouts for cutting bone and antler. Complete sets, showing the entire process of antler arrow point making from the unused antler to the finished point, are in the Museum collections from Kentucky and Ohio.

In regard to the cutting and shaping of these antler points, the well-known Adirondack guide, Charlie Sabattis (one-half Abenaki) informed the writer in 1903 that his father and the other Abenaki in general, always boiled antler for a very long time before attempting to cut it, and that this boiling reduced the antler to such a consistency that while hot it "cut just like cheese." In 1904 William Blueskye (Gá-nos-ho, His-nether-parts-are-wet), a Seneca Indian of great intelligence, gave exactly the same information, and later in the same year the writer found in the middens and refuse pits of an Erie Indian village site, at Ripley, Chautauqua County, New York, long shavings of antler, and antler from which such shavings had been cut, which seemed to bear out this statement. Mr. M. R. Harrington, who has tried experimenting with the process, declares it impracticable; but perhaps he did not boil the antler enough.

Fig. 5, Plate x, is an example of an antler pin or awl with a carved head, from Bowman's Brook site, Mariners' Harbor. It is the only example which has so far come to light. Fig. 4, Plate x, is an antler cylinder from the same place which was probably used as a "pitching tool" or fabricator in the finishing of chipped stone objects by pressure. Fig. 16, Plate x, shows a bone implement from the same site which perhaps had this use also. Figs. 1–2 are cylindrical implements of antler from Tottenville and Mariners' Harbor, of problematical use. Fig. 11, Plate x, shows a large antler prong, hollowed at the base, perhaps for a handle. This specimen comes from a shell pit on South Avenue, Mariners' Harbor, near the Arlington Station. Similar objects, apparently used as lance, spear, or pike points, have been found on ancient sites of the Iroquois, Seneca and Erie of Western New York.

---

[1] American Anthropologist, N. S., Vol. III, p. 431.

Fig. 15, 17, 18 and 19, Plate x, show various types of bone awls. These are found sparingly, and excavation would probably bring more to light on most of the larger sites. Their scarcity is attributable to their perishability, as none are ever found on the surface. All those illustrated come from Mariners' Harbor, mainly from the Bowman's Brook site. While called "awls," these tools may have had various uses. From their abundance in fire and refuse pits on some Algonkin sites (notably at Shinnecock Hills, Long Island), it has been suggested that they may have been used as forks for handling hot food or removing it from the cooking pot when eating. The writer has found a similar instrument used as the striking pin in the cup and ball game among the Northern Cree of James Bay, Canada. Fig. 7, Plate x, a bone arrow point found with the antler and stone points noted above at Burial Ridge, Tottenville, is hollow, and probably the shaft was inserted. Fig. 14, Plate x, represents a bone scraper or flesher probably for removing hair or fat from skins. This specimen was excavated at Tottenville by Mr. Pepper. The writer has heard of no other examples.

Cups or vessels made of tortoise shell which is usually the carapace of the box tortoise, *Tranene carolina*, still common in Staten Island woods, are to be found on most sites. The inner ribs are removed by cutting and scraping as may be observed. Owing to the tendency for the shells of these tortoises to crack apart along the sutures, very few perfect specimens are found. Fig. 22, Plate x, is an unusually perfect example from the Burial Ridge at Tottenville. Perforated tortoise shells, or shells used as rattles, etc., seem never to have been reported from this region.

Fig. 34, Plate vi, is a fossil which has been kindly identified by Dr. Louis Hussakof, of the Department of Palaeontology, as a tooth of *Carcharodon rondeletii* (Müller and Henle), a living species of shark whose fossil remains are found in the Pliocene deposits of Italy, Sicily and England, and in the Miocene and Eocene beds of the Ashely River, South Carolina, in this country, from whence this specimen, found at Watchogue, probably came. A fossil shark tooth has been found by the writer at Shinnecock Hills, Long Island, in an Indian grave; and another notched and fashioned into an arrow point, from Central New York, has been published by Beauchamp. Evidently these objects were known to the aborigines and were perhaps brought by them from the Ashely River deposits. Another has been seen from a New Jersey Lenapé site near Trenton.

Pottery. While the modern Lenapé of Canada and elsewhere still use wooden bowls and spoons, splint and bark baskets, etc., for culinary purposes, and while we have records of such objects from the immediate vicinity of the region in question, nevertheless no such specimens have come down to us. Only the imperishable potsherds and fragments of stone vessels now remain.

While steatite fragments occur in Staten Island equally well distributed, they are rare, and naturally so, as there are no known steatite quarries nearer than Connecticut. The fragments found seem to be of the regular New England type of vessel, having knobs at the ends for handles. Such knobs seem to have been usual on the steatite vessels of this region.

The clay artifacts are exceedingly limited as to form, pottery vessels of four types and clay pipes of several varieties being the only articles found. The typical pottery vessel of the local Lenapé was wide mouthed, with sides narrowing gradually to the pointed base, in some cases giving the impression of an elongated cone. In size these jars ranged from those capable of holding about a quart to several gallons. The pointed base precluded the possibility of standing alone unless stuck up in the sand or propped up with stones. These vessels were ornamented with incised lines on the outside swell of the rim, and rarely a little way down the inside.

A second type of typical Algonkin vessel possessed a more rounded bottom, with sides somewhat swollen about the middle, and neck slightly constricted before reaching the mouth which flared a little though never being quite as broad as the middle. Sometimes the lip or rim was turned a little outward. These vessels were almost invariably decorated with stamp or roulette. The decoration frequently extended for a little way about the inside of the mouth, and on the outside as far down as the central bulge.

A third type is an intermediate mixed form. It is a vessel showing modified Iroquoian influence. The characteristics of this form are a rounded bottom, constricted neck, and thin and narrow collar. This form like the above is always decorated by stamp or roulette and in the same manner, it is fairly common, usually on sites where the typical Iroquoian form is found.

The fourth and last form found is the typical Iroquois vessel of the Mohawk valley and elsewhere. It is well known that the Mohawk, or more properly Kanienga, tribe of the Five Nations subjugated all the local Algonkin of this region for many miles, and there are deeds on record of sales by them of parcels of Staten Island land to the whites. Certainly their influence was very great, and it is not surprising that the æsthetic value of their bold and graceful pottery should impress itself upon their subjects.

The Iroquoian vessels found here possess a round bottom, constricted and rather narrow neck, and thick and heavy collar, which at intervals bears curious humps. The striking angles and square mouths so characteristic of true Iroquois pottery are absent, however. Decoration is usually, but not always, by incised lines, and the lower edge of the collar is invariably notched. This has been called "the hallmark of Mohawk pottery." In some instances a wash or sizing of finer, lighter clay has been used. This seems never to have been used on the true Algonkin pottery; at least, the writer has never observed it. One specimen has the collar stamped by the impression of the fluted edge of a scallop shell.

One other curious form of Iroquois influence has been noted. Representations of the human face, not infrequent in Western New York, have never to the writer's knowledge been found heretofore on Lenapé clay work, pipes or vessels; but fragments of a single specimen of a typical Algonkin pointed based vessel, decorated with incised lines and rude raised human faces, was found a few years since by the writer at the Bowman's Brook site, Mariners' Harbor, where the more usual Iroquois forms occur with the typical Algonkin type. A single fragment of a vessel showing a knob or handle has been found at Watchogue.

From fragments found it is patent that these vessels were usually built by the coil process, but the junctures were carefully smoothed over with a pebble or shell and rarely a wash or sizing of a lighter clay was given to conceal the coils and give a brighter appearance to the pot. The coil work was under no circumstances allowed to show in a finished vessel, as in some specimens from the southwest. Clay was tempered with burnt and ground granite or other rock, or shell calcined and ground, probably with a stone mortar and pestle or muller. On rare occasions, cut grass or bark, or perhaps some other substance, was used for tempering; at least, in some specimens found, the subsequent firing has caused the tempering material to entirely disappear, leaving marks and cavities much like those to be found in some pottery from the south, which was fibre tempered.

It is impossible to learn how the coiling process was begun in moulding vessels in this region, nor the exact methods of firing; probably the vessel was first built up, smoothed over, and allowed to dry. It was then, in the case of typical Algonkin vessels of this vicinity, decorated almost, if not always, by combinations of incised lines and dots, and never by a stamp or roulette nor allowed to remain plain. Professor W. H. Holmes gives a description of this operation collected by James Mooney among the Catawba in North Carolina,[1] as follows: —

"After the vessel had dried until the afternoon of the third day, in the sun, as far as possible, the surface was again rubbed inside and out with the polishing stone. This work occupied half an hour. After this the vase was placed before the fire where not exposed to drafts and dried or baked for half an hour.— It was then ready for firing which was conducted indoors. Oak bark was used for firing; Sally Wahuhu stated that poplar bark gave superior color and finish. Bark was preferred to wood, because it was more easily broken up and was more convenient. A heap of bark

---

[1] 20th Annual Report, Bureau of American Ethnology, p. 54.

was laid on a bed of living coals; the vessel was filled with broken bark and inverted over the pile of ignited bark and then completely covered with the same fuel. The exterior bark was fired and the supply renewed for an hour, when the red-hot vessel was taken out. It was kept away from the drafts during the burning and the first part of the cooling to prevent cracking. It was allowed to cool near the fire until the red heat had disappeared, when it was removed to the open air. On examination it was found that the inside had been colored a deep, glistening black by the burning; but the exterior, save in spots where the bark had been dense and the fire much smothered, was of grayish and reddish tints."

Staten Island pottery is often as light colored within as without. Some specimens have been fired too much, others too little; in both cases, the result is a very crumbly and brittle ware. When a vessel was cracked or broken in a simple manner, parallel holes were drilled on either side of the fracture, and the vessel was "laced" together with sinew, thongs or cord, and, though no longer serviceable to hold liquids, was at least good enough for the storage of corn, etc. Figs. 26, A and B, Plate VI, show pottery fragments drilled for this purpose.

Foods were boiled in the pointed vessels probably in two ways: the first consisted in propping the vessel up in the middle of the fire, an easy matter when the fire was built in a pit, and the second method was by dropping heated stones into the water until it boiled. The Lenapé women were sometimes slovenly housekeepers, for often fragments of pottery may yet be found bearing the traces of soot and grease on their sides that were not scrubbed off in Indian days.

Pottery vessels are never found buried with skeletons here, as elsewhere. They are, however, rarely found in graves, not near the skeleton but at some distance from it, and always broken; sometimes stones lie on and among the sherds as though cast upon the pot to break it. The frequent occurrence of charcoal, deer-bones, mollusk shells, etc., nearby would suggest a "Feast of the Dead" and a subsequent destruction of the vessels used, rather than an offering to the spirit of the departed.

Pipes. The clay pipes of the local Lenapé were abundant and throughout typically Algonkin in form and decoration. Three types have come to our notice. The first type is not at all common, and is merely a perfectly straight, plain or nearly plain pipe; the stem is tubular and rather short, expanding at one end to form the bowl. Fig. 7, Plate IX, from Mariners' Harbor, shows a plain straight clay pipe of this type. Fig. 1 is a fragment showing the entire stem and part of the bowl of a very short rude pipe of this class from Rossville. The second type is about the same size, but the bowl bends off from the stem at a slight angle or curve, as in Fig. 8 from Mariners' Harbor. This type is often highly ornamented, and is the most abundant form. The third and last type noted has a broad, flat, rather short stem, a cross section of which resembles a long-sided rectangle with bulging sides, the bowl is set on this at a slight angle, and is usually of greater capacity than in the other types, as in Fig. 13 from Tottenville. Pipes of this class are not uncommon.

Staten Island clay pipes are rarely if ever tempered; they seem, however, to be made of finer clay than the average pottery, and are more often sized or washed with a light clay paste. The ornamentation is usually done by incision and the designs resemble those of the pottery vessels; but there is more originality. While the human face or form never appears as in the Iroquois country, yet specimens have been found whose ornamentation suggested conventionalized life forms, and one or two fragments of stems appear not unlike the famous Iroquois snake pipes in which a snake is coiled about the stem and bowl. However, on no occasion has enough of one of these pipes been found to show whether or not this was the case. The perforation in the stem was probably secured by moulding the clay around a twig or reed which subsequently disappeared in firing. Apparently twists of grass were never used for this purpose as among the Iroquois.

A single specimen of a pipe stem showing secondary use as a bead has been found at Watchogue. In this case the broken ends were carefully ground or smoothed off. Several incised designs representing a man, a fish, etc., appear to have been scratched on at a later date, perhaps by the finder, though they may be aboriginal. (Fig. 10, Plate IX.)

Stone pipes were invariably made of steatite of various colors. Two types occur. The most abundant of the two (and both are rare) is the typical monitor type, as in Fig. 6, Plate IX. A number of these have been found at Tottenville; one, which had been broken, was mended by boring and lashing, as in the case of the pottery vessels. One specimen in the collection of Mr. Almar Decker of Tottenville, is of unusual size and has a tiny stem or mouth piece fashioned at one end. The second class is what McGuire calls the trumpet pipe.[1] Only one specimen of this form has been recorded. It was found in an Indian grave in the Burial Ridge, at Tottenville by Mr. Max Bedell of Pleasant Plains.

No stone pipes have been recorded from any of the sites on the north shore of the Island, with the exception of a broken red catlinite pipe of typical rectangular western style, now in the collection of the Staten Island Association of Arts and Sciences. It is undoubtedly a case of mistaken locality, as it belongs to a period far later than any of the other stone pipes from this locality, and is of a type and material which are never found in this region.

---

[1] McGuire, Annual Report, Smithsonian Institution, 1897, p. 494.

The curiously repeated references by early contemporaries to pipes of copper used by local aborigines are doubtless erroneous, as there is no archæologic evidence of this fact. Perhaps the red or yellow clay of which some pipes were made misled the casual observer.

Copper. Metal was probably never worked by the Staten Island Lenapé. In the grave of a child opened by Mr. George H. Pepper at Burial Ridge, Tottenville, in 1895, copper stains were found about the skull and upper part of the skeleton. Some *olivella* shell beads were also discolored in the same way, the inference being that beads of native copper had been used as a necklace. This is the only record of native copper for this region, and the beads were probably exotic in origin. A very few recent metallic objects are later described under the next head.

Trade Articles. Objects of European manufacture are surprisingly rare. Old deeds and records make very frequent mention of such things, but they seem to have disappeared as almost everything now found belongs to the prehistoric period. Some of the lists of objects received by the Indians from the Dutch and English in exchange for land grants will serve to show the kind of material to be expected on Staten Island Lenapé sites. The Island was sold a number of times by the Indians to the Dutch, and at least once to the English. In the Indian deed of Staten Island to the Dutch, dated July 10th, 1657,[1] the following goods are to be imported from Holland for the Indians, many of whom may not have lived upon Staten Island proper although belonging to the tribes inhabiting it: — 10 boxes of shirts; 30 pairs of (ferousse) socks; 10 muskets; 10 bars of lead; 10 ells of red (dousyns) cloth; 2 pieces of duffel; 30 kettles; 50 axes, large and small; 30 pounds of powder; some awls; 25 adzes; some knives. Again, in the deed to the English Governor Francis Lovelace, in 1675, we find: — 400 fathoms of wampum; 30 Match coats; 30 Flints; 20 Guns; a firkin of powder; 60 bars of lead; 30 Hose; 50 knives.

As stated before, however, few or none of these articles are now extant. A brass arrow point (Fig. 29, Plate VI) comes from Watchogue; it is long and narrow, and perforated near the centre. Another (Fig. 30, Plate VI) is of a different type, and was found at Old Place. Perhaps both specimens may have been made from brass trade kettles. Fig. 23 represents a small fragment of brass or copper found in a shell pit at Old Place. It is perforated for suspension. Fig. 31 represents a pewter trade ring from Old Place. Several glass beads have been found, and Mr. Isaac Wort, Sr., of Rossville, says that, when he was a boy, trade axes, or tomahawks, were numerous near his home in the sandy fields. Glass beads were also abun-

---

[1] E. B. O'Callaghan, Documents Relating to the Colonial History of the State of New York, Vol. XIV, p. 393.

dant. A single specimen from this vicinity, was noted by the writer. On Mr. Wort's farm, several small, apparently aboriginal shell-heaps and pits yielded Indian pottery, flint chips, a bone awl, fragments of china and split and cracked cow and sheep bones. As the last living Staten Island Indians dwelt in this vicinity, no doubt some of their historic settlements were hereabouts. Not far from here the writer has picked up many brass thimbles (for example, Fig. 33, Plate VI), on an Indian site; these are abundant on early historic Indian sites in Western New York.

Clay pipes stamped "R. Tippet" occur on several sites; a fragment of a pewter kettle has been found. One or two iron arrow points have been reported, and Captain Wainwright reports having found a portion of a Dutch pottery vessel in an Indian grave at Burial Ridge, Tottenville. Short as it is, this is an almost complete list of the trade articles now in existence.

History and Ethnography of Staten Island.

The aboriginal inhabitants of Staten Island at the time of its discovery seem to have belonged to the Lenni Lenapé, or Delaware Indians. There is apparently no reason why we should not accept as genuine the famous "Walum Olum," or Red Score,[1] of the Lenapé from which we derive the Delaware migration legend given here in abstract.

At some ancient mythical period, the first Lenapé lived on tidewater in the far Northeast, perhaps in Labrador. Thence they journeyed southwest to a broad body of water, containing many islands and full of fish, possibly the St. Lawrence at the Thousand Islands. Crossing this, they stayed for some time in the forest lands of New York at war with the Snake people and the Talega, who were sedentary agricultural people living to the southeast in Ohio and Indiana. The Snake people they expelled, but the Talega continued to hold the Upper Ohio River and its branches.

Wishing to join their kindred in the east, the New England Algonkin, the Lenapé united with the Talamatan (Huron) to drive out the Talega, perhaps the Cherokee or Tsalaki. They did not succeed in this until the historic period; but they managed to reach the Delaware Valley, though they never gave up their claims to the western country.

During the sixteenth century the Iroquoian Conestoga, or Susquehannock, erupted into the Susquehanna Valley, thus forming a barrier between the eastern and western Algonkin, and eventually forcing many Lenapé bands across to the east bank of the Delaware, where they remained until well within the historic period.

---

[1] D. G. Brinton, The Lenâpé and Their Legends, p. 169.

The Lenni Lenapé or Delaware Indians were divided into three great bands and were located, when first known by the whites, in what are now the States of New York, New Jersey, Pennsylvania and Delaware.

The most northerly of the great Lenni Lenapé divisions, the Minci, or Muncey ("mountaineers," Brinton), held the mountains near the headwaters of the Delaware above the Forks at the junction of the Lehigh. They had an important rendezvous at Minisink Plains above the Water Gap, and another on the east branch of the Delaware ("Namaes Sipu, Fish River," Brinton). Their hunting grounds covered territory in the three colonies of Pennsylvania, New Jersey and New York. Bands of this division held the western bank of the Hudson River for some distance.[1]

Aside from the three great divisions geographically considered, there were numerous local bands usually called after the localities in which they resided, and these divisions had nothing whatever to do with the clans and great divisions or sub-tribes. Hrdlička,[2] describes and locates, on a map of his making, the Lenapé bands of the vicinity of Trenton, New Jersey, according to John Smith, De Laet, Evelyn, N. J. Vischer and N. Vischer, Campanius, Acrelius and Proud; these agreeing in the main with locations of bands placed on the accompanying map by the author. Some of Hrdlička's names are not given here, however, as, according to Brinton, who commented upon the original sources, they are unimportant and sometimes doubtful. Hrdlička's map also splits the bands into finer divisions than is here necessary. Brinton, quoting from Evelyn, Heckewelder and Rafinesque, mentions some others which are not given in the following list by Ruttenber (page 89 *et seq.*) of the local bands from north to east.

Muncey.

1. Esopus, west bank of Hudson River near Kingston.
2. Waoranoecks, east bank of Hudson River, opposite the Esopus.
3. Pachami, east bank of Hudson River, south of the Waoranoecks.
4. Wappingers, both banks of Hudson River, south of the Pachami.
5. Mamekotings, Mamakating Valley, west of Shawangunk Mountains.
6. Wawarsinks, these with the Katskills and Mamekotings have no history separate from the Esopus of whom they were neighbors.
7. Minnisinks, west of the Esopus and inhabiting the headwaters of the Delaware.
8. Waranwankongs, west bank of Hudson River, opposite the Wappingers.

---

[1] D. G. Brinton, The Lenâpé and Their Legends, p. 37.
[2] A. Hrdlička, The Crania of Trenton, Bulletin, American Museum of Natural History, Vol. XVI, Article III, pp. 34–40.

UNAMI.

9. Haverstraws, west bank of Hudson, south of the Waranawankongs, and in the locality now known as Haverstraw.
10. Tappans, west bank of the Hudson, from Hackensack River north. They claimed at one time a part of Staten Island.
11. Aquackanonks, from the vicinity of Paterson, N. J., westward.
12. Hackensacks, Valleys of the Passaic and Hackensack Rivers, south to the northern shore of Staten Island.
13. Raritans or Assanhicans, from Trenton, N. J., up the Delaware and Raritan River Valleys to the southern end of Staten Island.
14. Navesincks, Highlands south of Sandy Hook, N. J.
15. Assiscuncks, vicinity of Assiscunck Creek above Burlington, N. J.
16. Rancocas, Rancocas Creek, just south of the Assiscuncks.
17. Okahoki, opposite the Rancocas, on the west bank of the Delaware.
18. Shackamaxon, west bank of the Delaware, near Philadelphia and northward.

UNALACTHTIGO.

19. Chikelacki, vicinity of Wilmington, Delaware.
20. Narraticons, near Jersey shore of the Delaware River, opposite the Chikelacki.
21. Manteses, south of the Narraticons and north of the Kechemeches.
22. Eromiex, at Pensaukin Creek.
23. Kechemeches, Cape May, New Jersey, and above.
24. Sikonesses, or Seconesses, at Cohanses Creek.
25. Axion, at Burlington.

Besides the bands here given and located on the accompanying map, we have record of the following who are not located, either because of insufficient information as to locality, or from lack of importance.

MUNCEY.

Neshamini.
Passayouk (Passaic — ?).
Calcefar,
Asomoclus,
Mosilian,

Nanttunexts.
Hickory Indians (?).

These names are very corrupt, according to Brinton.[1]

---
[1] D. G. Brinton, The Lenâpé and Their Legends, p. 41.

UNCLASSIFIED.

Wapings, Opings or Pomptons (synonymous with Aquakanonks — ?).

On the map, the location of these bands and the great divisions of the Lenapé, at the time when they were first known to the Whites, is given as nearly as is now possible, with special reference to the Unami Lenapé of Staten Island. There are, doubtless, many mistakes, and it should be remembered that the Lenapé were soon displaced by the Whites, especially along the coast, and by the Iroquois; so that their territory during later colonial times was much farther west. As the Whites still advanced, they were driven first from the Susquehanna to the Ohio; then into Canada on the one hand, and south and west into Kansas and the Indian Territory on the other. Most of the Lenapé now remaining are either in Canada or Indian Territory.

Bands of the Lenapé are here and again located and plotted on old maps by contemporary writers; but the better and more complete lists of the various divisions have been compiled from these sources by Ruttenber and Brinton. Hrdlicka's map, as has been stated, is too involved, and covers only a small part of the territory under consideration.

The old papers and documents which have been available show that Staten Island at one time was held by at least two local bands of the Unami Delaware, the Raritans on the southern, and Hackensacks probably on the northern shore, while a third band, the Tappans, had at least some claim upon it. Ruttenber says, "The Raritans occupied the valley and river which still bears their name. They were first called Sanhikans, or Fire Workers. They were divided, it is said, in two sachemdoms and about twenty chieftaincies. From their title deeds it would appear that the two sachems were Appamauskoch and Mattano or Mattenon. Their territory on the Hudson included the valley of the Raritan, and from thence to the sea,"[1] which included Staten Island.

In O'Callaghan, we find that: — "The district inhabited by a nation called Raritangs, is situated on a fresh water river, that flows through the centre of the low lands which the Indians cultivate. This vacant territory lies between two high mountains, far distant the one from the other. This district was abandoned by the natives for two reasons; the first and principal is, that finding themselves unable to resist the southern Indians, they migrated further inland; the second, because this country was flooded every spring."[2]

---

[1] Ruttenber, Indian Tribes of Hudson's River, p. 90.
[2] O'Callaghan, Vol. IV, p. 29.

References to the Raritans as owners and inhabitants of Staten Island are frequent, but the presence of the Hackensacks and Tappans has been entirely ignored by local historians. Ruttenber says "Staten Island, by the Indians called Eghquaons, appears to have been owned in partnership by the Raritans, Tappans and Hackensacks," [1] and in a deed to Van der Capellen, dated July 10, 1659, the name of a sachem of the Tappans, "Taghkospemo," appears.

In a letter from Governor Lovelace, dated February 24, 1665, we find an account of a visit made by him to "Perewyn lately made Chief of Hackensack, Tappan and Staten Island, and states that they reviewed and acknowledged the peace between them and the Maquas and Senecas, the which they say they are resolved to keep inviolate." [2]

Little seems to be known about the Indians during the period between the writings of Dankers and Sluyter and 1640. It is probable that they were at first friendly with the Dutch, then tolerant, and finally, as will be shown, hostile. The first recorded case of hostility was occasioned as follows: —

In the spring of 1640, some servants of the Dutch West India Company, while passing Staten Island on their way to the South River settlements, landed long enough to steal a sloop and make way with some hogs. The Raritan Indians, though wholly ignorant of the theft, were promptly accused of it. The hot-headed Kieft, then Governor of New Amsterdam, showed his approval of the charge by sending out his Secretary Van Tienhoven and seventy men, with instructions to invade the Indian cantons on Staten Island, to capture as many savages as possible, and to burn and destroy all that fell in their way. When the party arrived at their destination, they became insubordinate and vowed they would have the blood of every Indian taken. Van Tienhoven, who seems to have been a liberal and humane man, found all his arguments of no avail and finally in despair left the party. The blood-thirsty soldiers, relieved of all restraint, proceeded and soon came upon the unsuspecting savages. The fight was probably sharp and severe, the Indians apparently resisting the enemy with all their power. During the action, several savages were killed, and a brother of the local chief was taken prisoner by one Govert Lockermans. The troops then fired the village, and cut the standing corn. They then slew their prisoners (though De Vries says [3] he was grievously maltreated, but not killed), and retreated in triumph, leaving dead on the ground a comrade named Ross, who had been supercargo of the ship "Neptune."

The Raritans were not slow to avenge the wrong done to them. The

---

[1] Ruttenber, p. 91.
[2] Ruttenber, p. 00.
[3] De Vries, Journal, p. 143.

De Vries plantation on Staten Island went up in smoke, although the owner had always been a friend to the Indians. Governor Kieft, fuming in impotent fury, promptly offered a bounty of ten fathoms of wampum for every Raritan scalp brought in, and twenty fathoms more for the head of every Indian engaged in the Staten Island troubles. He built also a small fort near the present Fort Wadsworth. Matters then lapsed into a state of inactivity, but the Dutch complained that the Indians grew daily more and more insolent.

About this time the Hackensack Indians, stirred up by Miantenimo, Sachem of Sloops of Narragansett Bay,[1] killed an Englishman, and a few days later shot a Dutchman in Myndert Meyndertz's colony near Newark Bay, where the Hollander had settled contrary to the wishes of the Indians. Director Kieft demanded the murderers from the head men who were, however, unable to produce them, for the guilty wretches had fled elsewhere. To show their good will, the Sachems offered to indemnify the relatives of the dead men by liberal presents of wampum; but Kieft desired blood vengeance. De Vries, who was an able and humane man, pleaded in behalf of the Indians, but the Director was inexorable.

As there appeared to be no immediate way for the genial Director to satiate his desire for revenge, he was obliged to bide his time. It came only too soon. The Mahicans residing below Fort Orange (not the Mohawks, as Fiske and so many others have supposed) suddenly fell upon the Indians dwelling about the mouth of the Hudson. The terrified unfortunates fled through the deep snow to the Dutch stronghold at Manhattan. As they had succored the Whites in times gone by, they expected the Whites to succor them.

Apparently the Dutch received them well, at first. For about two weeks the fugitives were cared for and then they returned to their homes; but scarcely had the Indians done so, when another raid was made upon them and, rememberng their former kind treatment, they fled once more to New Amsterdam. The fugitives, mainly Hackensacks, formed two divisions, one of which camped at Pavonia, while the other crossed over to Manhattan Island and occupied the fields at Corlear's Hook on East River, near the present Grand Street Ferry.

Some of the "twelve men" in Kieft's Cabinet were now inspired with a truly magnificent scheme for vengeance. They went to the Director and requested him to grant them permission to attack the Hackensacks at night while they rested unsuspectingly under his protection. Kieft desired them to put their request on paper. When this was done, he granted their request, despite the passionate protests of De Vries.

---

[1] O'Callaghan, Vol. I, p. 183.

At midnight, February 25th, 1643, Sergeant Rodolf suddenly appeared with a band of soldiers amid the lodges at Pavonia. The flashes and reports of guns, the yelping of warriors, the shrieks of women and children, and the glare of burning lodges made an Inferno of the spot. Meanwhile one Adriensen attacked the hapless wretches at Corlear's Hook. The warriors were ill-armed and unprepared. The annals of this night are bloody beyond description. No band of Indians ever perpetrated more ferocious atrocities upon their enemies than these "civilized" Dutchmen. It would be sickening to repeat here the diabolical tortures inflicted upon women, children and wounded who fell into their hands. Suffice it to say that eighty Indians were murdered at Pavonia, forty more at Corlear's Hook, and many prisoners were taken. The Indians unfortunately succeeded in killing but few of their assailants. It is related that a man and woman who came to Pavonia in order to plunder the dead next morning, were shot by the survivors.[1]

Now, indeed, the Indians were aroused. On every hand, tribes took the warpath against the Dutch, the Raritans and Hackensacks having prominent parts. The farms on Pavonia and Long Island were almost entirely destroyed. An old chronicle says, "Staten Island, where Cornelius Melyn settled, [1643] is unattacked as yet, but stands hourly expecting an assault."[2]

In 1644, Joachim Pietersen Kuyter with forty burghers, thirty-five Englishmen under Lieutenant Baxter, and several soldiers from the Fort, under Sergeant Pieter Cock, all under the command of Councillor La Montagne, attempted an expedition against the Staten Island Indians. The little army embarked after nightfall, and landed on the Island at a late hour. As day dawned, they emerged upon a clearing in which were huddled the thatched lodges of the Indians; but, in some mysterious way, knowledge of the approaching foe had preceded them, and the place was deserted. The troops burned the village and withdrew, taking with them about five or six hundred skepels of corn, a skepel equalling about three pecks. The war was finally ended by the destruction of about seven hundred Indians at or near Greenwich, Conn., by a force under Capt. John Underhill, an Englishman of Pequot war fame. Thus, a wilderness having been made, it was called peace.

In early September, 1655, a Dutchman named Henry Van Dyck, ex-Schout-fiscal of New Netherland, who lived on the west side of Broadway, not far above Bowling Green, shot and killed an Indian woman who was helping herself to peaches. No notice of this murder was taken by the

---

[1] O'Callaghan, Vol. I, p. 184.
[2] O'Callaghan, Vol. I, p. 190.

white authorities, and the Indians decided to take the matter into their own hands. On the 15th of September, early in the morning, nearly two thousand warriors from Hackensack, Tappan and Stamford suddenly appeared on the streets of New Amsterdam. Consternation seized the Whites; but the Indians at first committed no personal violence, although they burst into various houses on a pretended search for their hereditary enemies, the Mohawks, and destroyed a great deal of property.

The City Fathers managed to persuade some of the head men to enter the Fort where they tried to treat with them. At last, it was arranged that the Indians should leave the city, and forthwith they withdrew to Governor's Island; but they returned with the nightfall. A party of warriors appeared before Van Dyck's door, and, when he appeared, he was shot through the heart with an arrow. A neighbor, Paulus Linderstien Van der Grist, was tomahawked on coming to his aid. The swift arrival of white men, armed with guns, forced the Indians to withdraw to the mainland, where they fell upon and destroyed Hoboken, Pavonia, and finally Van der Capellen's settlement on Staten Island. In the short space of three days, one hundred people were killed, one hundred and fifty taken prisoners, and vast quantities of livestock, property and grain were destroyed.

This loss fell heavily on Staten Island, where, according to Van der Capellen, fifteen people were killed and twelve hundred skepels of grain destroyed, to say nothing of cattle and personal property lost. Governor Stuyvesant succeeded in ransoming most of the prisoners and after a time the country was secure again. This outbreak, generally known as the "Peach War," was the last notable struggle in which the Staten Island Indians took part.

In 1675 Governor Lovelace in behalf of the English government bought the Island for the last time from the Indians. The original deed is in existence. Its preamble states that it was made between "Francis Lovelace, Governor General under James, Duke of York and Albany, and the Indians Aquepo, Warrines, Minqua, Sachemack, Permantowes, Qurvequeen, Wewareca, Oneck and Mataris, on behalf of theirselves, as the true owners and lawful Indians, proprietors of Staten Island."[1] Conveyance was executed by the affixing of the hands and seals of all parties and attesting witnesses.

The Indians had the privilege of remaining on the Island until the following May, when they were to surrender it to such persons as the Governor saw fit to receive it.

On the first of May, Thomas Lovelace and Matthias Nicoll paid to the

---

[1] R. M. Bayles, History of Richmond County, p. 78.

Indians: — 400 fathoms of Wampum; a Firkin of Powder; 30 Match boats; 60 Bars of Lead; 30 Flints; 30 Axes; 30 Kettles; 30 Hoes; 20 Guns; 50 Knives.

It was further covenanted that the Sachems or their deputies should appear once a year to ratify this sale. As several young Indians were not present at the sale, the deed was shown to them for their approval, and they witnessed it. Their names, according to the ancient orthography are Pewowahone, a boy about five years old; Pokoques, a girl about eight years old; Shirjuirneho, a girl about twelve years old; Kanarekante, a girl about twelve years old; Mahquadus, a young man about fifteen years old; and Ashehanewes, a young man about twenty years old.

After this sale, most of the Staten Island Indians withdrew to the mainland, and encamped, according to local tradition, about South River, a branch of the Raritan. It is said, while perfectly friendly with their kindred who had always lived there, they never encamped with them; but always pitched their lodges, though not far distant, on the other side of the river from the Raritans proper. This may, perhaps, have been on account of some clan custom. As the years passed, they with their neighbors withdrew to the Kittatinny Mountains, later joining the Stockbridges in New York. Thence they removed to Green Bay, Wisconsin, where perhaps some survivors may still be found among the Oneida and Stockbridge.

A few Indians lived on the Island for many years after the departure of the main body. The best known of these people were an old couple called Sam and Hannah, and their daughter Nance. They lived on the Seaman farm at Fresh Kill Road, and gained a precarious existence by basket-making, drinking up most of their earnings. Hannah disappeared one day, and it was usually supposed that she was killed during a drunken brawl with her husband. When the old man died, the daughter vanished and is generally thought to have left the Island.

There were other Indians on the Island who survived for many years, and at the time of this writing we are credibly informed that some people by the name of Story, living near Rossville, or Kreischerville, are at least one-quarter part Indian blood. The story runs that an old Indian named Captain Jack had seven daughters all of whom married white men, and that these people are the descendants of his daughters. At Bogardus Corners, several negroes now living (1907) claim to have Indian blood. Homer H. Harris is said to be the son of a half-Indian father and a mulatto woman. The last nearly-full blood, and old man, died in 1906. He lived near Gifford's on the shore and wore long hair. Wooden mortars and pestles were used to grind corn, up to within ten years of the present writing, by negroes at Bogardus Corners.

Before closing this historical summary, the writer would like to insert part of a deed of Staten Island to Michael Pauw (August, 1630) for, although chronologically out of place, it is of interest as preserving several more of the old Staten Island Indian names: —

"We the Director and Council of New Netherland residing on the Island of Manhatas under the jurisdiction of their High Mightinesses the Lords States General of the United Netherlands and the General Incorporated West India Company at their Chambers at Amsterdam Witness and declare by these presents that on this day the date underwritten came and appeared before us in their own proper persons Krahorat, Tamckass, Tolemakurmama, Wieromies, Lierarewach, Lachweuoen, Wissepoack, Laheinsios (a boy), Inhabitants owners and heirs of the land by us called Staten Island on the West shore of Hamels Hooftden [hills] and declared that for and in consideration of certain parcels of goods which respectively before passing of these presents acknowledge to have received into their hands, etc. —
Done at Fort Amsterdam aforesaid on this 10th day of August, 1630." [1]

Evidently the Island was overrun by the Mohawk Iroquois from time to time, both in the prehistoric period (as shown by their influence on local pottery, etc.) and in the later historic times. In the County Clerk's office at Richmond, there is recorded in Liber B, a deed dated February 10th, 1698–9, in which we find reference to a "Certain Tract or Parcel of Land Lying and being at Sagoddiochguisatt, which by deed of gift has been granted unto the said John Mangilson by the Maquase Indians in the year 1681–2 the said Land Running from the marked tree whereon ye name of the sd John Mangilson Stands and also the mark of the Maquase Indians unto the Creek that Lyeth Westward the line of the sd Land Running into the woods direct North upon a straight Line, Together with all houses, Barnes, Stables, orchards, fencings, Feedings....." [2]

CULTURAL RECONSTRUCTION.

Since a résumé of the preceding chapters will make it clear that, with few exceptions, the objects found on Staten Island belong to one culture and that the historical data enables us to identify the known inhabitants as a part of the Lenapé, the writer feels justified in attempting a partial reconstruction of the aboriginal culture practised by the Staten Island Indian. To be specific, he has drawn upon two sources of data: first, the available writings of contemporary Dutch and English; second, the archæology of the island as presented in local collections, both private and public, as well as from personal field experience. Naturally, this is far from satisfactory; but by

---

[1] Manual of the Corporation of the City of New York, 1869, p. 880.
[2] Liber B, op. cit., p. 322.

combining these various sources, enough has been obtained to give a fair exposition of several aspects of their culture.

Personal Appearance and Costume. In the Journal of David Pieterz De Vries (1665), occurs the following description of Algonkin Indians in the vicinity of Fort Amsterdam: —

"The Indians about here are tolerably stout, have black hair, with a long lock, which they let hang on one side of the head. The hair is shorn at the top like a cock's comb,* * * * Some of the women are very well featured, having long countenances. Their hair hangs loose from their head; They are very foul and dirty."[1]

In regard to shaving the head and roaching the hair, Wickham Cuffee, an aged Shinnecock Indian, still living in 1902 on the Shinnecock Reservation, Shinnecock Hills, Long Island, New York informed the writer that, prior to the advent of the whites with their metallic tools, the hair was burned or singed off the head by means of hot stones. He stated that hot stones were actually rubbed on the head which was doubtless a lapse of memory or an error. No doubt they were merely used to singe the hair and not brought into absolute contact with the head. Catlin[2] states that among Osage, Pawnee, Sac, Fox and Ioway, the custom of head shaving occurred, and among no others that he knew of. On the following page, he adds: —

"I found these people cutting off the hair with small scissors, which they purchase of the Fur Traders; and they told me that previous to getting scissors, they cut it away with their knives; and before they got knives, they were in the habit of burning it off with red hot stones, which was a very slow and painful operation."

On the 22nd of September, 1676, the two Labadist preachers, Dankers and Sluyter, after a voyage of nearly four months, from Amsterdam, in the good ship Charles, met at the Narrows off Staten Island, "some Indians upon the beach with a canoe, and others coming down the hill. As we tacked about we came close to the shore, and called out to them to come on board the ship. The Indians came on board and we looked upon them with wonder. They are dull of comprehension, slow of speech, bashful, but otherwise bold of person and red of skin. They wear something in front of them over the thighs, and a piece of duffels like a blanket around the body, and that is all the clothing they have. Their hair hangs down from their head in strings, well smeared with fat, and sometimes with quantities of little beads twisted in it out of pride. They have thick lips and thick noses, but not fallen in like the negroes, heavy eyebrows or eyelids, brown or black

---

[1] De Vries, op. cit., p. 154, *et seq.*
[2] North American Indians, Vol. II, p. 23.

eyes, and all of them black hair and thick tongues. After they had obtained some biscuit and had amused themselves climbing here and there, they also received some brandy to taste which they drank excessively, and threw it up again. They then went ashore in their canoes, and we having a better breeze sailed ahead handsomely."

In the "Remonstrance of New Netherland, and the Occurrences there, Addressed to the High and Mighty Lords States General of the United Netherlands, By the People of New Netherland,"[1] we find: —

"The natives are generally well limbed, slender around the waist, broad shouldered; all having black hair and brown eyes; they are very nimble and swift of pace, well adapted to travel on foot and to carry heavy burdens; they are dirty and slovenly in all their habits; make light of all sorts of hardships, being by nature and from youth upward accustomed thereunto. They resemble Brazilians in color, or are as tawny as those people who sometimes ramble through Netherland and are called Gipsies. Generally, the men have very little or no beard, some even pluck it out; they use few words, which they previously well consider. Naturally they are quite modest, without guile and inexperienced, but in their way haughty enough, ready and quick witted to comprehend or learn, be it good or bad, whatever they are most inclined to."[1]

In the same paper, it is stated regarding the Indians in the vicinity of New Amsterdam: —

"The clothing as well of men as of women consists of a piece of duffels, or of deerskin leather or elk hide around the body, to cover their nakedness. Some have a bearskin of which they make doublets; others again, coats of the skins of racoons, wild cats, wolves, dogs, fishers, squirrels, beavers, and the like; and they even have made themselves some of turkey's feathers; now they make use for the most part of duffels cloth which they obtain in trade from the Christians; they make their stockings and shoes of deerskins or elk hides, some even have shoes of corn husks, whereof they also make sacks.* * * * * They twine both white and black wampum around their heads; formerly they were not wont to cover these, but now they are beginning to wear bonnets or caps, which they purchase from the Christians; they wear Wampum in the ears, around the neck, and around the waist, and thus in their way are mighty fine. They have also long deers-hair which is dyed red, whereof they make ringlets to encircle the head; and other fine hair of the same color, which hangs around the neck in braids, whereof they are very vain. They frequently smear their skin and hair with all sorts of grease."[2]

In De Vries' Journal we also find the following: —

"I will state something of the nations about Fort Amsterdam; as the Hackinsack, Tapaense, and Wicquas-geckse Indians; and these are embraced within one, two, three, or four miles of the entrance of the river.* * * * Their clothing is a

---

[1] O'Callaghan, op. cit., Vol. I, p. 281.
[2] O'Callaghan, op. cit., Vol. I, p. 281 et seq.

coat of beaver-skins, over the body, with fur inside in winter, and outside in summer; they have, also, sometimes a bear's hide, or coat of the skins of wild cats, or *hefspanen* (raccoons).* * * * *   They also wear coats of turkey's feathers, which they know how to put together; but since our Netherland Nation has traded here, they trade their beavers for duffels cloth, which we give for them, and which they find more suitable than the beavers, as they consider it better for the rain; and take two and a half length of duffels, which is nine and a half quarters wide." [1]

Children were carried upon the back, and held secure by a piece of duffels or skin.

In Arnoldus Montanus' "Description of New Netherland" (1671), the following occurs: —

"The women ornament themselves more than the men. And although the winters are very severe, they go naked until their thirteenth year; the lower parts of the girls' bodies only are covered. All wear around the waist a girdle made of the fin of a whale or of seawant. The men wear between the legs a lap of duffels cloth, or leather, half an ell broad and nine quarters long; so that a square piece hangs over the buttocks and in front over the belly. The women wear a petticoat midway down the leg, very richly ornamented with seawant, so that the garment sometimes costs three hundred guilders. They also wrap the naked body in a deer skin, the tips (edges) of which swing with points (fringe). A long robe fastened at the right shoulder by a knot, at the waist by a girdle, serves the men and women for an upper ornament, and by night for a bed cover. Both go, for the most part bare headed. The women bind their hair behind in a plait, over which they draw a square cap, thickly interwoven with seawant. They decorate the ornaments for the forehead with the same stuff. Around the neck and arms they wear bracelets of seawant, and some around the waist. Shoes (moccasins) and stockings (leggings) were made of Elk hides before the *Hollanders* settled here. Others even made shoes of straw, but since some time they prefer Dutch shoes and stockings." [2]

In the grave of a child, opened for the Museum at "Burial Ridge," Tottenville, Mr. George H. Pepper found about the neck many *olivella* shells in which a perforation had been worn by rubbing (Plate XI). In the Plate are represented a number of these shells imbedded as found. A single tiny discoid bead occurs with the rest. The double-holed stone gorget (Fig. 1, Plate VIII), occasionally found on Staten Island, is still used by the Lenapé Indians of Munceytown, Ontario, Canada, as a hair ornament, and is bound on the hair. One of these is shown in Fig. 2, Plate VIII. It was called by them "Lita-pum-bla-wan." They claim also to have used similar "gorgets" of bone and wood in the old days. Fig. 6, Plate VIII, shows what appears to be one of these objects in the process of manufacture.

---

[1] De Vries, op. cit., p. 154, *et seq.*
[2] O'Callaghan, op. cit.

The single holed gorget or pendant (Figs. 3 and 4, Plate VIII), apparently worn suspended as a neck ornament, also occurs. Both specimens here illustrated come from Tottenville. Fig. 5 shows an irregularly shaped fragment of mica, in which a perforation, evidently for suspension, has been started.

Wampum was undoubtedly used for ornament and as a medium of exchange, but none has ever been found. On most sites occur those inner columns of the conch (Plate XI), called locally "wampum sticks," from which the outer whorls have been broken away in the process the next steps of which were polishing, cutting off disk-like sections and perforating to make the finished wampum. Ninety-five were found in a grave at Burial Ridge, Tottenville. A single wampum or discoid bead was found with perforated *olivella* shells near the neck of a child's skeleton at Tottenville, by Mr. George H. Pepper.

"Their pride is to paint their faces strangely with red or black lead," * * * * * The women "sometimes paint their faces, and draw a black ring around their eyes." [1]

"Their ornaments consist of scoring their bodies, or painting them of various colors, sometimes entirely black, if they are in mourning; but mostly the face." [2]

Fragments of limonite and red ochre showing marks of scrapers, etc., and which were probably used to obtain pigment, are sometimes found on Staten Island.

Vegetable Resources. Practically all traces of primitive agriculture on Staten Island have vanished. An occasional rude stone hoe, usually well polished from continual use is found. Two varieties of these occur, neither one at all common. Two (Figs. 14 and 15, Plate V), from Kreischerville and Tottenville respectively, represent the notched type, and one (Fig. 16, Plate V) illustrates the plain unnotched form. These are mentioned by Dankers and Sluyter.

The long stone pestle (shown in Fig. 18, Plate V, from Arrochar) is not uncommon, owing to the fact that the wooden pestle may have taken its place, although this type was undoubtedly less common here than among the not far distant Iroquois. The long stone pestle seems to be a peculiarly Algonkin form in the east. The stone pestle was invariably used in a wooden block or mortar. Dankers and Sluyter say (again of the Canarsie of Fort Hamilton), "Their bread is maize pounded in a block by a stone, but not fine. This is mixed with water and made into a cake which they bake in the hot ashes."

De Vries remarks, "They pound it [maize] in a hollow tree"; doubtless referring to the tree trunk mortar. He also adds: —

---

[1] De Vries, Journal, p. 155.
[2] O'Callaghan, op. cit., Vol. I, p. 281.

"When they travel they take a flat stone, and press [grind] it [maize] with another stone placed upon the first, and when it is pressed, [ground] they have little baskets, which they call *notassen*, which are made of a kind of hemp, the same as fig-frails,— which they make to serve them as sieves, [as do the Delaware and Iroquois of to-day] and thus make their meal. They make flat cakes of the meal mixed with water, as large as a farthing cake in this country, [Holland], and bake them in the ashes, first wrapping a vine-leaf or maize-leaf around them. When they are sufficiently baked in the ashes they make good palatable bread. The Indians make use of French [doubtless aboriginal] beans of different colors, which they plant among their maize. When the maize (which is some three or four feet apart, in order to have room to weed it thoroughly) is grown one, two, or three feet high, they stick the beans in the ground alongside of the maize stalks, which serve instead of poles which we use in the Fatherland, for beans to grow on." [1]

Two types of stone mortars occur. One is a large thin slab of stone, generally with a depression or hole on each side showing the action of considerable friction. The other type is larger, and usually has but a single cup or depression. Obviously these are far too heavy to be used for transportation. They seem never to occur except upon the larger sites, and not at a distance from them as De Vries' statement would lead one to believe. Pebbles, showing much use as grinding or crushing tools or mullers (Figs. 5 and 6, Plate v) are not infrequent.

Certainly tobacco must have been raised, or some substitute used, judging from the number of pipes and fragments found. Nuts (which were sometimes dried and preserved), ground nuts, pumpkins, watermelons, melons and wild grapes are mentioned by De Vries. He also mentions wild hemp.

"The Indians use a kind of hemp, which they understand making up, much stronger than ours is, and for every necessary purpose, such as notassen (which are their sacks and in which they carry everything); they also make linen of it. They gather their maize and French beans the last of September and October, and when they have shelled the corn, they bury it in holes which they have previously covered (lined) with mats, and so keep as much as they want in the winter while hunting. They sow the maize in April or May." [2]

Charred corn (kernels and cobs) and charred beans and hickory nuts have been found in shell pits at the village site at Bowman's Brook, Mariners' Harbor. In early records, mention is made of large quantities of corn destroyed at Staten Island Lenapé towns by the Dutch soldiery.

Hunting. Hunting and fishing, probably more than agriculture, were the mainstays of the Hackensack and Raritan. At the present day, stone arrow points are to be found in considerable numbers on the various sites,

---

[1] De Vries, Journal, p. 156, et seq.
[2] De Vries, Journal, p. 158.

and may occasionally be picked up anywhere. They vary greatly in form and size (Plate XII). Needless to say the notched and stemmed varieties are by far the most abundant. The triangular points were possibly used entirely for warfare in this region, though elsewhere this was certainly not the case, as among the Iroquois who used no other form but the triangle. Points of antler and bone (Figs. 7 to 10, Plate X) may have been used for hunting; but so far the only ones on record have come from Burial Ridge, Tottenville, associated with the triangular stone type in and among the bones of skeletons.

Old records go to show that the long bow was used. De Vries describes their methods of hunting, and says that, in companies of a hundred or more, they would range the woods driving the deer and game before them. The Indians would proceed about one hundred paces apart, and, holding a "flat thigh bone" in one hand, beat upon it with a stick and thus drive the game into the river. As the hunters approached the river, they would draw closer together so that any animal between two of them was at the mercy of their bows and arrows or had to take to the water. Any creature so unfortunate as to have to swim was captured by Indians who lay in wait in canoes, "with snares which they throw around their necks, and drag them to them, and force the deer down with the rump upwards, by which they cannot draw breath." [1]

Very probably the black bear was treated with veneration as among many Algonkin peoples. Certainly this animal must have been slain in quantities on Staten Island by the Indians, as they were killed at a later date by the whites; but equally certainly no bear's teeth or bones appear ever to have been found on any of the sites. The modern Cree of the Southern Hudson's Bay region always destroy the bones of the black bear for fear the dogs will get them and thus offend the spirit of the dead bear, and so injure future hunts.

Fishing. Large quantities of irregular, natural pebbles, notched usually once on two opposite sides (Figs. 10 and 11, Plate V, from Tottenville), have been found on Staten Island, particularly on the plowed fields and shell heaps of Tottenville in the vicinity of Burial Ridge, where they may yet be found in great numbers. In this and some neighboring localities, they are actually more abundant than stone arrow points. This is not true, however, of the North Shore sites. Some of these net sinkers show a primary or secondary usage as pitted hammerstones.

Another type, not uncommon, but by no means so abundant, is the grooved sinker. Sinkers are usually made of pebbles of a more round and

---

[1] De Vries, Journal, p. 159.

choice shape, and in some instances considerable pains has been taken in their manufacture (Figs. 8 and 9, Plate v, from Tottenville and Mariners' Harbor respectively). These have been found associated with the ordinary notched variety in some numbers at Tottenville as though they had been attached to a net which was subsequently cast aside. Some show battering on the edges and may have been used as mauls or hammers instead of sinkers. Fig. 7, Plate v, from Tottenville, shows a fragment split from the side of a grooved axe which seems to have had a secondary use as a net sinker.

De Vries, in his Journal, states: —

"Striped bass are caught in large quantities and dried by the Indians,— for at this time the squaws are engaged in sowing the maize, and cultivating the land, and the men go a-fishing in order to assist their wives a little by their draughts of fish. Sometimes they catch them with seines from seventy to eighty fathoms in length, which they braid themselves, and on which, in place of lead, they hang stones, and instead of corks which we put on to float them, they fasten small sticks of an ell in length, round and sharp at the end. Over the purse, they have a figure made of wood, resembling the devil, and when the fish swim into the net and come to the purse, so that the figure begins to move, they then begin to cry out and call upon the *mannetoe*, that is, the devil, to give them many fish. They catch great quantities of this fish; which they also catch in little set nets, six or seven fathoms long, braided like a herring net. They set them on sticks in the river, one and one-half fathoms deep."[1]

No bone fish hooks have been found, on the Island, and the long narrow notched arrow points so generally called "fish spears" and "fish points" seem to be about the most useless type of all for this purpose. A broad barbed point would hold the fish much more securely. Bone harpoons have not yet been reported, but two or three jagged barbed "stings" or "spines" from the sting ray (Figs. 20 and 21, Plate x), found in a shell pit at Bowman's Brook site, Mariners' Harbor, may have had such a use.

Shell fish in vast quantities were taken, as attested by the great heaps of shells at Tottenville and elsewhere, and the numerous shell pits on sites all over the Island. We have no records as to how they were taken, but doubtless they could easily be obtained at low tide almost anywhere along the shore. There is considerable historic and archæologic evidence that great quantities were dried for future use as well as those eaten on the spot.

Food Materials. The following is an incomplete list of the food materials that have thus far been noted during our investigations. Thanks are due Mr. Wm. T. Davis for assistance in identification. Almost all the mammals, birds, shell-fish, vegetables, etc., have been identified from specimens obtained at the sites at Bowman's Brook, Old Place, and other north shore

---

[1] De Vries, op. cit., p. 162.

Hackensack sites. There are probably plenty of similar remains at Tottenville and the south shore.

Mammals: Virginia deer (*Odocoileus americanus*), very abundant; Raccoon (*Procyon lotor*), not common; Wild Cat (*Lynx ruffus*), common locally; Muskrat (*Fiber zibethicus*), fairly common; Beaver (*Castor canadensis*), frequent; Rabbit (*Lepus floridanus*), common; Domestic dog (*Canis vulgaris*), common; Timber wolf (*Canis occidentalis*), common; Red (?) fox (*Vulpes fulvus* — ?), common locally.

Birds: Wild turkey (*Meleagris gallopavo silvestris*), abundant; and others which are unidentified.

Reptiles, Fishes and Crustaceans: Box Tortoise (*Terrapene carolina*), common; Diamond-back Terrapin (*Malaclemmys centrata*), common; Snapping Tortoise (*Chelydra serpentina*), common; Sting-ray (*Dasyatis*, sp. ?), rare; Sturgeon (*Acipenser*, sp. ?), common locally; Common lobster (*Homarus americanus*), rare; Blue crab (*Callinectes sapidus*), rare; there are also bones of other fishes and reptiles in abundance which are unidentified.

Shell-fish: Oyster (*Ostrea virginica*), very abundant everywhere; Pear conch (*Fulgur carica* and *F. canaliculata*), very abundant everywhere; Hard clam (*Venus mercenaria*), common locally; Soft clam (*Mya arenaria*), common locally; Scallop (*Pecten irradians*), common locally; Mussel (*Mytilus edulis*), common locally; Natica (*Polynices heros* and *P. duplicata*), common locally.

Sea snails and "Fairy boats" are not common. They were probably present by accident only, having been brought in with clams and oysters, and were not an article of diet. In the spring of 1901, while excavating in the shell pits at Old Place, in company with Mr. Wm. T. Davis, we had the good fortune to collect a great number of the shells of land snails (*Helix alternata* and *H. thyroides*); but at the time we doubted their use as food. More recent discoveries, however, have proved the case. While exploring an ancient village site of Shinnecock Indians at the Shinnecock Hills, Long Island, in the summer of 1902, for the American Museum of Natural History, we discovered a large deposit of the shells of both species of snails under such conditions as to render further doubt impossible.

The following vegetables and seeds have been found in prehistoric fire pits and lodge sites: Indian corn (*Zea mays*), common locally; Hickory nuts (*Hicoria*, sp. ?), rare locally. The Indian corn we have found differs in many ways from the modern variety. The cobs are very much shorter and more pointed, and contain fewer and larger kernels.

Habitations. There are at this late date no records of the types of habitations used by the Staten Island Lenapé, and the archæological remains now to be found prove little in that direction. The Shinnecock Indians of Long Island, now practically extinct, who were similar in many respects to the natives of the area now under discussion, built lodges of the following type, according to some of the surviving old men interviewed by the writer in 1902 while working for the Museum at Shinnecock Hills. A dome-shaped framework of bent boughs with cross pieces tied on at intervals, and averaging perhaps thirty feet in circumference, was erected. Openings were left at the top for a smoke hole and at one side for a door. Then the framework was thatched with grass from the salt meadows. Around the interior about one foot from the ground was a raised bench upon which the inhabitants reclined or sat. The fire was built in the interior of the wigwam, or "wickom," as they called it. Such lodges were built up to within thirty or thirty-five years ago (1908).

Another type of lodge, resembling the "Long House" of the Iroquois, is described by Dankers and Sluyter as having been observed by them (in September or October, 1676) at "Najack," now Fort Hamilton, Long Island. This is just across the Narrows of New York Bay, and the Indians here mentioned were the Canarsie, who like the Shinnecock were of Mohegan, rather than Lenapé, origin, yet probably very closely resembled the latter in material culture.

"We soon heard a noise of pounding like threshing, and went to the place whence it proceded, and found there an old Indian woman busily employed beating Turkish beans out of the pods by means of a stick, which she did with astonishing force and dexterity. Gerrit (their guide) inquired of her in the Indian language, which he spoke perfectly well, how old she was, and she answered eighty years; at which we were still more astonished that so old a woman should still have so much strength and courage to work as she did. We went thence to her habitation, where we found the whole troop together, consisting of seven or eight families, and twenty or twenty-two persons. Their house was low and long, about sixty feet long and fourteen or fifteen feet wide.

"The bottom was earth, the sides and roof were made of reed and bark of chestnut trees stuck in the ground and all fastened together. The ridge of the roof was often about a half a foot wide from end to end, in order to let the smoke escape, in place of a chimney. On the sides of the house the roof was so low that you could hardly stand under it. The entrances which were at both ends were so small that they had to stoop down and squeeze themselves to get through them. The doors were made of reed or flat bark. In the whole building there was no iron, stone, lime or lead.

"They build their fire in the middle of the floor, according to the number of the families, so that from one end to the other each boils its own pot and eats what it likes, not only the families by themselves, but each Indian alone when he is hungry, at all hours, morning, noon and night. By each fire are the cooking utensils, consisting of a pot, a bowl or calabash and a spoon, also made of calabash. These are all that relate to cooking. They lie upon mats, with their feet towards the fire on each side of it. They do not sit much upon anything raised up, but, for the most part, sit upon the ground or squat on their ankles."

Quoting again from the "Remonstrance": —

"Their dwellings are constructed of hickory poles set in the ground and bent bow fashion, like arches, and then covered with bark which they peel in quantities for that purpose. Some, but principally the chief's houses, have, inside, portraits and pictures somewhat rudely carved. When fishing and hunting, they lie under the blue sky, or little better. They do not remain long in one place, but remove several times a year and repair, according to the season, to wherever food appears to them, before hand, best and easiest to be obtained." [1]

In De Vries' Journal, it is stated in regard to the sudatory or sweating lodges: —

" When they wish to cleanse themselves of their foulness, they go in the autumn, when it begins to grow cold, and make, away off, near a running brook, a small oven, large enough for three or four men to lie in it. In making it they first take twigs of trees, and then cover them tight with clay, so that smoke cannot escape. This being done, they take a parcel of stones, which they heat in a fire, and then put in the oven, and when they think that it is sufficiently hot, they take the stones out again, and go and lie in it, men and women, boys and girls, and come out so perspiring that every hair has a drop of sweat on it. In this state they spring into the cold water; saying that it is healthy, but I let its healthfulness pass. They then become entirely clean, and are more attractive than before." [2]

Small beds of cracked stones and pebbles, without relics, often at some distance from other remains are not infrequently found. The broken appearance of the stones seems to indicate that they were first heated and then were plunged into cold water, or that water was thrown upon them. These may be the remains of old sweating lodges.

Transportation. Owing to the fact that the canoe birch does not range so far south, the birch bark canoe was unknown to, or at least unused by, the Indians of Staten Island. Instead, the wooden canoe or dug-out took its place. Such canoes were made by the process of charring and cutting, fire being the active agent. Canoes of elm or other bark may perhaps have been made. In the "Remonstrance of New Netherland" occurs this passage: "They themselves construct the boats they use, which are of two sorts: some, of entire trees excavated with fire, axes and adzes; the Christians call these Canoes; others again, called also canoes, are made of bark, and in these they can move very rapidly." [3] Dankers and Sluyter, speaking of the Canarsie of Fort Hamilton, state that they have "for fishing a canoe

---

[1] O'Callaghan, op. cit., Vol. I, p. 282.
[2] De Vries, op. cit., p. 155.
[3] O'Callaghan, op. cit., Vol. I, p. 282.

without mast or sail, and not a nail in any part of it, though it is sometimes fully forty feet in length, fish hooks and lines, and scoops to paddle with instead of oars." A wooden dug-out, probably of Indian make, was found in the mud of Hackensack River near Hackensack, New Jersey, some years ago, and is now the property of Dr. F. G. Speck of the University of Pennsylvania.

Beauchamp, in his "Aboriginal Use of Wood in New York," gives a description and figure of a wooden dug-out canoe. He says: —

"In what is considered the earliest view of New York City in 1635, attributed to Augustine Hermann, is a strange form of the dug-out which may possibly be the artist's fancy. It is a long boat, manned by five men, which has sloping ends rising far above the sides. From the highest point are long horizontal projections, terminating in large balls. There are smaller canoes of a common type. Figure 27 shows this form from an engraving of 1673, precisely like the former, but propelled by women. The figure is entitled *Navis ex arboribus trunco igne excavata*. No early writer has described this in New York, nor does it at first seem probable that the Indians would have made one of this form. Moulton accepted it, and suggested a fair explanation. He described the earlier figure. There was at each end, he said, 'what may be termed a bowsprit finished by a spherical head about the size of a man's. These bowsprits or handles seem an ingenious contrivance for lifting the canoe and carrying it on the land, by two men hoisting it on their shoulders, and thus as on a pole, carrying it from place to place with ease and expedition.' *Moulton*, vii.

"If it were light, two men might suffice, but for a heavier one four men might use crossbars, one at each end, and the balls would prevent these from slipping. When left by the tide, something of the kind might have proved very useful. Pictures and descriptions, however, usually represent a heavy and clumsy boat, useful but neither handsome nor swift, with straight sides and sloping ends, rather a trough than anything else."[1]

The form above described is no doubt a truly aboriginal type. Mr. M. R. Harrington found dug-out canoes of a very similar form among the Muskhogean Indians of the Southeast, and the ends were used for the purpose suggested. We have met with no records of land transportation. Doubtless pack straps and baskets of a type similar to those now found among the surviving Lenapé were in use.

Mortuary Customs. Three methods of burial seem to have been common among the Lenapé Indians of Staten Island. They are: (a) flexed burials without objects, (b) flexed burials with objects, and (c) bone burials. A fourth method, that of burying the body at full length, seems to have occurred occasionally at Tottenville.

In regard to the first of these forms, the flexed burial (i. e. the body laid

---

[1] New York State Museum, Bull. 89, Archæology 11, p. 144.

on one side and the arms and legs flexed, the knees and hands drawn up to or near the chin) is probably most common. The average depth for such a burial is from one and a half to three feet. Some are very near the surface and the writer has exhumed at least one that was very deep down.

Apparently it was the custom to hold a "Feast of the Dead" at the time of interment, as in almost all instances the earth above and about the skeleton contains particles of charcoal, fire-cracked stones, split and charred animal bones, potsherds, bivalve shells and the like. Sometimes a foot or more above the body will be a pit containing great quantities of oyster shells, etc., as though, when the departed was out of sight of the living beneath a thin layer of earth, a feast was held and the refuse, etc., cast into the still open grave. In one very deep grave, at a depth of seven and a half feet, and some distance below the skeleton, the remains of a pottery vessel were found upon which lay stones, apparently thrown in to break it, possibly that it might never be used again. Animal bones lay about; then, in a layer of dark and practically refuse-free earth, the flexed skeleton; and above this again a bowl-shaped deposit of oyster shells, etc., extended to the surface. On rare occasions, thick layers of oyster shells, the sharp cutting edge up, have been found packed regularly above the skeleton, perhaps to prevent the wolves or dogs from digging up the body.

As a general thing, burials occupy a knoll or section near to, but not among, the dwelling sites. However, skeletons are sometimes found in shell or fire pits, and this may perhaps be accounted for by the fact that, if the death occurred in winter when the ground was frozen, digging graves with the primitive tools at the command of the Lenapé was a serious if not impossible matter; hence, the corpse may have been placed in a refuse pit and covered with débris, an easier process than grave digging. All the graves seen, opened by, or reported to, the writer on the north shore of Staten Island were of this type of "Bone Burials," and contained no objects whatever except such discarded tools, etc., as may have found their way by accident into the grave.

Flexed burials with objects are in every respect, save the placing of objects with the dead, the same as the first form described. On Staten Island, these seem to have been confined to the Burial Ridge at Tottenville, described elsewhere in this paper, and to one or two graves on the Wort Farm at Woodrow. Mr. George H. Pepper informs the writer that graves with objects have been disinterred at Morgan's Station on the New Jersey mainland opposite Tottenville; but apparently such burials are rare throughout the Algonkin region of southeastern New York, Long Island and neighboring New Jersey, in marked contrast to the Iroquoian cultural area to the north and west.

Almost as common as the first class described are "bone" or "bunched" burials. In this case the flesh has rotted or been removed from the body before interment, and the dry bones thrown or laid in a hole, usually without order and generally with the skull on top. The writer has opened graves of this type at Bowman's Brook site, Mariners' Harbor, under conditions which precluded the taking of photographs. At the same site, a single grave was found to contain the heaped-up bones of a number of individuals, perhaps as many as half a dozen. Burials at full length are said to have been found at Tottenville, in Burial Ridge or the immediately adjacent fields.

At the famous Bowman's Brook site at Mariners' Harbor, the writer found the skeleton of a dog which had received regular interment. A few inches above this skeleton (which, by the way, was in the heart of the village proper and not in the cemetery) was a deposit of oyster shells such as was often found above human remains on the same site. Perhaps this was the skeleton of some pet animal. Dogs' skeletons have also been found at Tottenville. The writer believes those who have attributed a ceremonial origin to these dog burials, which are not uncommon on New York Algonkin sites, are in error. With the skeleton of an old woman, found by the writer at Bowman's Brook site, were the remains of a tiny lynx (*Lynx ruffus*) kitten, still with its milk teeth.

Quoting again from De Vries' Journal, we learn: —

"They make a large grave, and line it inside with boughs of trees, in which they lay the corpse, so that no earth can touch it. They then cover this with clay, and form the grave, seven or eight feet, in the shape of a sugar loaf, and place palisades around it. I have frequently seen the wife of the deceased come daily to the grave, weeping and crying, creeping over it with extended body, and grieving for the death of her husband. The oldest wife by whom he has children does this; the young wife does not make much ado about it, but looks about for another husband. They keep a portion of the dead in the house. * * * * * They then bury the bones in the grave, with a parcel of Zeewan (wampum), and with arrows, kettles, knives, paper, and other knick-knacks, which are held in great esteem by them, and cover them with earth, and place palisades around them, as before related. Such is the custom on the coast in regard to the dead. The chief doctrine held among them is the belief in the immortality of the soul by some. Others are skeptical on this point, but not far from it, saying, when they die they go to a place where they sing like the ravens; but this singing is entirely different from the singing of angels." [1]

The fact that "they keep a portion of their dead in the house" may account for subsequent "bone burials."

Social and Religious Organization. In the "Remonstrance of New Netherland," we find: —

---

[1] De Vries, op. cit., p. 164, *et seq.*

"Traces, and nothing more, of the institution of marriage can be perceived among them. The man and woman unite together without any special ceremony, except that the former, by agreement previously made with the latter, presents her with some wampum or cloth, which he frequently takes back on separating, if this occur any way soon. Both men and women are exceedingly unchaste and lascivious, without the least particle of shame; and this is the reason that the men so frequently change their wives and the women, their husbands. They have, usually, but one wife; sometimes even two or three, but this mostly obtains among the chiefs. They have also among them different ranks of people, such as noble and ignoble. The men are generally lazy and will not work until they become old and of no consideration; then they make spoons and wooden bowls, traps, nets, and various other such trifles; in other respects, they do nothing but fish, hunt and go to war. The women must perform the remainder of the labor, such as planting corn, cutting and hauling firewood, cooking, attending the children, and whatever else has to be done.

"They are divided into various tribes and languages. Each tribe usually dwells together, and there is one among them who is chief; but he does not possess much power or distinction, except in their dances and in time of war. Some have scarcely any knowledge of God; others very little. Nevertheless, they relate very strange fables of the Deity. In general, they have a great dread of the Devil, who gives them wonderful trouble; some converse freely on the subject and allow themselves to be strangely imposed upon by him; but their devils, they say, will not have anything to do with the Dutch. Scarcely a word is heard here of any ghost or such like. Offerings are sometimes made to them, but with little ceremony. They believe, also, in an Immortality of the soul; have, likewise, some knowledge of the Sun, Moon and Stars, many of which they even know how to name; they are passable judges of the weather. There is scarcely any law or justice among them, except sometimes in war matters, and then very little. The next of kin is the avenger; the youngest are the most daring, who mostly do as they like.

"As soldiers they are far from being honorable, but perfidious, and accomplish all their designs by treachery; they also use many stratagems to deceive their enemies and execute by night almost all their plans that are in any way hazardous. The thirst for revenge seems innate in them; they are very pertinacious in self defence, when they cannot escape; which, under other circumstances, they like to do; and they make little of death, when it is inevitable, and despise all tortures that can be inflicted on them at the stake, exhibiting no faintheartedness, but generally singing until they are dead. They also know right well how to cure wounds and hurts, or inveterate sores and injuries, by means of herbs and roots indigenous to the country, and which are known to them." [1]

Of marriage customs, De Vries says, after stating that the women are marriageable directly after arriving at puberty: —

"Whoever gives the most zeewan is the successful suitor. They go home with him, and remain sometimes one, three, or four months with him, and then go with another; sometimes remaining with him, according as they are inclined to each other. The men are not jealous, and even lend their wives to a friend. They are fond of meetings to frolic and dance; but the women are compelled to work like asses, and

---

[1] O'Callaghan, op. cit., Vol. I, pp. 281–2.

when they travel, to carry the baggage on their backs, together with their infants, if they have any, bound to a board.

"The girls consider themselves to have arrived at womanhood when they begin to have their monthly terms, and as soon as they have them, they go and disguise themselves with a garment, which they throw over their body, drawing it over the head so they can hardly see with their eyes, and run off two or three months, lamenting that they must lose their virginity; and they therefore do not engage in any diversion by night, or other unseasonable time. This period being over, they throw away their disguise, and deck themselves with a quantity of zeewan upon the body, head, and neck; they then go and sit in some place, in company with some squaws, showing that they are up for a bargain." [1]

In speaking of a "Long House" and its inhabitants at Fort Hamilton, Long Island, Dankers and Sluyter observed that the dwellers in such a communal house were "all of one stock, as a father, mother and their offspring."

Mythology. Naturally little of the folk lore and mythology of these people has come down to us, but to Dankers and Sluyter we are again indebted, this time for the Hackensack creation myth which is as follows: —

"16 Oct., 1679. In the morning there came an Indian to our house, a man about 80 years of age, whom our people call Jasper, who lived at Ahakinsack [Hackensack] at Akinon.* * * * * We asked him where he believed he came from? He answered from his father. 'And where did your father come from?' we said, 'and your grandfather and great grandfather, and so to the first of the race?' He was silent for a little while, either as if unable to climb up at once so high with his thoughts, or to express them without help, and then took a piece of coal out of the fire where he sat, and began to write upon the floor. He first drew a circle, a little oval, to which he made four paws or feet, a head and a tail. 'This,' said he, 'is a tortoise, lying in the water around it,' and he moved his hand round the figure, continuing 'this was or is all water, and so at first was the world or the earth, when the tortoise gradually raised its round back up high, and the water ran off it, and then the earth became dry.' He then took a little straw and placed it on and in the middle of the figure, and proceeded, 'the earth was now dry, and there grew a tree in the middle of the earth, and the root of this tree sent forth a sprout beside it, and there grew upon it a man, who was the first male. This man was there alone, and would have remained alone; but the tree bent over its top and touched the earth; and there shot therein another root, from which came forth another sprout, and there grew upon it the woman, and from these two are all men produced."

Art as shown in Pottery. In the absence of their fabrics, leather or wooden utensils, the sole remaining place where we may seek to reconstruct the art of the Staten Island Lenapé is in their pottery. Considering first the forms used by these prehistoric potters, we find by examination of fragments and the reconstruction of vessels that at least five classes of pottery may be

---

[1] De Vries, op. cit., p. 155, et seq.

differentiated: of these, three are distinctly native; a fourth exotic; and a fifth intermediate, representing a transitional stage between the native and foreign types.

On one site, considered by the writer to be the oldest of all the Algonkin remains on Staten Island, situated at the junction of the Shore Road and Western Avenue at Bowman's Point or Holland Hook, Mariners' Harbor, pottery is exceedingly rare, only four or five sherds having been found. However, these were enough to show that the vessel from which they were broken was of rude and heavy workmanship, possessing a plain undecorated rim and sloping downward to a pointed bottom. They were accompanied by large fragments of steatite vessels, and a large scraper of very unusual form described elsewhere in this paper. The general appearance of the site itself suggested relative antiquity and the writer is inclined to consider it the oldest Algonkin site on the Island. It is situated about a quarter of a mile from the great Hackensack village on Bowman's Brook, which was evidently a much more recent settlement. On all the older sites this type of vessel occurs, sometimes plain, but often ornamented, while fragments are also found on sites having undoubted traces of the historic period. In form, it is a cone with the sides below the apex somewhat swollen and rounded. From what the writer has seen among the local collections from the Muncey and Hackensack region and from Mr. Ernest Volk's splendid collection made for this Institution in the Delaware Valley, this type must be considered the typical Lenapé vessel. It was not restricted to those people, however, as it was comparatively universal among the coastal Algonkin from Virginia northward to New England.

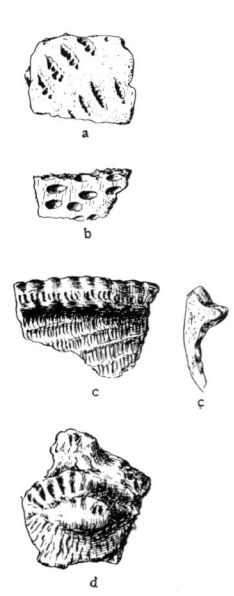

Fig. 2. Fragments of Pottery, Staten Island Museum.

A second type found in this region and apparently derived from the former, intermediates being found, has a slightly more rounded base and an overturning flaring lip with a slightly constricted neck.

The third and last typically Algonkin type has a still more rounded bottom and a somewhat constricted and narrow neck with a flaring lip, the latter feature being somewhat less conspicuous than in the second type.

The fourth type is found only on sites showing historic traces or advanced degrees of prehistoric culture, and is more abundant on the northern than on the southern shore. It is a somewhat modified form of the graceful vessels found throughout the Iroquois country of central New York, more especially, perhaps, in the Mohawk Valley, inhabited by a people who, during the latter part of the prehistoric and the historic existence of the coastal Algonkin of New York, are known to have had great influence over them. This

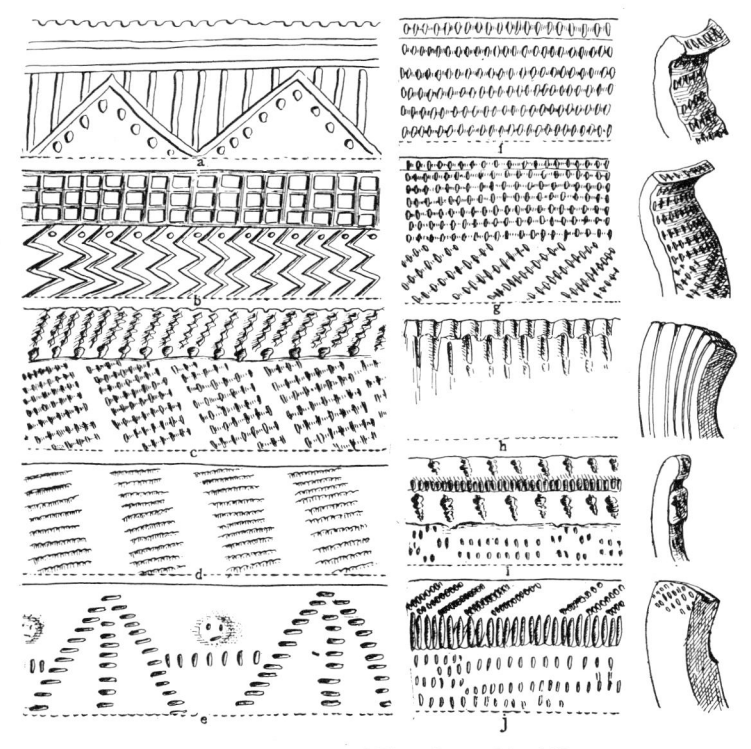

Fig. 3. Pottery Designs and Rims, Staten Island Museum.

form in the Mohawk Valley is characterized by a bottom so rounded that it can stand by itself, a deeply constricted neck, a raised collar or rim, often square in shape with an angle at every corner and a raised point at every angle. In some instances the mouth is rounded, which obliterates the corner angles; but the raised peaks or points are still present at regular intervals. This type occurs, as has been said, on Staten Island sites where historic articles are found or where the comparatively high quality of the ware suggests a later period of prehistoric development. It is not present on the older sites, nor is it found so plentifully as we progress southward in Lenapé territory through the Island into the mainland where Iroquois influence was perhaps less keenly felt. The variety having the rounded rather than the square and angular mouth, is apparently the only type found here.

The fifth and last form is an intermediate between the Iroquoian and Algonkian type. It occurs only on sites where the Iroquoian form is found, and so far as the writer has been able to ascertain possesses a rounded bottom, constricted neck, and thin collar with no peaks or humps. The resemblance seems to lie between the third Algonkin type described and the

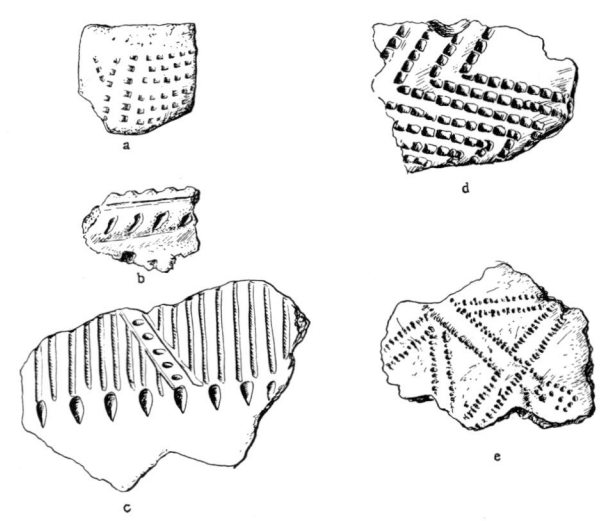

Fig. 4. Fragments of Pottery, Staten Island Museum.

Iroquoian. A single fragment of a clay vessel possessing an ear, lug, or knob (Fig. 2d), comes from Watchogue.

Before proceeding further, it may be said that the vessels of Iroquoian type are usually better made than the others, and are often washed or sized with colored clay before firing. In size, the vessels from Staten Island vary in capacity from a few pints to a number of gallons.

Unfortunately, in treating the designs applied to earthenware in this region, we must at once eliminate one interesting and important element, that of symbolism. There is now nothing whatever to show how greatly this element influenced design. So far as the writer is aware, no painted pottery has been obtained from Staten Island; although we have been shown some sherds, possibly painted with red ochre, from Hackensack territory near what is now Bayonne. The forms of decoration now to be found were applied by incision and stamping, the latter process including the roulette. Only the rim was decorated, usually outside, but quite commonly inside as well. Throughout this region, life forms are exceedingly rare. A single example (Fig. 3e), has been obtained, showing a design found upon a vessel of the first Algonkin type mentioned, where rude raised faces (probably human) were found at intervals in connection with a crude pattern of incised lines running an unusually long way down the rim. The specimen is unique, not only from Staten Island, but from the coastal Algonkin region of the Eastern United States. While probably Lenapian, it may show Iroquoian influence; since, on Iroquois sites, whole series of similar heads and faces may be found from the crudest conventional forms to those which approximate portraiture.

The typical decoration applied to Lenapé jars of the first type was the incised chevron design and its variations, as shown in Fig. 3a from the Bowman's Brook site. The writer has but rarely seen stamp or roulette designs on vessels of this type. Fig. 3i demonstrates this form, however, and in addition appears to have a raised design in stucco parallel to the edge. Fig. 3c shows a rather ornate design from Old Place made with a stamp or roulette. All the incised designs from this region are straight or angular, no rounded forms being known. Fig. 3b from Tottenville shows a combination of net and zigzag designs not found elsewhere. Fig. 3d shows a design made by marking with a clam shell the edge of a plain Algonkin pot in parallel lines.

The second Algonkin type described is not so common as the first and the designs applied were both incised and stamped. Fig. 3h shows an incised pattern from a vessel obtained from the Bowman's Brook site, Mariners' Harbor, as does Fig. 3j. Fig. 3f is decorated with impressions apparently made with a twine-wrapped stick, as was Fig. 2c. Fig. 2b shows a fragment of vessel apparently decorated by gouging or by small incisions made in the clay.

Fig. 3g represents the design on a vessel of the third Algonkin type, from a grave at Bowman's Brook site, Mariners' Harbor. It was decorated by pressing cord-wrapped sticks on the clay when still wet. Fig. 3f represents the design of a vessel of Algonkin type, made by the cord-wrapped stick process, consisting of a series of parallel impressions around the rim and neck.

Fig. 5i shows a design taken from a partially restored Iroquoian vessel excavated years ago in the Tottenville shell heaps by Mr. William Oliffe. In Iroquoian pottery hereabouts, the angle where the collar leaves the neck is usually notched, a characteristic of the true Iroquois potter's art, especially in the Mohawk valley. Figs. 5f and 4c represent specimens of this type from Watchogue, and Fig. 4b is an Old Place specimen having an unusually narrow rim. Fig. 5g from Watchogue resembles Fig. 4c also from that site; but the latter has a design apparently made with a carved stamp, while the former is decorated by incision. Fig. 5h from Bowman's Brook site, Mariners' Harbor, shows a very rude incised design and the collar is less thick than usual. Fig. 5e is a design taken from the rim of an Iroquoian vessel, black without, but sized within with a bright red wash, and decorated by the typical coast Algonkin method of pressing the fluted edges of a scallop shell into the wet clay. This is from Mariners' Harbor. Fig. 4a from Old Place shows roulette decoration on an Iroquoian rim.

Figs. 5a, b, c, and d show four designs taken from the vessels of the fifth, or intermediate class. They are all decorated by means of a cord-wrapped stick, save Fig. 5d. Fig. 2c shows a curious profile from an otherwise typical vessel. In Fig. 2a, from Mariners' Harbor the method of decoration is indeterminate but was probably done by stamping.

Steatite or soapstone vessels are very rare in comparison with pottery, and such vessels must have been brought a long way. One specimen from Lake's Island is unique in being rudely decorated by scratching or incising along the edge. These seem to be of the Atlantic Coast Algonkin type, oblong with a lug, or handle, at each end. As steatite is not native to Staten Island, it must have been transported from some distant point, the nearest aboriginal quarries being in Connecticut.

Résumé.

In reviewing the archaeological remains from Staten Island, one is struck by a few slight, though perhaps significant, differences in culture between the sites probably occupied by Hackensack on the northern shore and Raritan sites on the southern. The great shell heaps at Tottenville are nowhere duplicated; but facilities for shell fishing were far greater in this neighborhood than elsewhere. However, the sites on the south shore are far more abundant in net sinkers and hammerstones than those of the north where the former are rare and the latter not at all common. On the other hand, arrow points, deer bones, etc., though occurring in both places, seem comparatively more abundant on the north shore sites, which may indicate that these sites were inhabited more by a hunting population, and those on the south by a fishing people. The ungrooved axe, hatchet, or celt, is exceedingly uncommon on all north shore sites, some of the largest,

Fig. 5. Pottery Designs, Staten Island Museum.

as Bowman's Brook site, having none at all; whereas celts are found, though not in great abundance, on almost all south shore sites. Pottery showing Iroquoian influence occurs on south shore sites; but it is much more abundant on those of the north shore. The Hackensack, throughout their range were much more on the line of travel for Iroquois war parties than the Raritan.

In no graves on the north shore, so far opened by the writer or reported by reliable authority, have there been found objects intentionally placed with the dead for spirit use; but at Tottenville, in Burial Ridge, and at Woodrow, Mr. George H. Pepper and others found some splendid material — a fact most unusual in Algonkin burials of coastal New York. Mr. Pepper informs the writer that at Morgan's Station, New Jersey, nearly opposite Tottenville, similar objects were found in graves some years ago. This is also in Raritan territory.

Stone pipes, of which a number have been found on the south shore, have never been reported from the north; and so far no bone or antler arrow points come from the latter region; yet this is negative evidence, for the conditions under which so many were found at Tottenville may not occur on the north shore. In the main, however, all other articles are more or less common to both districts.

The archæological remains, taken as a whole, differ from those of the Mahican of the Hudson Valley, and the tribes speaking Algonkin dialects in New England and Long Island in a number of ways. The stone gouge and adze, so typical of those regions occur but rarely; one gouge and four or five adzes being known. The typical stone pestle is more common, but is rarely so long or well made as the typical New England article. Again, bone and antler implements are apparently more common in this region than in the New England area. Steatite is quite uncommon, while the abundant pottery differs in form and decoration from that of Long Island and New England.

The region of Manhattan Island and the nearby mainland was anciently the point of contact between the Lenapé and New England Algonkin peoples, who doubtless differed culturally as their archæological remains testify; and it is in this Manhattan region that we find many evidences of a mixed culture. When, however, we examine remains from the Hackensack region, both on the mainland and Staten Island, it appears that as we draw southward the typical Lenapé culture begins to assert itself until in the Raritan remains on the south shore of Staten Island and on their sites along the Raritan River on the New Jersey mainland, we find the influence of the New England culture entirely wanting, Iroquois traces faint, and the material in question almost identical with remains found by Abbot and Volk in the Delaware Valley at Trenton.

On the whole, by comparison with such contemporary writers as De Vries, Van Der Donck, Dankers and Sluyter, and later with Heckewelder, we find that the prehistoric culture of Staten Island Indians was that of the coast Algonkin of the middle states and typically that of the Lenapé or some people of very similar culture. Comparison with the ethnology of still existing Delawares of Canada has shown many similarities and doubtless, if a complete study of the Lenapé of Indian Territory and the West were made, still further evidences of unity might be found. In summing up, therefore, it is apparent from this study of archæological remains of the region in question, that the prehistoric culture of Staten Island was identical with that of the Algonkin Lenapé, Hackensacks, Raritans and Tappans of the historic period.

BIBLIOGRAPHY.

In preparing this paper, the writer wishes to acknowledge his indebtedness to the Staten Island Association of Arts and Sciences for the loan of specimens, the permission to reproduce photographs for illustration, and the details of the text, especially in regard to many of the sites; to Mr. William T. Davis of New Brighton, for the loan of specimens for illustration, the use of personal notes and many other courtesies; to Mr. George H. Pepper of the University of Pennsylvania, for the loan of personal notes and information; to Mr. Peter Decker of Watchogue for information, specimens and assistance; and to Messrs. Isaac, Sr., Isaac, Jr., George and Samuel Wort of Woodrow, Rossville, for the loan of specimens for illustration, personal notes and information. The writer also wishes to acknowledge the kindness of Messrs. Charles Benedict, Almar Decker, Max Bedell, and Isaiah Merrill for information and the privilege of viewing their collections. The following additional sources of information may be noted:—

ABBOTT, C. C. Primitive Industry. Salem, 1881.
ALLEN, DR. J. A. Identification of animal bones found in shell pits, etc.
BEAUCHAMP, REV. WM. New York State Museum Bulletins. Ar. 1–13.
BRINTON, D. G. The Lenape and their Legends. Philadelphia, 1885.
BAYLES, R. M. History of Staten Island.
CALVER, W. L. Personal notes and information.
CLUTE, J. J. Annals of Staten Island. New York, 1877.
DANKERS and SLUYTER. Journal of a Voyage to New York, etc., in 1679–80. (Memoirs of Long Island Historical Society, Vol. I., 1875.)
DAVIS, WM. T. (a) Papers in Proceedings Natural Science Association of Staten Island.
(b) "Staten Island Names; Ye olde Names and Nicknames."
DE VRIES, DAVID PETERSON. Voyages from Holland to America. New York, 1853.
HARRINGTON, M. R. Letters to writer.
HECKEWELDER, JOHN. An account of the History, Manners and Customs of the Indians, etc. Philadelphia, 1876.
HOLLICK, DR. A. Papers in Proceedings Natural Sciences Association of Staten Island.
LOSKIEL, GEORGE H. History of the Missions among the Indians of North America. London, 1794.
MONTANUS, ARNOLDUS. Description of New Netherland, Amsterdam, 1671.
OCALLAGHAN, E. B. Documentary History of New York.
PARKER, A. C. Personal notes and letters.
PEPPER, G. H. Papers in Proceedings Natural Science Association of Staten Island.
RUTTENBER, E. M. History of the Indian Tribes of the Hudson River. Albany, 1872.
SLUYTER and DANKERS. See Dankers.
WAINWRIGHT, CAPT. N. Papers in Proceedings Natural Science Association of Staten Island.

ABORIGINAL REMAINS ON MANHATTAN ISLAND

BY

JAMES K. FINCH.

INTRODUCTION.

The first field work done on Manhattan Island is of very recent date. Doubtless many articles of Indian manufacture and evidences of their occupation were found as the city grew up from its first settlement at Fort Amsterdam, but of these specimens we have very few records. The first specimens found which have been preserved, to the knowledge of those now interested in the subject, were found in 1855, and consisted of a deposit of Indian arrow points found in Harlem during excavation for a cellar on Avenue A, between 120th and 121st Streets. Some of these are spoken of by James Riker [1] as being in the author's cabinet. Riker also speaks of shell heaps near here.[2] The next specimens preserved were found at Kingsbridge Road (now Broadway) and 220th Street in 1886, and are in the John Neafie Collection at the Museum.[3] These consist of an arrow point and a few bits of pottery. The next work was begun in 1889 by Mr. W. L. Calver of this city, and has led to the discovery of much valuable material which has been preserved.

The following account of the work is taken mainly from Mr. Calver's note-book:—

In the autumn of the year 1889, while exploring the heights of Bloomingdale (now called Cathedral Heights) for any relics that might have remained from the Battle of Harlem, Mr. Calver discovered one arrow point at 118th Street, east of Ninth Avenue, and immediately afterwards a circular hammerstone. On a later trip to the same locality, he found a small grooved axe or tomahawk.[4] In February, 1890, while hunting for Revolutionary relics in the vicinity of Fort Washington, he made a trip to the northern part of the Island in search of British regimental buttons, many of which were said to have been found in that vicinity. There he met an old acquaintance, Mr. John Pearce, a policeman then on duty there, by whom he was introduced to Mr. James McGuey, a youth residing in the vicinity of 198th Street and Kingsbridge Road. To Mr. Calver, Mr. McGuey presented several relics

---

[1] History of Harlem (1881), footnote, p. 137.
[2] Ibid., p. 366.
[3] Catalogue 20, Nos. 2558–2559.
[4] The writer found an arrowhead on South Field, in front of Columbia University Library, on September 30, 1904.

found by himself on camp sites and made an appointment to meet him early in March to explore for Indian remains. The same day, Mr. Pearce took Mr. Calver to be introduced to Mr. Thomas Reefe who resided near Kingsbridge Road and Isham Avenue, and, while crossing the orchard at Academy Street and Seaman Avenue, Mr. Calver saw that the ground was thickly strewn with shells which afterwards proved to be of Indian origin.

The first Sunday in March, Messrs. Calver and McGuey explored this part of the Island for Indian remains. At the junction of Academy Street and Prescott Avenue, they found an Indian potsherd whose importance Mr. McGuey seemed to realize, for, a week later, Mr. Calver met him again and was presented by him with a number of fragments of Indian ware. He assured Mr. Calver that he had found it by digging in an Indian graveyard. The two men dug again at this place, now known as "the Knoll," and found more pottery. They then went to Cold Spring, a point on the extreme northern end of the Island, and in a shell heap there they found more Indian work. Mr. Alexander C. Chenoweth, an engineer, then on the Croton Aqueduct, hearing of these discoveries, obtained a permit from the property owners and began to explore "the Knoll" for Indian remains. Having finished here, he went to Cold Spring and made some further discoveries. All his specimens were purchased in 1894 by the Museum, and some of them are now on exhibition.[1]

Since this time, several interesting relics have been found and, as the work of grading streets, etc., at this part of the Island is carried on, more relics will probably come to light. An account of the recent finds will be found in another part of this volume, the time of this writing having been 1904.

LOCATION OF ARCHAEOLOGICAL SITES.

The only Indian remains left on the Island, so far as known to the writer, are situated at the extreme northern end at Inwood and Cold Spring.[2] They consist of the so-called shell heaps or refuse piles from Indian Camps, and three rock-shelters at Cold Spring. But we have evidence to show that this was not the only part of the Island occupied by the Indians. Mrs. Lamb[3] says that the Dutch found a large shell heap on the west shore of Fresh Water pond, a small pond, mostly swamp, which was bounded by the

---

[1] Catalogue 20, Nos. 2066–2069, 3407–3533 and 6579–6602.
[2] Mr. Reginald Pelham Bolton, in coöperation with the American Scenic and Historic Preservation Society, has been trying to have the site at Cold Spring included in a small park. This would save the last traces of the primitive Manhattanite and it is to be hoped that the plan will go through. See 9th Annual Report of the Society.
[3] History of New York City, p. 36.

present Bowery, Elm, Canal and Pearl Streets, and which they named Kalch-Hook or shell-point. In course of time, this was abbreviated to Kalch or Collect and was applied to the pond itself. This shell heap must have been the accumulation of quite a village, for Mrs. Jno. K. Van Rensellaer [1] speaks of a castle called Catiemuts overlooking a small pond near Canal Street, and says that the neighborhood was called Shell Point. Hemstreet refers to the same castle as being on a hill "close by the present Chatham Square," and says that it had once been an "Indian lookout." [2] Excavations at Pearl Street are said to have reached old shell banks.[3] "The Memorial History of New York" says that a hill near Chatham Square was called Warpoes, which meant literally a "small hill." [4] According to the same authority, "Corlear's Hoeck was called Naig-ia-nac, literally 'sand-lands.' It may, however, have been the name of the Indian village which stood there, and was in temporary occupation." This is the only reference we have to this village, but there are references to another on the lower end of the Island. Janvier[5] says that there was an Indian settlement as late as 1661 at Sappokanican near the present Gansevoort Market. According to Judge Benson,[6] Sapokanican was the Indian name for the point afterwards known as Greenwich. "In the Dutch records references are made to the Indian village of Sappokanican; and this name .... was applied for more than a century to the region which came to be known as Greenwich in the later, English, times. The Indian village probably was near the site of the present Gansevoort Market; but the name seems to have been applied to the whole region lying between the North River and the stream called the Manetta Water or Bestavaar's Kill." [7] Benton says that the name of the village was Lapinican.[8] Going back to the old Dutch records might lead to some results in finding the actual names, etc., of these places.

Most of the specimens found on Manhattan Island, as already stated, come from the northern part. We have a few from the central portion, however. There are the arrow-heads spoken of by Riker, and in Webster Free Library there is a fine specimen of a grooved stone axe found at 77th Street and Avenue B. Mr. Calver has found an arrow-head at 81st Street and Hudson River and the specimens from Columbia College have been already mentioned.

---

[1] Goede-Vrouw of Manahata, p. 39.
[2] Hemstreet, Nooks and Corners of Old New York, p. 46.
[3] Bulletin, N. Y. State Museum, Vol. 7, No. 32, p. 107, Feb. 1900.
[4] James G. Wilson, op. cit., p. 52.
[5] Evolution of New York.
[6] N. Y. Historical Society Collection, S. II, Vol. II, Pt. I, p. 84, 1848.
[7] Thos. A. Janvier, In Old New York, pp. 85–86.
[8] New York, p. 26.

Doubtless the northern part of the Island was inhabited for the longer period; but it is probable that all along the shore, wherever one of the many springs or small brooks, shown on old maps, emptied into the Hudson or East River, there were small, temporary Indian camps. It is likely that these camps were used only in summer, while the primitive occupant of Manhattan retreated to the more protected part of the Island, as at Inwood and Cold Spring, during the winter. Or it may be possible that, as Ruttenber[1] states, the villages on Manhattan Island were only occupied when the Indians were on hunting and fishing excursions, while their permanent villages were on the mainland. Bolton,[2] however, says their principal settlement was on Manhattan Island.

Fort Washington Point. There is a small deposit of shells, on the southern edge of the point, in which the writer found some small pieces of pottery and a few flint chips, thus proving its Indian origin. This was probably a summer camp as it was too exposed for winter use.

The Knoll. "The Knoll" was the name applied to a small rise of land, at the southwest corner of Dyckman Street and Sherman Avenue, which ran out into Sherman Creek from the eastern edge of the hill at that place. As already stated, Messrs. Calver and McGuey found potsherds here; then Mr. Chenoweth obtained permission of the property owners to make excavations. He found numerous fragments of arrow points and pottery in some refuse deposits from an Indian camp and also uncovered what were thought to have been "paved fireplaces." The newspapers of the time had accounts of the finds, with pictures of the pottery and other objects found.[3] Mr. Chenoweth also uncovered a number of skeletons. It is stated that these graves were marked with rough headstones, and there are pieces of a coffin from here in the Terry Collection in the American Museum, as are also a number of lead buttons found with one interment. Everything seems to point to these as being burials of early settlers, but Mr. Chenoweth holds that they are Indian. Several of the skeletons have been preserved in the Museum. So far as is known the only Indian burials yet discovered in this locality were found by Mr. J. Bradley James, Jr., at Van Cortlandt Park.[4] A parallel condition to this at the Knoll was found at 211th Street and will be spoken of later. The Knoll site had undoubtedly been an ancient Indian camp. Probably Sherman Creek was open up to this point to Indian canoes.

Cold Spring. Cold Spring is situated at the extreme northern end of

---

[1] Indian Tribes of Hudson's River, p. 78.
[2] History of Westchester County, p. 25.
[3] New York Herald, January 14, 1894; also Illustrated American, September 19, 1901.
[4] Popular Science News, August, 1896, and April, 1897.

Manhattan Island on the southern shore of Spuyten Duyvil Creek. The Indian remains consist of three rock-shelters and three refuse heaps. The rock-shelter is a formation where the overhanging rocks form a small cave or shelter which the Indians used as a dwelling place. All their rubbish, such as oyster shells, broken pottery and broken arrow-heads, were dumped near by, forming the so-called shell heaps. Messrs. Calver and McGuey explored the shell heaps; but Mr. Chenoweth was the first to suspect the existence of the shelters. There is only one which is likely to have been used as a dwelling place, the others being places where food was stored or shelters for fires used in cooking. These shelters face east, and are at the foot of the hill (formerly called Cock Hill) which forms the most northern part of Manhattan Island. The largest one was formed by several of the rocks breaking off the cliffs above and falling in such a manner that, by digging out some of the earth from beneath them, the Indians could make a small shelter. Probably it was occupied by one family, while the others lived in bark wigwams near by.[1] Another of the shelters is simply an excavation under the end of a huge fragment which also dropped from the cliffs above, and the third is a large crevice in the foot of these cliffs. When Mr. Chenoweth first explored them, all these shelters were completely filled with earth which had gradually worked its way in since their occupation, and much credit is due him for suspecting their presence. In them he found fragments of pottery and stone implements, together with the bones of turkey and deer. The largest of the refuse heaps is situated on a rise directly in front of these shelters. It consists of a layer of shells, in places several inches thick, found under a layer of fine loam, a black earth which has been deposited since the shells which are scattered over the original sandy yellow soil. The sheltered position of this place made it an especially desirable camp site. The hills to the south and west formed a protection to the camp from winds, and by Spuyten Duyvil Creek access could be had to either Hudson or East Rivers; while the Cold Spring, from which the place takes its name, furnished an abundant supply of fresh water.

Inwood Station Site. At the foot of Dyckman Street and Hudson River, there existed a large deposit of shells most of which were removed when the rocks on which they lay were blasted away for grading the street. A few arrow points and bits of pottery, as well as several Revolutionary objects, were found here. Part of the deposit is still left on the northern shore of the small bay just below Inwood station. There are photographs of this deposit in the Museum.

---

[1] Memorial History of New York, Vol. I, p. 33, for picture of houses, and p. 39 for description.

Harlem Ship Canal. Formerly at 220th Street and Kingsbridge Road was a large deposit of shells on the westerly side of the road. This was destroyed when the ship canal was put through. As with the Inwood Station site, no systematic examination of this place was ever made. Mr. John Neafie found some potsherds here in 1886, and Mr. Chenoweth also has some potsherds from here.[1] Mr. Calver says that this was a large deposit, and that the peculiar thing about it was that the shells were so wedged and packed together that a pick would hardly penetrate them. They lay on the bare rock surface in cracks in the rock.

Harlem River Deposit. Mr. Calver says, "Extending from 209th Street to 211th Street on the west bank of the Harlem River and almost on a line with Ninth Avenue was another large deposit of oyster shells lying just beneath the top soil of the field. These shells had nearly all been disturbed by the plow and are interesting only for their color, which was red. Pieces of horn of deer and split bones of the same animal were common among the shells; but, in spite of the apparent antiquity of the deposit, there was, even in the lowest strata of it, some small fragments of glass which proved that either the whole mass had been disturbed or else the shells had been left during the historic period. There are several stone sinkers and hammerstones from this spot in Mr. Calver's collection and at the Museum.

Isham's Garden. This is a large garden about on the line of Isham Street and Seaman Avenue. The soil is white with small fragments of shells. A number of arrow points, flint chips, hammerstones, sinkers and a few bits of pottery have been found here. Mr. Calver has found several shell pockets with small deposits of pottery, etc., on the hill to the south of this garden.

Academy Street Garden. This is a small garden between Academy and Hawthorne Streets, running through from Seaman Avenue to Cooper Street. It was a British camp site during the Revolution, and a number of buttons, gun-flints and bullets have been found there as well as numerous Indian remains. It seems to have been the workshop for a red jasper-like stone of which no finished implements have been found but numerous chips. The shells at this point were first noticed by Mr. Calver in 1890. They may not all be of Indian origin as some may be due to soldiers.

Dog Burials found in 1895. In January, 1895, Mr. Calver found two interesting "dog burials." The first burial was unearthed at the summit of a ridge of soft earth at 209th Street, near the Harlem River. The ridge, which was about twelve feet high, had been partly cut away for the grading of Ninth Avenue. It was at the highest part of the hillock that a pocket of oyster and clam shells was noticed, from which a few fragments of Indian

---

[1] John Neafie Collection, 20-2558; Chenoweth, 20-3498.

pottery which lay on the face of the bank had evidently fallen. The shells, upon inspection, were found to have served as a covering for the skeleton of a dog or wolf. Another burial was found on May 18th within fifty yards of the first burial. It had been covered with shells just as the first one, but had been disturbed by workmen. Mr. Calver says: "The two canine burials were situated at a point just without the borders of the Harlem River shell heap and were distinct from it. The shells were found to be matched, hence it was concluded that they were thrown in unopened or eaten on the spot. As the skeletons were intact and the bones uninjured, all probability of the animals having been eaten is disposed of." These burials are common in this vicinity. No satisfactory explanation of them has been given; but Mr. Calver thinks they were for some religious purpose, and suggests a relation to the "White Dog Feast" of the Onondagas of this State.[1] It is certain that the pockets were in many cases used as fireplaces.

Shell Pockets at 211th Street. In March, 1903, there was considerable excitement over the reported discovery of an Indian graveyard at 211th Street.[2] The graveyard proved to have been that of some slaves, and was situated on the western end of the rise between 210th and 211 Streets, on the eastern end of which is the old Neagle Burying Ground. This discovery was interesting because under the negro graves several shell pockets of undoubted Indian origin came to light. The workmen, in grading Tenth Avenue, cut into this hill to obtain material for filling, and uncovered the graves and pockets. It seems almost certain that the deposits were made some time ago; then the wind blew the sand over the deposits to a depth of four or five feet, and negroes later used this place as a burial ground. In support of this theory is the fact that the pockets were four or five feet under the surface, that the soil above showed no signs of having been disturbed, and that this rise is put down on the Government maps of this section as a sand dune.[3] During the summer of 1904, Mr. Calver with Messrs. Hall and Bolton uncovered nine more pockets to the southwest of the graveyard.[4] These pockets all seem to have been of the same period as the others, and all appear to have been on the original ground surface, although those farther up the hill were some four feet under the present surface. In one of these pockets, Mr. Calver found the complete skeleton of a dog; in another, a turtle shell; two others contained complete snake skeletons; while a fifth held the fragments of a small pottery vessel. The pockets were small, being about three feet in diameter and of equal depth, showing no

---

[1] N. Y. Herald, May 26, 1895.
[2] Evening Telegram, March 14, 1903.
[3] New York Geologic Folio.
[4] New York Tribune, Oct. 30, 1904, and New York Sun, Dec. 14, 1904.

signs of having first been used as fireplaces and then filled up, though charcoal was scattered among the shells. Almost all the relics from Van Cortlandt Park were found by Mr. James in pockets similar to these.

HISTORICAL REFERENCES.

Historical references to the Indians who occupied this territory in the early days are very confusing and contradictory. There seems to be a great deal of trouble in the use of the word Manhattan. Van der Donck in 1633 classified the Indians of this section by language, and said, "Four distinct languages — namely, Manhattan, Minqua, Savanos and Wappanoos" — are spoken by Indians. "With the Manhattans we include those who live in the neighboring places along the North River, on Long Island, and at the Neversinks."[1] It is probable that "it was....this classification by dialect that led the Dutch to the adoption of the generic title of Manhattans as the name of the people among whom they made settlements."[2] De Laet wrote that "on the east side, on the mainland, dwell the Manhattans," and in 1632 Wassenaer adds that they are "a bad race of savages, who have always been unfriendly to our people" and that "on the west side are the Sanhikans, who are the deadly enemies of the Manhattans."[3] "When Hudson returned from his trip up the River which now bears his name, he was attacked by Indians in birch or dug-out (?) canoes at the mouth of Spuyten Duyvil Creek. These Indians were a sub-tribe of the Wappingers or Wapanachki, called the Reckgawawancs."[4] This name seems to have been given to the Indians who inhabited Manhattan Island, while the term Manhattans as already stated was a classification of dialect only. Ruttenber says that the Reckgawawancs were named after their chief Rechgawac;[5] and the name also seems to have been applied to part of the Island for Riker says that,— "The Indians still [in 1669] laid claim to portions of the Harlem lands,....one of the tracts being their old and favorite haunt Rechewanis, or Montagne's Point. The chief claimant was Rechewack, the old Sachem and proprietor of Wickquaskeek, who, as far back as 1639, had been a party to the sale of Ranachqua and Kaxkeek."[6] This sale was made to Bronck by "Tackamack"[7] and his associates and

---

[1] Wilson, Memorial History of N. Y, Vol. I, p. 34.
[2] Ibid., p. 49.
[3] Ibid., p. 34.
[4] Ibid., p. 46.
[5] Ruttenber, op. cit., p. 78.
[6] History of Harlem, p. 287.
[7] This should be Tackarew, according to Ruttenber who says that his descendants were residents of Yonkers as late as 1701: see, Indian Tribes, p. 78.

included a "large tract of land called by them Ranachqua, lying between the great Kill [Harlem] and the river Ah-qua-hung, now the Bronx."[1]

During Indian troubles in 1675, the Wickquaskeeks at Ann's Hook, now Pelham Neck were told "to remove within a fortnight to their usual winter quarters within Hellgate upon this island." Riker says, "This winter retreat was either the woodlands between Harlem Plains and Kingsbridge, at that date still claimed by these Indians as hunting grounds, or Rechawanes and adjoining lands on the Bay of Hellgate, as the words 'within Hellgate' would strictly mean, and which, by the immense shellbeds found there formerly, is proved to have been a favorite Indian resort."[2] A little later the Indians asked to be allowed to return to their maize lands on Manhattan Island and the Governor said that they, "if they desire it, be admitted with their wives and children, to plant upon this Island, but nowhere else, if they remove; and that it be upon the north point of the Island near Spuyten Duyvel."[3]

Mrs. Mary A. Bolton Post, in writing to the editor of "The Evening Post," June 19th of the year of the opening of the Harlem Ship Canal (1895), speaks of some Indians who were allowed to camp on the south side of Spuyten Duyvil Creek on the Bolton property in 1817. Ruttenber says that the Reckgawawanos had their principal village at Yonkers, but that on Berrien's Neck (Spuyten Duyvil Hill) was situated their castle or fort called Nipinichsen. This fort was protected by a strong stockade and commanded the romantic scenery of the Papirinimen, or Spuyten Duyvil Creek, and the Mahicanituk (Hudson River), the junction of which was called the Shorackappock. It was from this castle that the Indians came who attacked Hudson on his return down the river.[4] Some small shell deposits occur on Spuyten Duyvil Hill, but as yet this "castile" has not been definitely located. The village site at Yonkers, according to Mr. James, is now covered by buildings; but several relics found near the site years ago are now in the Manor Hall at that place (1904).

Judging from these references, we might conclude that the territory occupied by the tribe commonly known as Manhattans included Manhattan Island and that part of the mainland which is west of the Bronx River north to Yonkers, and that these Indians were a sub-tribe of the Wappinger division of the Mohicans.

---

[1] History of Harlem, p. 151.
[2] Ibid., p. 366.
[3] Ibid., p. 369.
[4] Ruttenber, pp. 77–78.

THE INDIANS OF WASHINGTON HEIGHTS.

BY

REGINALD PELHAM BOLTON.

INTRODUCTION.

The earliest history of the City of New York is especially associated with the northern portion of the Island of Manhattan, and it is a remarkable fact that the long-retarded development of the locality has preserved to this late date many of the actual evidences of aboriginal life, of which, in the lower and middle part of the island, all traces were long since swept away. It is therefore, not only with a particular degree of definiteness, but with the peculiar interest attaching to many visible remains of the past, that the history of Washington Heights is fraught. Three hundred years have elapsed since that period when, prior to the advent of Henry Hudson, Manhattan was the undisturbed domain of the Red man. The rugged heights from Manhattanville to Spuyten Duyvil, which bore the native name of "Penadnic," or perhaps more properly, "Pen-atn-ik," "the sloping mountain," whose densely wooded sides formed a refuge for innumerable wild beasts and birds, were traversed by the natives on a trail, which, following the line of least resistance, mounted from Harlem, on the present general course of Avenue Saint Nicholas, to 168th Street, and thence, as Broadway now runs, to Dyckman Street. At this point, it is most probable that the trail divided, leading in several directions to the residential localities or camp-sites of the natives around the Inwood valley, two of which paths probably extended to the Spuyten Duyvil Creek, at points available for crossing to the mainland. Of these, one was a shallow place long thereafter known as "The Wading Place," close to the present Kingsbridge, at that portion of the creek which was known to the natives as Pa-pir-i-nemin, "the place where the stream is shut," a term which was applied to the water way, as well as to the abutting lands on Marble Hill, and at Kingsbridge.

Another, and perhaps a more important path, led to that secluded and still undisturbed dell below the east side of the end of Inwood Hill, which is now known locally, as the "Cold Spring Hollow," where, among overhanging masses of rocks detached from the lofty cliff, a secure refuge was afforded from winter's storms and from hostile observation, a spot known to the Red Man as, Sho-ra-kap-kok, or "the sitting-down place." This has been rendered, "a portage," and may well have been so, since it was in direct line between the Harlem and the Hudson River. The marshy bed through which the creek then wound (and in part still winds) its devious way, was shallow enough near the spring to permit communication with the mainland at Spuyten Duyvil Hill, on the crest of which was a large native village, strongly protected by a girdle of palisades and known as "a small water-place," or Nip-nich-sen.

The native occupants of this part of the Island of Manhattan were members of a local band, known as Weck-quas-kecks or Wick-quas-keeks. Their speech was Algonkian, their group Mohican, their tribe, Wapanachi, their sub-division, Siwanoy, and they and their neighbors, the Reck-ga-wa-wancs, divided the nomadic occupation of lower Westchester County and of the Upper part of Manhattan Island.

The term Manhattans, it may be noted, was merely indicative of those Indians from whom the name was learned, and to whom it was applied, being the men encountered upon Man-ah-atn, "the island of hills."

The Reck-ga-wa-wancs, whose chief in 1639 was Rechewack, seem to have made their headquarters at Ran-ach-qua, a considerable village on the Acquehung, or Bronx River, and at a fishing headquarters, of which they made great use in certain seasons, at Rech-a-wan-is or Montagne's Point, on the shore of the Bay of Hell Gate, near 110th Street, and also at another site at 121st Street and Pleasant Avenue, in the same locality.

The Wick-quas-keeks' chief village was Nip-nich-sen, the defensible and palisaded position on the summit of Spuyten Duyvil Hill, which was located where the public school building now stands; but recent discoveries indicate that a large part of the band made their home, and their resort for oystering, fishing and ceremonial observances, in the sheltered valley of the Dyckman tract, now generally known by its modern title of Inwood.

This favored valley, affording several very desirable positions for native residence, bore among them the general title of its tribal occupants, Wick-quas-keek, or, as the name became corrupted in colonial times, Wickers-creek. Situated between the noble Mai-kan-e-tuk, or Hudson, the great "river of ebb and flow," on the west, and placid Muscoota, or Harlem, on the east, and lying in a basin surrounded by the Pen-atn-ik Hills to the south and west, the Nip-nich-sen and Papirinemin Hills on the north, and the range of Kes-kes-kick, or Fordham Heights, to the east, no more ideal place could well be found for native occupancy. It is not therefore surprising, that at a number of points in and around this valley, the remains of Indian occupation have been, and at this date are still numerous, and that it appears to have been inhabited by quite a considerable population, and for a great length of time.

As in later years of military strife, the commanding heights of Fort George Hill overlooked the entire scene, and afforded a wide range of vision in all directions. Native objects taken from the soil in the area between 191st and 196th streets, and Amsterdam and Eleventh (or St. Nicholas) Avenue, indicate its use as a place of residence and probably of observation while a large crevice in the rocks on Fort George Avenue, may have afforded a shelter for an outlook. Across the vale to the west, at 181st Street, was a large clearing in the woods, on which the natives raised maize to such an extent, that it was known to the early settlers as the "Great Maize Land," or Indian Field, and on Jeffrey's Hook, now known as Fort Washington Point, deposits of shells, in which fragments of native pottery have been found, attest the use of this bold promontory as a place of occupation.

The little brook, rising in the high ground at 180th Street just west of Fort Washington Avenue, made its way down the present line of Bennett Avenue, to 194th Street, and crossing the trail at that point, entered the marshy lowland on its way to that deep indentation of the Harlem below Fort George Hill, the Dutch Half-kill, now known as Sherman's Creek, into which another stream entered, rising in the neighborhood of Seaman Avenue.

Where the brook and trail crossed at 194th Street and Broadway a favorable sloping bank still used for truck farming, was utilized as a camp-site by natives, and perhaps the massive overhanging rocks below Fort Tryon between 194th and 198th Street on the west side of Broadway, may have afforded them some shelter in winter.

Along the east side on Inwood Hill, from Academy Street to the Creek, numerous remains indicate a considerable occupation, easily traced at present along the recently-opened line of Seaman Avenue. Between Academy and Hawthorne Streets, many evidences of the work of native artificers in the manufacture and repair of spear and arrow-heads point to long continued residence. In the field, still farmed upon the estate of Mr. William B. Isham, at Seaman and Isham Avenues, a planting ground was evidently cultivated, the native tools therein found, the rich soil and favored location combining to indicate its use.

In the middle space of the valley, in full sight of the surrounding heights, and of the Nipnichsen village, the tribal ceremonies were probably held, for at 211–213 Streets, just west of 10th Avenue, pits containing oyster shells, packed over and around the remains of a dog, and accompanied by broken pottery, suggest the observance of the long-surviving aboriginal ceremony of the White Dog feast and burial.

Along the bank of the Spuyten Duyvil Creek, now largely wiped out by the ship canal, were, and in some places are still, certain shell deposits, and along the west bank of the Harlem, at 219th, 213th, 210th and 202nd Streets various objects of interest attest the one-time presence of the Indians. Another such favorite spot for the fisherman of the tribe, as it was long after

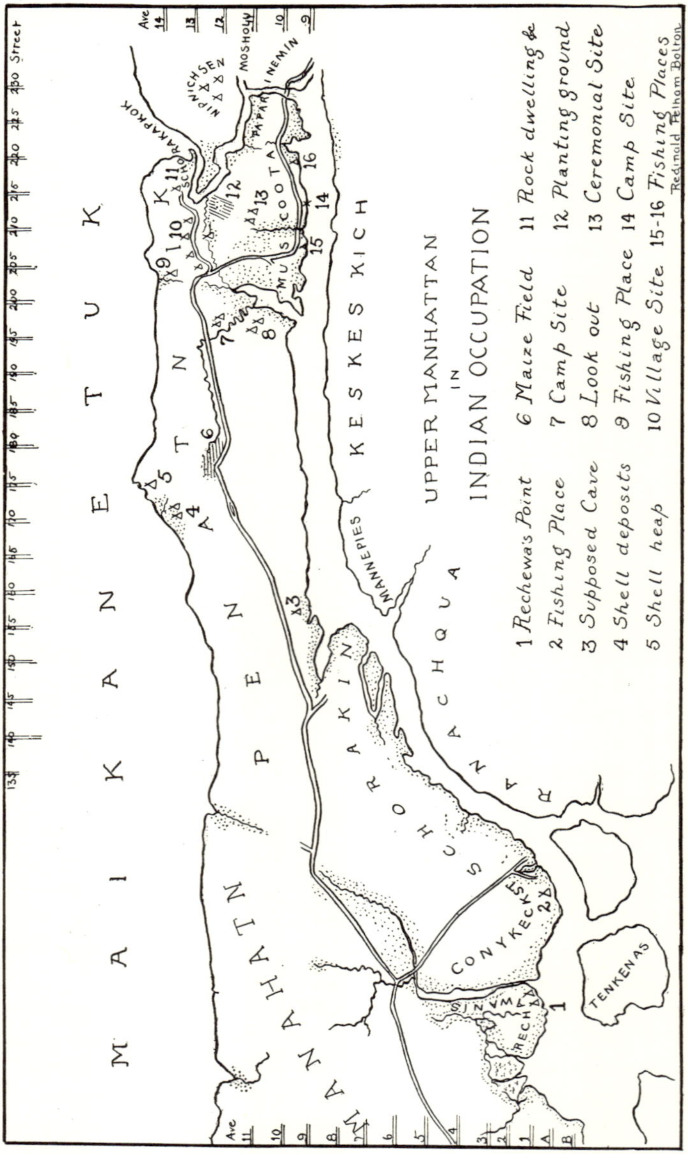

for his colonial successors, was the "Little Sand Bay" at Tubby Hook, just south of Dyckman Street, on the east side of the Hudson River Railroad, where, amid the still existent remains of primeval occupation, and surrounded by the same wild rocks that sheltered their rude huts of bark, the interested visitor may stand to-day and view the same noble scene of flowing river and palisaded background. It is, however, at Shora-kap-kok, among the romantic tangle of wildwood and precipice, through which a woodland foot-path winds towards the "Spouting Spring," that the most extensive shell deposits may be found, massive heaps covered by the acres of brushwood, out of which, hard by the spring, a magnificent tulip tree has reared its lofty form, the largest and perhaps the oldest tree in the upper part of the island. Here too, the interested investigator will find the actual rock-shelters under the cliff, from which were taken by Mr. Alexander Chenoweth, in 1895, successive layers of aboriginal pottery and implements, and remains of food which are now in the Museum.

Here, in the solitude of wild nature, it will take but little efforts of the imagination to bring before the mind the scene, when the bustling horde of Wick-quas-keeks swarmed about the rocks, through the woods, and along the bank of the creek, the men hauling from their log canoes, "napsia" baskets filled with oysters, opening and drying their succulent contents for the purpose of food or trade; the squaws mending grass nets and fishing lines, filling the cooking pots with red-hot stones from the wood fires, the smoke of which blackened and the heat of which split the sides of the rocks beneath which they were kindled; the children bearing water from the spring, playing games of skill with knuckle bones, or shooting with favorite toy bow and arrow, while the papooses, with baby stolidity, were perched near the crackling fires, sucking the bones of the latest toothsome addition to the larder, be it deer or dog. Or amid the wintry snows, when the fires were kindled inside the rock-shelters, and in the bark-huts erected on the shell heaps, one can readily picture the same occupants wrapped in furry bear, downy beaver, or silky deerskins, huddled around the crackling logs pounding corn, boiling sapsis, scraping hides, splitting pebbles and flints, and longing for the spring's return.

Into this peaceful and simple existence, one bright afternoon in September, in 1609, came the astonishing news of the advent, on the broad bosom of the Mai-kan-e-tuk, of the Sea-Monster or devil-canoe, which had arrived ten days before in the lower bay, and of which no doubt stories, almost unbelievable, had already reached their band, on which craft were reported to be white-faced men dressed in strange clothing, and possessing the most fascinating objects, hatchets and knives, alluring to mankind, and colored beads fascinating to squaws, which might be procured from them by exchange. The "Remonstrance" of 1649, recites that "even at the present day, the natives of the country (who are so old as to remember the event) testify: that on seeing the Dutch ships on their first coming here, they knew not what to make of them, and could not comprehend whether they came down from Heaven, or whether they were Devils. Some among them, on its first approach even imagined it to be a fish, or some sea-monster, so that strange rumor concerning it flew throughout the whole country."

As the Halve Maen floated up with the tide towards Nip-nich-sen, the community no doubt turned out in a body and swarmed to points of vantage on Inwood and Spuyten Duyvil Hills, under shelter of trees and rocks, as the vessel came to an anchor off the shore, probably at a point just south of Fort Washington Park, in view of the loftiest point of the Palisades up-stream, "which showed out to us," as the ship's log runs, "bearing north by east five leagues off us." The next morning, before the southeast breeze, she went up river, followed by many a wondering gaze; and then came news from the native neighbors on the lower part of the island that two of their number had been detained on the ship, and were now carried off upon her, while another, who had been taken in similar manner had escaped.

On the first of October, the vessel re-appeared, coming down the river before a northwest wind, but, meeting the flood tide off the mouth of the creek, came to anchor there. The occurrences which followed, are told in detail by Robert Juet, in the Journal of Hudson's Voyage. "Then came one of the savages that swamme away from us at our going up the river, with many others, thinking to betray us, but we perceived their intent, and suffered none of them to enter our ship."

The revengeful nature of the Red Man, however, had been aroused by the detention of the hostages whom Hudson had seized, and, as the ship lay with her head down-stream, waiting the turn of the tide, they made an attack upon the vessel. "Two canoes full of men, with their bows and arrows shot at us after our sterne: In recompence whereof we discharged six muskets, and killed two or three of them."

Thus was started the blood feud between the Red and White man on our island, and the stupidly revengeful action, immediately aroused the whole local community, so that, as the ship weighed and slowly floated down river on the ebb, "above an hundred of them came to a point of land to shoot at us." The ship would have passed close to Fort Washington Point, so that the natives swarmed the woods at close range. "There I shot a falcon at them," the first cannon that ever woke the echoes of our hills, "and killed two of them, whereupon the rest fled into the woods," scared no doubt by the thunderous explosion. "Yet they manned off another canoe with nine or ten men," "which came to meet us," probably from the little cove below the Point, "So I shot at it also a falcon, and shot it through and killed one of them. Then our men with their muskets, killed three or foure more of them. So they went their way."

We may well imagine the excitement and rage of the Wick-quas-keeks after this affair, and the descriptions of it which would be spread abroad and handed on to the younger members of the tribe, to perpetuate a distrust and enmity which would bear fearful fruit a third of a century later.

We are not without detailed description of our primeval predecessors upon the island of Manhattan, for the Hollanders recorded many of their impressions of aboriginal peculiarities. We may assume that they possessed the usual characteristics, the stolid demeanor, the crafty methods, and revengeful nature of the Indian, all of which were exhibited in their dealings with the White intruders. These local bands appear to have had, in addition, some particular local habits. They painted their faces with red, blue, and yellow pigments, to such a distortion of their features, that, as one sententious Dominie expressed it, "They look like the devil himself." Their dependence on supplies of game and fish caused their removal from one place to another, semi-annually, and we read of their removal to a summer "hunting-ground" in Westchester, whence the band returned to "Wickers Creek," for the winter shelter, and to resume their occupation of oystering and fishing in the Harlem and Spuyten Duyvil Creek.

As for dress, "They go," said Juet, "in deerskins, loose well-dressed, some in mantles of feathers, and some in skins of divers sorts of good furres. They had red copper tobacco pipes, and other things of copper they doe weare about their neckes."

No copper objects have been found in upper Manhattan, probably their metallic stock was bartered away with the early colonists, for in 1625, De Laet described their use of "Stone pipes for smoking tobacco."

As regards their food, the evident abundance and size of the local oyster shells shows that they possessed in them a ready source of subsistence. As soon as Hudson's ship reached the neighborhood of Greenwich, where the Indian Village Sappokanikan, was located, the natives "brought great store of very good oysters aboard, which we bought for trifles." De Laet (1625) says, "their food is maize, crushed fine and baked in cakes, with fish, birds and wild game." Van der Donck and others wrote in 1649: —

"Their fare, or food, is poor and gross, for they drink water, having no other beverage; they eat the flesh of all sorts of game that the country supplies, even badgers, dogs, eagles and similar trash, which Christians in no way regard; these they cook and use uncleansed and undressed."

"Moreover, all sorts of fish; likewise, snakes, frogs and such like, which they usually cook with the offals and entrails."

"They know also, how to preserve fish and meete for the winter, in order then to cook them with Indian meal."

"They make their bread, but of very indifferent quality, of maize, which they also cook whole, or broken in wooden mortars."

"The women likewise perform this labor, and make a apa or porridge called by some, Sapsis, by other, Duundare, which is their daily food, they mix this also thoroughly with little beans, of different colors, raised by themselves; this is esteemed by them rather as a dainty than as a daily dish."

Their weapons were, of course, the usual aboriginal bow, arrow, spear, club and tomahawk, though but a few years later, they had acquired from the settlers enough fire-arms to become exceedingly expert in their use. "Now, those residing near, or trading considerably with the Christians, make use of fire-locks and hatchets, which they obtain in barter. They are excessively fond of guns; spare no expense on them, and are so expert with them, that in this respect they excell many Christians." Many of their discarded neolithic weapons have been found, and these exhibit a wide variety of material and workmanship, indicating considerable acquisitions from other tribes and localities. Their household utensils included "mats and wooden dishes," and Juet refers to their "pots of earth to dresse their meats in," and speaks also of the women bringing "hempe." The character of the grass mats which the women wove is to be seen in the imprints made with such material upon the outer surface of some of the local pottery. They also made the grass baskets, often referred to in early records, as "napsas." The pots of earth were the large earthenware vessels made by the Indian women, on the decorations of the rims and upper portions of which, these poor creatures expended all their ingenuity and sense of art.

Of these objects, there remain a number of interesting examples discovered in upper Manhattan, the most complete, and at the same time, most artistic, being the fine Iroquoian vessel discovered by Mr. W. L. Calver, on the south side of 214th Street, about 100 feet east of 10th Avenue, in the fall of 1906. The large vases found in broken condition in the cave at Cold Spring, are of the cruder and therefore, earlier design of the original Algonkian inhabitants, who at a later period, probably by barter, and perhaps by inter-marriage, acquired or learned the art of Iroquoian design and decoration.

Of the period during which the race occupied this locality, we can only make conjectures. The extent and character of the shell heaps at Cold Spring and the pits and burials at Seaman Avenue, certainly indicate a settlement of large numbers or of considerable age. The ceremonial pits at 212th Street, and certain remains of aboriginal feasting, such as fish bones and oyster shells, appeared to exist at a level below the graves of the slaves of the settlers, buried at that place.

While these conjectures may carry back the period of occupancy to antiquity, the tools and weapons are all of the modern order, and no objects of true paleolithic character have been discovered, so that we have as yet, nothing definitely reaching back into the remote ages of the most primitive mankind, although on Hunt's Point in the Bronx, at no great distance away from our island, a very interesting rude ax and a hammer were discovered by Mr. Calver in a gravel-pit, near the old Hunt burying-ground.

ABORIGINAL REMAINS ON WASHINGTON HEIGHTS.

The objects of an aboriginal character, which have been discovered upon the upper part of Manhattan Island, afford a good deal of information as to the nature and habits of the natives. The story of the first discovery of aboriginal objects in this locality is worth preserving, and may show on how slight a matter may hinge the direction which is given to archæological attention, which in this instance, if not given at the time, would in all probability have resulted in the destruction, by building and street opening, of most of the evidences of primeval life, which the work of Mr. W. L. Calver has preserved. It was in the spring of the year 1890, that, during a search for Revolutionary relics, he became acquainted with James McGuey, a resident of Inwood, with whom a casual observation of the ground at Seaman Avenue and Academy Street was made. Here, a number of arrow-heads and a hammerstone, were discovered together with a fragment of Indian pottery. This little surface find started the explorers' interest in this direction and McGuey extended his investigations to the land on the south side of Dyckman Street which was then being opened, where he secured a number of fragments of pottery. At this place, which is known as "The Knoll," there were a number of rude stones set in such positions as to indicate the presence of graves. The information of these finds spreading, they were dug into by several residents who found therein a number of skeletons which the newspaper accounts described as aboriginal. The presence of buttons and other colonial objects, however, disproved this fanciful theory, and the discovery of the first indisputable Indian burial was not made until 1907 by W. L. Calver and the writer, in Seaman Avenue. (Fig. 6.)

The wanderings of the first two explorers led them to the shell heaps at Cold Spring Hollow where their search was soon rewarded by many objects of aboriginal character. Others were found by them, at the foot of Dyckman Street near the Hudson River bank, and at large shell heaps near the then Kingsbridge Road (Broadway) on the line of the present

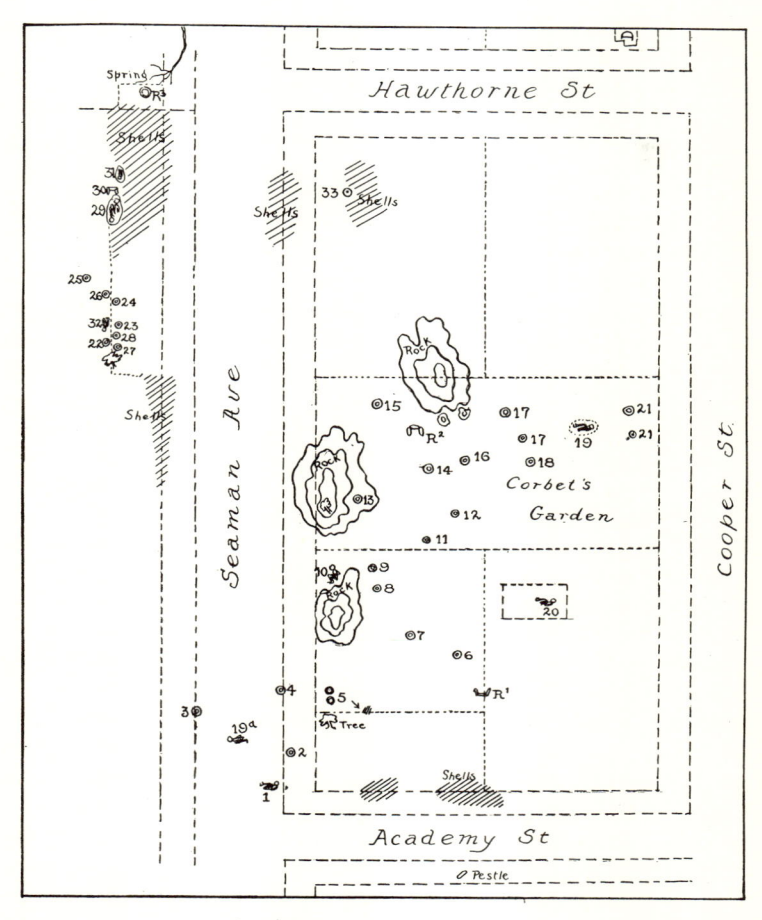

Fig. 6. Location of Burials, Pits and Shell-beds near Inwood. 1. Human remains. 2. Shell pit, deer antler. 3. Shell pit. 4. Shell pit, pottery. 5. Shell pits. 6. Shell pit, sturgeon below. 7. Shell pit, sturgeon scales. 8. Shell pit. 9. Shell pit. 10. Human remains. 11. Fire pit. 12. Shell pit. 13. Dog burial, puppy. 14. Shell pit. 15. Part of a jar. 16. Shell pit, fish and meat bones. 17. Shell pits. 18. Two dogs in shell pit. 19. Human skeleton, 1907. 19a. Female skeleton, 1908. 20. Human remains when house was built. 21. Small fire pits, Revolutionary. 22. Large shell pit. 23. Large shell pit. 24. Shell pit. 25. Dog burial. 26, 27, 28. Shell pits. 29. Two human skeletons, male and female. 30. Revolutionary fireplace "Royal Mariners" and "17th" 31. Skeleton and infant, female. 32. Skeleton (Chenoweth, 1908). 33. Revolutionary fireplace, 71st, officers' buttons. D, Dyckman dwelling. R1, R2. Revolutionary fireplaces. R3. Revolutionary well.

Ship Canal. The soapstone pipe, Plate XVII, Fig. 4, was also found near the same highway, bearing upon it a rude representation of a human face. At 209th to 211th Streets along the shore of the Harlem River, a number of shell deposits proclaimed the one-time presence of the Indian, and with them were found bones of deer and split bones of other animals, although the surface of these deposits had been much disturbed by the plows of the Dyckmans.

Near this spot, on January 27, 1895, Mr. Calver found the first of the dog burials (250)[1] which have since then been discovered in a number of places around Inwood Vale. This skeleton, together with fragments of pottery was found beneath a compact mass of oyster shells about eighteen inches deep. The skeleton was incomplete and evidently disposed at the

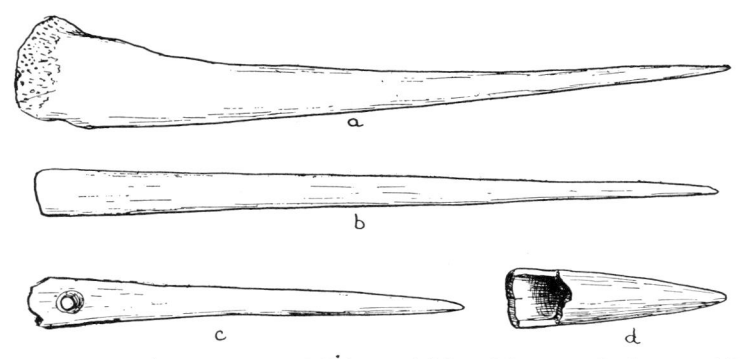

Fig. 7 *a* (1–3942), *b* (1–3944), *c*, *d* (Bolton and Calver Collection). Implements of Bone and Horn, Van Cortlandt Park. Length of *a*, 14.5 cm.

bottom of the pit with intention and care, probably indicating that the animal was sacrificed in some such ceremonial as the "White Dog Feast" of the Onondagas, which has survived to recent times. Of these burials one (250) was found at 209th Street and 9th Avenue, another (251) at 210th Street and 10th Avenue, another among a series of pits around the base of the hillock in which were found the remains of the negro slaves of the early settlers, at 212th Street and 10th Avenue. This latter was opened by Messrs. Edward Hagaman Hall and W. L. Calver and was found to contain with the skeleton of a dog, fragments of a vase, Fig. 8. Other pits at this place contained the bones of a turtle and a snake, and one contained large fish bones (281), possibly the remains of a necklace.

During the year 1907 Mr. Calver and the writer discovered numerous

---

[1] Reference numbers are those of the Calver Collection.

shell pits in Seaman Avenue, (Plate XIII), one of which, not far from the first human burial (291) contained the skeletons of two dogs (252), one much smaller than the other, which, together with some pottery, lay under a mass of oysters, and nearby was a rather shallow pile of oyster shells, below which lay the remains of a puppy (253). Across the avenue, close to the human burials (291, 292) a shallow pit of shells and debris contained the skeletons of two puppies (254). These dog burials may have been not an uncommon feature of the aboriginal life of a local tribe.

The opening, by Mr. Alexander Chenoweth, of the interior of the cave at Cold Spring, disclosed a large number of objects, showing its extended occupation by the Red man. These objects are now in the Museum, where they form an interesting collection. Around this spot many other objects were found indicating the use of this sheltered glade by the wild animals of the forest, by the Indians, and by their successors, the soldiery of the Revolution. The mixed character of such objects is shown by No. 268, a group of aboriginal and civilized debris taken at one time from the soil beneath an overhanging rock, the surface of which still bears traces of the fires it once sheltered.

One of the most interesting places, which was examined with considerable thoroughness, is the site of the one-time "Century House," or the Nagel homestead, and perhaps also the site of the home of Tobias Teunissen, the first white settler in this locality (p. 98). Here, on the river bank at 213th Street, around and below quantities of colonial, Revolutionary and more modern relics, were found many evidences of Indian occupation. The interesting "banner stone" or ceremonial (Plate XVII, Fig. 6) was found here, almost two feet below the ground in 1906; its state indicating long use, its fracture and repair, and final second breakage. Among oyster shells of abnormal size and shape were found a fine stone tomahawk (Plate XVII, Fig. 11) which appears to have been utilized as a rubbing stone or pestle, a beautifully formed war arrow-head of black chert, a flint boring-tool (211) and the small paint cup (229) in the form of a hollow pebble such as are found on the beaches of Long Island, but having two distinct nicks on its edge. Quite near this cup was a piece of brown ochre or paint stone. A pestle (212) was found in one wall of the old building, long buried within its foundation, and close to the dwelling, but well below the sods was the bone needle (Fig. 7c). Another curious find of a needle was number 239, which was found in the shell pit which contained the remains of the two puppies on Seaman Avenue (254).

These finds culminated in the discovery, by Mr. W. L. Calver, at 214th Street, about one hundred feet east of 10th Avenue, of a fine jar of Iroquois pattern, about 13 inches in diameter and height. This interesting object slightly protruded from the surface of a newly graded bank and had been missed by the spades of the laborers by no more than an inch (Plate XIV). It lay upon its side, about eighteen inches below the sods and was quite intact. It has an old break in the rim which may have been utilized as a spout, and a hole about three quarters of an inch in diameter in the body. This jar has the four characteristic prominences of rim, around which the decoration is incised in diagonal and vertical lines, with a band of four lines following the contour (Plate XV).

These finds and particularly those of the dog burials, stimulated interest in the search for some traces of the actual aboriginal residents of this section; and many were the laborious efforts made to locate such remains. These were not rewarded until the grading away of the base of the east side of Inwood Hill for the opening of Seaman Avenue, disclosed a large number of shell pockets or pits and the hasty operations of the laborers threw out with these a few fragments of human bones. By the number and variety of objects found on the line of Seaman Avenue, it would appear that this favored spot was the site of a considerable encampment or village. It occupies the sandy slope at the base of the east side of Inwood Hill, and is sheltered from north and west winds and from observation from the Hudson River.

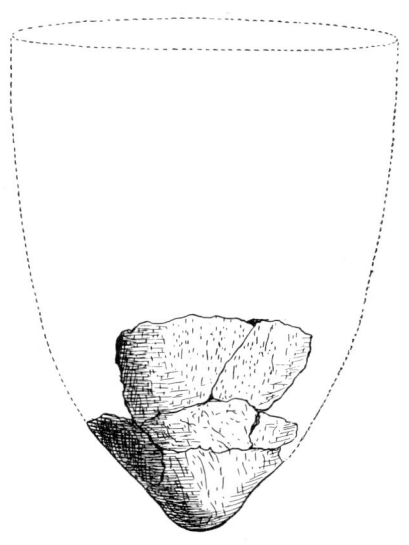

Fig. 8 (Bolton and Calver Collection). Bottom of an Algonkin Vessel, Showing a Peculiar Point. Manhattan Island.

Its advantages were recognized in the Revolution by its selection as one of the largest camps of that period; where we learn from Washington's own observations, upwards of a hundred tents were placed. So, remains of Revolutionary warfare, buttons, badges, weapons, missiles and camp debris are found scattered over the same area with aboriginal stone weapons, implements and pottery, while the camp fire of the British soldiery trenches upon the fire pit of the Red man, or may even be found to have been dug into the shallow grave of an Indian warrior. All around this place were found, in recent years, numerous surface indications of Indian occupation, including a large number of fragments of the red indurated shale of New Jersey, worked in part into weapons, while arrow-heads of varied material and character were scattered over the same space (99–102 to 110, 168) a good club-stone (193) was found here. Here also were found articles of less sinister character such as stone axes (125–142) hammerstones (111 to 114–120–141) used for pounding nuts and corn, sinkers (118–144–145) used for fishing nets, pestles (150), a celt (119), a gouge (149) and a tool (158) of unknown character. These objects were scattered over the area extending westward from Academy Street to and beyond Isham Street and were particularly in evidence in a strip of ground, extending from Seaman Avenue to Cooper Street, cultivated by a gardener named Corbett. The excavations referred to (1907) destroyed a number of shell pits or pockets ere they could be investigated, but enough remained to establish the long continued use of the location by the aborigines.

At the bottom of several of these shell pits were found quantities of

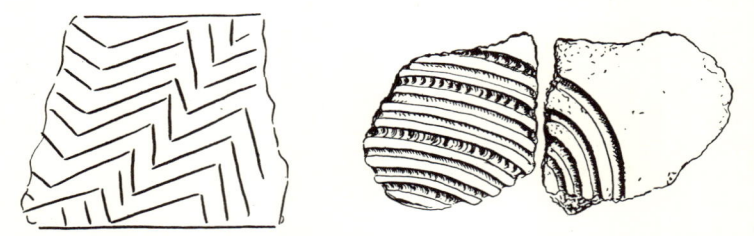

Fig. 9 a (20–3461), b (20–6586). Incised and Stamped Fragments of Algonkin Pottery. Manhattan Island.

sturgeon scales (225 and 259) accompanied by deer prongs in one case and by pottery in another. Other pits contained evidences of fire, firestones, pottery and animal bones (260 and 261). Among the debris thrown into the street, the writer found the first evidence of human remains (284), a fragment of a skull and a vertebræ. The find excited attention and other fragments were soon found at the corner of Academy Street and Seaman Avenue (283). Among them were a tooth and a fragment of a jaw. A few other fragments (285) were thrown out at Hawthorne Street. It thus became evident that there were human interments in the vicinity, and in August 1907 the first burial (291) was discovered under a shell pit in Corbett's garden. The grading process had been extended only about eighteen inches below the sod, but had sufficed to destroy the jaw of the skeleton which extended upwards, as did also the foot bones. The bones lay in and upon a close mass of oyster shells, some of which were unopened, the skeleton reclined on its right side, facing west. The arms were flexed and crossed, the knees bent and the head thrown back. No traces of weapons were found, nor were there any other objects found, save a fragment of an animal bone.

The location and position led to further exploration which early in 1908 led to still more interesting discoveries. Sunday, March 22nd, being the first day in the field for exploration for the season for 1908, W. L. Calver and the writer met at Seaman Avenue and Hawthorne Street, Manhattan, to discuss plans for further excavations on this Indian village site. The rains of the winter 1907–8 had washed the west bank where the layer of oyster shells and black dirt lay along the hill, and a patch of red burnt earth was observed, which on digging out, disclosed a fireplace, evidently of the period of the Revolution, having some large burnt stones, ashes, wood charcoal, brick, broken rum bottles, a wine glass nearly complete, a large open clasp-knife with bone handle, a hoop-iron pot-hook, various forged head nails, and a curious folding corkscrew. Gold buttons of Revolutionary pattern and an officer's silver button of the Royal Mariners, together with pewter buttons of the 17th Regiment disclosed who had occupied the spot.

At one part of this fireplace, we came upon a pocket of oyster shells, evidently Indian, about two feet deep, and on removing some of these had the good fortune to uncover a human thigh-bone. We worked carefully into the shells and under the pocket, gradually disclosing the complete remains of a full grown man (293) lying on its right side, feet to the north, head facing east, knees doubled up, the left arm extended down through the thighs. The feet had been within the area of the hole in which the Revolutionary fireplace had been made, and only one or two foot bones were found. At a later period other foot bones were found on the opposite side of the Revolutionary fireplace, evidently having been displaced in its construction. The right arm was flexed, and the hand was under the head, the latter was intact and every tooth was in place. Shells had been packed over the body, and some around it. We were much puzzled by a number of human bones, lying compactly together by the skeleton, in a position that would have been in its lap had it been upright (Plate XVI).

We removed the skull, covered the remains, and on Sunday, March 29th, renewed the work. We went carefully to work upon the cluster of mixed bones (293b) in front of the large skeleton, and soon found them to be rather compactly arranged in a rectangular form about 14 by 26 inches, the long bones parallel. The vertebræ abruptly ended parallel with the head of the larger skeleton, and after working some time, we found a skull placed below, beneath the pile of bones in a vertical position, facing north, the lower jaw of which was disengaged, and was placed sideways in front of the face. The back of the skull was broken in, and was black with marks of burning. The lower jaw was burned, and some of the teeth split by fire. The arm and leg bones were charred at the joints. Inside the skull was a burned toe bone. There were some oyster shells among the charred remains.

A significant fact was that the right arm bones of the large skeleton were below the pile of burned bones. This feature, and the compact arrangement of the latter within the space in front of and at the same level as the large skeleton, seem to point strongly towards an intentional arrangement of these bones, in front of the large corpse and to indicate the simultaneous burial of the two bodies. On examination, the large skeleton proved to be that of an adult male, and the dismembered remains those of a female of about 35 years of age. No implements were found with the remains but a part of a stone pestle (231) and a rude celt (232) lay under the sod among the oysters above the large skeleton.

On Sunday, June 14, 1908, another burial was found about 20 feet north of the above. This burial consisted of an adult skeleton doubled up and its back much curved, and was apparently that of a female of mature age. Between the knees, the remains of a small infant were laid, the skull of the latter being fragmentary. The right hand of the adult was below the infant and the left hand around the throat. The skull was intact and had nearly all the teeth. One finger bone had grown together at the joint in a crooked position apparently due to disease. On lifting the ribs of the right side, an arrow-head of flint fell out between the fourth and fifth bones. These skeletons lay about two and a half feet below the grass, and a pocket of oyster shells was over the head. The woman's remains lay within a space about 31 inches long by 50 inches wide, flat in the hard red sand bed facing east.

Shortly after these remains were discovered, Mr. Chenoweth extended the excavation previously made by the explorers at the side of a large oyster shell pit in the same bank of sand, and uncovered a male skeleton of which he preserved the skull. Some small fragments of the skeleton (287) were afterwards found by the writer on this spot. Contractors for the sewer in Seaman Avenue also uncovered the remains of a young female (290) close to the position of several of the shell pits previously described.

These interments have some curious features. The position of the remains facing east, sometimes west, the absence of weapons or other objects and the oyster shells packed with or above them are subjects for interesting discussion on which future finds may throw much light, as also upon the peculiar double burial and the burnt state of the female remains.

The general result seems to indicate that the Wick-quas-keeks had special customs and ceremonies of which the dog-burial was one, and the possible suttee of the widow of a sachem, another. The use of the shell pits partly for shells only, partly for the debris of feasts, partly for dog or fish burials and partly to cover human remains is a subject open to conjecture.

The continued disturbance of the surface may yet bring to light other

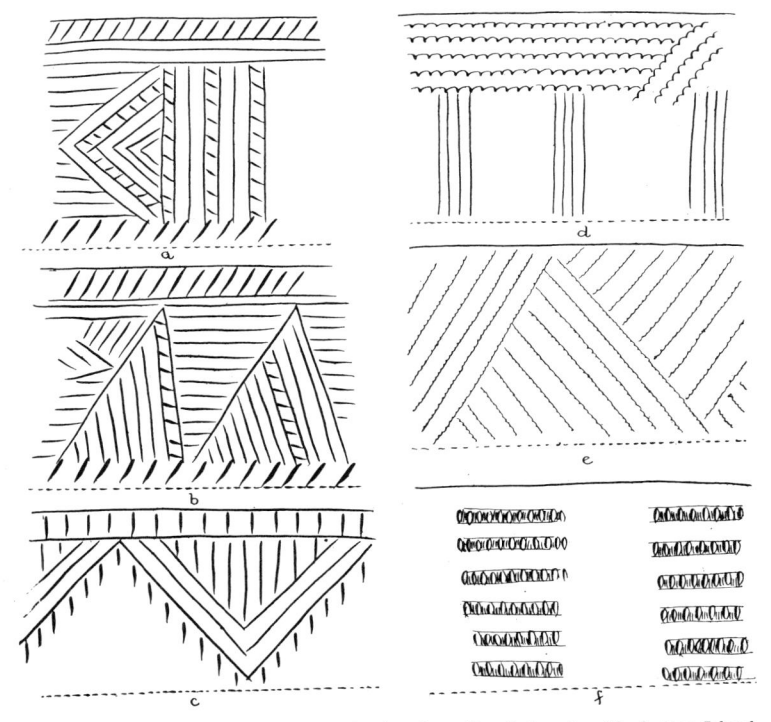

Fig. 10 (Bolton and Calver Collection). Designs from Vessels found on Manhattan Island.

remains and objects which may afford information as to the purposes of some of these discoveries, but enough has been found to indicate the characteristics of the early Manhattanites and to add to the interesting fact of their association with the island upon which our great city was founded; peculiarities, which in themselves are of particular interest to archæologists.

Relations with the First Settlers.

The story of the relations of the European settlers with these early owners of Upper Manhattan, is a tale with many of the same characteristics, as that of the contact of the two races in other parts of our country, where the White man, finding a foothold by courtesy, or by some nominal purchase, eventually excites the Indian's jealousy by his encroachments, and then pursues with the native, a course of expropriation, with or without warrant, returning an exterminating vengeance on every attempt of the native to resist the advance of "civilization." So, on Manhattan, the first White arrivals, by courtesy of the natives, who were "hospitable when well treated," as De Laet says, "ready to serve the White man for little compensation," became squatters at Battery place, a tenure which in 1626, was, by the so-called "purchase" of the island by Director Minuit, exchanged for an ambiguous ownership, the extent of which, as well as the authority of those Indians who entered into the bargain were promptly repudiated by the natives as soon as the White man advanced to their home locality, and made his appearance at Harlem and the Heights. It appears from their objections, frequently repeated from this time forward, that the Indians had at least regarded that sale as extending no further than Yorkville on the east and Manhattanville on the west, at which part of Manhattan in those early days, the watery marshes of Harlem plain, the deep indentation of Rechewa's creek on the east (the later Harlem Creek) and the rivulet in the Manhattanville ravine on the west, practically cut off the island from the Heights. That this view not only prevailed, but was recognized by those of the Hollanders, whose sense of justice was added to a consideration of self-interest, is shown by the fact that Stuyvesant entered, in 1649, into an additional deed of purchase of some portion of the upper end of the island, which deed also recognized the then, and future Indian title to ownership of the westerly half of the upper end of the present Borough.

It was in the year 1636, that Doctor de la Montagne, the first White settler of Harlem, arrived, in a dug-out canoe, at Rechewas' Point, or 105th Street, on the East River, bringing with him, his wife, two babies, and some farm hands, and soon made a clearing for a bark cabin, at 7th Avenue and 115th Street. His authority for settlement was a "grant" from Kieft, of about two hundred acres, extending from 109th to 124th Streets and from 5th to 9th Avenues, through which extended the Indian trail to the Heights. To this locality, De la Montagne gave the name of Vredendal or "Quiet Dale," and to it were soon attracted other hardy settlers who pre-empted practically all the large tract of low-land which is now covered by Harlem, all settling thereon without further consideration of, or consent by, the natives.

Jonas Bronck arrived in 1639, but crossing the Harlem to Morrisania, he made a new purchase of the tract then known as Ranachqua, now part of the Bronx, by a regular deed, in which Rechewac and other sachems joined.

One of the most important of these early squatters of Harlem was Bronck's friend and fellow-countryman, Captain Jochem Pietersen Kuyter, who secured from the Dutch authorities in July, 1639, the right to settle upon the Indian "Schorrakin," a large tract along the bank of the Harlem, from the line of 1st to 5th Avenue, which he re-named Zegendal, the "Vale of Blessing," and to which he added a sort of claim to the lower end of Washington Heights, which became known to the scanty settlers, as "Jochem Pieter's hills."

It was but natural, if the Red Men regarded these Harlem settlements as trenching upon their property rights, and as interfering with their very means of subsistence, that they would resent a continual enlargement of the settlement, and as each succeeding settler was followed by others, and their favorite haunts, fishing and oystering places were appropriated, their suspicious nature was aroused, and it only needed some overt act on the part of the White Man, to precipitate an outbreak. Every inducement of advantage, as well as of security, lay in the direction of conciliating the natives, who surrounded the pioneers on every side, and at first the accommodation of each to the other was mutually recognized. The settler often needed the Red Man's labor, his venison, oysters and furs, and at times even his maize, for all of which he paid in objects of small value, or bartered his old guns and ammunition. On the other hand, to the native, the settler represented a market for these materials, and a source whence could be obtained beads for his squaw, and fire-water for his own enjoyment. Thus the settlers had come to regard the Wick-quas-keeks as no novelty, and their visits to the bouweries or their appearance on the trail, or their passage on the broad waters, as matters of no special importance. Kuyter wrote, that the settlers "pursue their out-door labor without interruption, in the woods, as well as in the field, and dwell safely, with their wives and children, in their houses, free from any fear of the Indians." How different might have been the history of this locality, had this mutual confidence been maintained.

The breach was precipitated by Director Kieft's own ill-judged course of action. Attempting in 1639, to impose and collect a Tax upon the Red Men, he followed this futile act by an attack, with very slim excuse, on the Raritan Indians, by a force of soldiers, in July, 1640, which act excited all the neighboring tribes. A Wick-quas-keek, who from boyhood, had harbored a grudge against the Hollanders, because his uncle had been killed, and his beaver skins stolen by three of Minuit's men some years before, took a long-deferred revenge one mid-summer day, by murdering old Claes Swits, one of the Yorkville settlers, in his house at Turtle Bay, which stood "on the road over which the Indians from Wick-quas-keek passed daily." It was a brutal act, and the murderer was known, for he had worked for Swit's son, and it was accompanied too, by theft, for the savage, "stole all the goods," for some of which he was bargaining with the old man when the deed was done.

A yacht was sent to Wick-quas-keek to demand satisfaction, and the surrender of the murderer, but the Indians, regarding the act as entirely justifiable from their point of view, refused, and their head Sachem expressed the general feeling of their growing resentment, by saying that he "wished twenty Swannekins (Dutchmen) had been murdered," instead of the one who had fallen. No satisfaction could be obtained, and the more peaceable spirits among the Hollanders postponed action in revenge, urging that at any rate, an attack on the Indians should not be made, "till the maize trade be over," and should be attempted "in the harvest when the Indians were hunting."

When that period had arrived, a conference took place (November 1, 1641) as to the advisability of using force with the savages. Jochem Kuyter, whose bouwerie was the most advanced and exposed to retaliation, advised patience, and suggested that the Indians who were alert, should be lulled into security before an attack should be made upon them. So no action was taken, until scouts reported early in 1642, that the natives "lay in their village suspecting nothing," and the deplorable decision was then reached to seize this opportunity of sending an armed force upon them. Accordingly, a body of 80 men, commanded by Ensign Hendrick Van Dyck, marched to the neighborhood of Yonkers, under the guidance of Tobias Teunissen, a farmer employed by Montagne, who knew the locality. The expedition failed to surprise the natives, and losing their way in the darkness, the Hollanders returned, fortunately without conflict. Their appearance, however, had effected sufficient impression, to lead the sachems to agree to a peace treaty, which was formally entered into in Bronck's house in Morrisania.

The ties of mutual confidence had now been broken between the Red and White Man, and as the ill luck of both would have it, the enemies of the former, the Mohawks of the Albany district, chose the succeeding winter for an incursion upon the Wick-quas-keeks, for the purpose of reducing them to their ancient condition of tributary vassalage. An overwhelming horde of Mohawks, equipped with firearms, descended upon Westchester County, and slaughtered the unfortunate clansmen in Yonkers, Spuyten Duyvil and probably at Inwood, captured many of their women and children, and forced the survivors, a fugitive crowd, to make their way in the deep snow of that bitter winter season, to Fort Amsterdam, there to seek the protection of the White intruders.

To the everlasting shame of Kieft, of Tienhoven and others among the Hollanders, the White men repaid this confidence by a murderous act of treachery, of which the history of civilization contains few equally barbarous examples. On the night of February 25, 1643, the wretched Wick-quas-keeks, then huddled in temporary shelters at Van Corlear's Point, and at Pavonia, on the Jersey side of the Hudson River, were massacred in cold blood by "civilized" soldiers and citizens, and so indiscriminate was the slaughter, that even Indians of friendly tribes were put to death. The cruel act brought a prompt punishment. Joining hands, the outraged natives of all neighboring clans, took issue against the settlers, and all around the new City and especially at Harlem, they attacked the outlying settlements, slaughtered the farmers, captured their families, killed or drove off the live stock, and burned their houses, their grain and hay. The rest of the winter "passed in confusion and terror," but in the spring, a mutual desire for a truce, which would enable both parties to sow their fields, led to a doubtful peace, which was formally agreed to on April 22, 1643, a peace which, as soon as their crops were harvested, was broken by the Red Men, who again drove the settlers off their holdings, and chased them within sight of the walls of the fort. Privation, if not starvation, now stared the colonists in the face, so that even the most peaceful among them joined in expeditions, by which during the winter of 1644, the territory of the Wick-quas-keeks was scoured, and the natives driven from their homes by sword and fire.

Amidst all the destruction, Zegendal, the Harlem home of Captain Kuyter, had been preserved, protected as it was by a strong palisade, and a guard of men stationed within, but on March 5, 1645, it too was set on fire by a blazing arrow, and the house, barn and crops were entirely destroyed. This act was no doubt the crowning revenge of the tribesmen, directed against Kuyter, for his share in the conflict, as a Captain of troops, and the ineffectiveness of the guard and of the defenses of palisades in protecting this important property, created so widespread an impression, that all further efforts to colonize our locality, were, for the time being, abandoned. Nevertheless, a system of passive resistance to the active savages eventually wearied them to such an extent, that the tribes became willing to bury the hatchet, and on August 30, 1645, at a grand council in Fort Amsterdam, a peace was concluded, in which "Little Ape," the chief of the Mohawks, spoke as the representative of their tributary tribe, the Wick-quas-keeks and pledged them to the treaty obligations, of which that which most affected the local clan, was, that no Indian should "come with weapons on Manhattan Island, nor in the vicinity of Christian dwellings."

Adriaen Van der Donck, the first lawyer among the settlers, and a man of some substance, had, in 1647, received as a grant from Governor Kieft, but had also honorably secured by purchase from the Sachem Tacharew, that tract of marsh and meadow, some thirty or forty morgen in extent, bordering on the north side of Papparinemin, which we now know as Kingsbridge, intending there to build and till, "since his inclination and judgment led him to that place." The features of marsh and meadow, so dear to a Dutchman's heart, led others to look with interest upon the very similar features upon our Island, in the charming vale which to-day comprises the Dyckman tract.

It thus came about that the settlers had barely summoned the necessary courage to start back to their abandoned holdings, and the aborigines had recovered enough sense of security to return to their lair under the Inwood hills, ere, undeterred by the failure of his previous course of action, and disregardful of the unextinguished right of livelihood and residence of the Red Man, Governor Kieft, in 1646, entered upon a course of extended grants of unsettled lands, selecting the very centre of Indian home-life for distribution to the favored recipients.

To Matthys Jansen Van Keulen, he gave, August 18, 1646, a ground brief of all Marble Hill, the "Papparinemin," and to the same enterprising land-grabber and his friend Aertsen, a patent was issued for the entire 200 acres of the choice marshes of the Dyckman tract extending from 211th Street, south to Dyckman Street, a tract known later as the Ronde-vly, or Round Meadow.

On this land, which the patentees did not attempt personally to occupy, a hardy pioneer now took up his abode. Tobias Teunissen, who, as the representative or lessee of the patentees, thus became the first squatter at Inwood, had been employed by Dr. De la Montagne on his farm in Harlem, and now taking to himself a new Vrouw, the couple ventured into the very heart of the Red Men's home, and established themselves on the Harlem west bank, probably at or near the site of the later, Nagel or Century, house. There is some reason to suppose their little dwelling may have been that of which the writer discovered the foundation, fireplace and floor, beneath the surface of the garden ground in front of the site of the Century house, a little half basement built of rough stone, the upper part in frame, half sunk in the crest of the river bank, around which were also found a number of interesting Indian objects.

Teunissen's situation was not without peril, for he had been the guide in the unsuccessful expedition to Yonkers, in 1642 and was thus a marked man among his savage neighbors, with whom an injury was nursed but never forgotten. The appearance among them of this pioneer, and still more, the appearance of the surveyors, deliberately staking out these claims in the immediate vicinity of their winter home, must, we may well imagine, have filled the natives with forebodings of the inefficacy of the peace they had so recently concluded, and have stirred again in their breasts the sense of resentment.

Kuyter, whose bouwery at Zegendal lay still in ruin, had been engaged in a controversy with Kieft, which eventually resulted in the departure of the latter, and his replacement by Stuyvesant. The removal of Kieft, however, at first brought no improved policy towards the Indian rights, for his successor, following the same course, began by allotting to Isaac de Forest, another large section of Harlem lands, between that of Jochem Pietersen Kuyter, and the Van Keulen hook. Stuyvesant, however, eventually recognizing the ill-success and difficulty besetting these continued efforts to settle the lands of which the Red men still maintained their ownership, entered, in 1649, into a remarkable deed of purchase, evidently intended to quiet those claims and to avoid further restlessness on the part of the natives. This deed ran as follows: —

"On this day the date underwritten appeared before the Noble Lords the Director General and the Council, Megte-gich-kama, Ote-yoch-guo, Wegta-koch-ken, the right owners of the lands lying on the North River of New Netherland on the east shore called Ubiequaes hook in the breadth through the woods, 'till a certain Kill called Seweyrut diverging at the East River, from thence northward and southward to a certain kill named Rechawes, the same land betwixt two kils one half woods betwixt the North and East Rivers so that the western half to the aforesaid is still remaining and the other Easterly half with a south and north directions middle through the woods the aforesaid owners acknowledged that with the consent of the Chief Sachem they have sold the parcel of land and all their oystering, fish, &c. unto the Noble Lord Petrus Stuyvesant Director General of New Netherland for and in consideration of certain parcels of merchandize which they acknowledge to their satisfaction to have received into their own hands and power before the passing of these presents, viz:

6 Fathoms cloth for jackets	10 Harrowteeth
6 Fathoms Seawant	10 Corals or Beads
6 kettles	10 Bells
6 Axes	1 Gun
6 Addices	2 lbs. Lead
10 knives	2 lbs. Powder
	2 Cloath Coats.

In consideration of which the before-mentioned owners do hereby the said land convey transport and give over to the aforesaid Noble Lords the Director General and to his successors in full, true and free ownership.

To the said land We the Grantors neither now nor hereafter shall ever present any claim for selves, or heirs and successors desisting by these presents from all action, either of equity or jurisdiction, but conveying all the same to the said Director General and to his successors to do therewith as it may seem proper to them without their the Grantors, or any of them molesting the Grantee of the aforesaid land whether in his property or in his family.

It is also agreed that the most westerly half just as the Lord Director pleases, shall go with this for so many goods as in.... can be, and they the Grantors promise at all times to induce their Rulers on the North River to take the matter over and not to sell any without the knowledge of the Lord Director General; the Grantors promising this transport firmly to maintain as in equity they are bound to do.

Witness these presents by them respectively signed in the Fort Amsterdam in New Netherland this 14th day of July A. D. 1649.

>Meg-te-gich-kama
>Ote-yoch-guo
>Weg-ta-koch-ken

The land boundaries herein loosely defined, evidently covered some large portion of the upper end of the island, from a point on the north side of Rechewa's Creek (or Harlem Creek) at 109th Street on the East River and was intended perhaps to extend as far north as the Sherman Creek, though possibly only as far as the then inlet at 155th Street and 8th Avenue. In either case, the right of the natives to the "westerly half," the wooded hills of the Heights, was clearly conceded, and the consent of the Mohawks "their rulers on the North River," was required for any further concession.

This bargain still left, undealt with and unpaid for, the Dyckman tract and Marble Hill, and the continued presence of Teunissen and his little family of wife and child in that area, within sight of their winter home, and upon the very ground on which their crops were grown and their ceremonies conducted, must have kept alive a resentment which lost nothing by the passage of time.

In this connection, the following statements of Riker are worthy of notice: —

"The Indians were resolved upon expelling the Whites from this end of the Island, upon the ground that they had not been duly paid for their lands. It is certain that the Indians did not recognize the sale (to Minuit) as a surrender of all their rights and privileges on this part of the Island. Perhaps, grown wiser in a generation, they saw that the trivial price then paid them ($24.) was no equivalent for their rich maize land and hunting grounds."

"But they probably claimed to have reserved (as they often did in their sales) the right of hunting and planting, because in after years the Harlem people so far admitted their pretensions as to make them further compensation.

Well had it been for the Colonists had they earlier given heed to the dissatisfaction of the Indians, and done something to remove it."

Riker does not seem to have observed the foregoing deed of 1649, in which Stuyvesant did make an effort in part to effect such a settlement, though it evidently did not go far enough, and I think the secret of the continued dissatisfaction lay more in the trenching upon their home lands of Inwood, and in the practice of hunting within their wild woods on the Heights, than upon their expropriation from Harlem, though they must naturally have suffered from the loss of their important fishing and oystering stations (121st Street and Pleasant Avenue, and on Montagne's or Rechewa's point 105th Street and Avenue A). Be the immediate provocation one or the other, the dissatisfaction of the Red Men so increased, that their threats and evidence of hostility caused general alarm and distrust among the White settlers, and in the year 1654, a fresh outbreak of savage vengeance resulted.

Among those who had returned to their abandoned holdings was Kuyter. Finding difficulty in securing help for the restoration of his farm, as many of the settlers still feared a re-settlement of the outlying bouweries, "through dread of the Indians and their threats," he at last undertook to occupy his farm himself, and marked man as he was, it was little to be wondered at, that in March, 1654, he fell an early victim to the savages, whose growing resentment against the re-occupation of their property now broke out afresh.

An organized effort now began on the part of the Red Men to sweep away, once and for all, the White intruders. On September 15, 1655, hundreds of braves, gathered at Inwood, embarked in sixty-four canoes, and reaching New Amsterdam, scattered through the town before daybreak, intent on plunder and killing. Governor Stuyvesant was absent, but the leaders of the townspeople, parleying with the savages, induced them temporarily to withdraw, probably because the savages never loved a daylight engagement. A skirmish, however, ensued in the evening, in which the Dutch soldiers drove off the invaders, who, in the same dread night of darkness, took their revenge upon the helpless settlers in the outlying districts, and commenced a terrible slaughter. "Miserably surprised by the cruel barbarous savages," Tobias Teunissen, and full fifty others, were murdered, and more than a hundred terrified women and children were carried off into captivity, among them Teunissen's wife and child.

The recent settlers in Kingsbridge, on the land which had been bought by Van der Donck, and those also on Jonas Bronck's land across the river, were driven away and their lands laid waste. The canoes of the Red Men prowled about Hellgate, waiting favorable opportunities of attack by their favorite method of surprise, and ere a few days had passed, every settlement was denuded by death, captivity, or flight, of its White occupants. Glutted with revenge, and having fully accomplished their main purpose, the savages sent in two captives, in October, offering to return others for ransom. In this offer, the families of Teunissen and of Swits, the son of the unfortunate colonist whose murder had resulted from the old grudge, were not included, both significant of a particular resentment felt by the natives towards these settlers.

Stuyvesant returned, and a council was called, at which the weakness of the little colony in the face of Indian numbers, was weighed against the desire for vengeance. The soldiers were therefore sent out only to bury the dead and gather in the scattered herds. They were stricken to the heart by the scenes of slaughter, devastation and ruin which every bouwery presented. It was not until the end of November, that the widows of Teunissen and Swits, with their children, were ransomed from their savage captors. What tales the poor women could have told of the wild life, habits, shelter and fare, which they had been forced to share for those weary weeks of captivity.

Thus perished poor Teunissen, the first settler of our Heights, a man of humble but sterling character, whose very determination and fearlessness brought about the sacrifice of his own life and of many others.

So thorough was the effect of this dreadful massacre, that by an ordinance of January 18, 1656, all further settlement upon outlying farms was forbidden, and all attempt for the time being, to colonize the island by separate farms was definitely abandoned, and the Red Men were left for a time, in undisputed possession of their wild home among the rocks of Inwood hill and to their whilom undisturbed occupations of fishing, oystering, and hunting on Washington Heights.

The Town of New Haerlem and the passing of the Red Man.

"The Director General and Council of New Netherland guarantee hereby, that for the further promotion of agriculture, for the security of this Island, and the cattle pasturing thereon, as well as for the further relief and expansion of this City Amsterdam in New Netherland, they have resolved to form a New Village or Settlement at the end of the Island, and about the land of Jochem Pietersen, deceased, and those which are adjoining to it."

Thus was ordered the establishment of the Village of New Haerlem, and the inducements of allotments of ground, for a dwelling, for a garden, and for a farm, with an accompanying slice of salt meadow soon attracted a little body of settlers, whose homes were laid out in August, 1658, along the line of that branch of the Indian trail which led from McGown's Pass, at Central Park near 110th Street, and afforded a beaten track to the Harlem River at 125th Street and First Avenue.

Confidence was to be established by the community life, and the mutual protection it afforded against the treachery of the natives. The public, however, was doomed to further alarm when news arrived on September 23, 1658, of the fierce outbreak of savage warfare at Esopus, so that many fled from their newly established homes, into the city, and a state of unrest existed all that winter. Farming operations were brought almost to a standstill, notwithstanding the precautions which the settlers employed, of farming in common, even planting their contiguous fields in strips of similar crops, so that the workers could always be near each other, and always having their weapons handy.

In March 1660, a military company was formed in Harlem, under the command of Jan Pietersen Slot, as Sergeant, which was furnished with a supply of powder, and the inhabitants were thus prepared for defense.

Another Indian attack and massacre at Esopus was reported, January 7, 1663, and started a fresh alarm at Harlem. The village folk again assembled into military companies, and proceeded to place palisades around their little village home, within which, two 7-lb. cannon were mounted, and a strict military watch was kept. The savages at Esopus were soon put to rout by the Dutch armed force under Stuyvesant, and part of the Harlem force having volunteered, took part in the campaign.

In July, a body of Wick-quas-keeks, including about 80 warriors now professedly friendly, fearing an attack from the armed parties of Mohawks upon the war path, moved from their usual haunts, for their better security, into the woods of our Height, and caused alarm and panic among the settlers. Their Chief, Sau-wen-a-rack, with his brother, came into Harlem and explained the reason for their proximity, stating that they feared an attack by the Esopus Indians, who were advancing 50 or 60 strong, to attack them and also to wipe out the Harlem settlement. The threatened incursion failed of accomplishment, but the Sachem and his people, taking advantage of the common feeling of danger, seized the opportunity to ask permission to fish near the village, which was conceded, on condition that they should bear no weapons near the town. To identify the friendly from the hostile, they were given copies of the official seal of the West Indian Company, printed on wax in small billets, to be shown on necessary occasions.

In 1664, 16 May, a new treaty with the tribes of the Hudson, was concluded, and the Harlem people were relieved by the fact that Sau-wen-a-rack, head sachem of our local tribe, renewed his pledge of friendship, by signing it.

In September of this eventful year, the British fleet arrived, and the Dutch dominion was exchanged for the English, under the Governorship of Col. Richard Nicolls, one of whose first orders, addressed "to the Schout and present magistrates of Harlem," ran as follows:

"To the Schout and present Magistrates of Harlem:
A *Warrant* to the Magistrates of Harlem for the Prohibition of the sale of Strong Liquors to Indians.
Whereas: I am informed of several abuses that are done and committed by the

Indians, occasioned much through the liberty some persons take of selling Strong Liquors unto them;

These are to require you, that you take especial care that none of your Town presums to sell any Sort of Strong Liquors, or Strong Beer, unto any Indian, and if you shall find any person offending therein, that you seize upon such Liquor and bring such person before me, to make answer for the offense.

Given under my hand, at Fort James in New York, this 18th of March, 1664, (1665. New Style). Richard Nicolls."

Governor Nicolls, on October 11, 1667, issued to the growing township of New Haerlem, a charter, which, entirely ignoring any of the rights or claims of the aboriginal owners, granted to the new community the entire area of Upper Manhattan, northward from a line drawn across the island, from 74th Street at the East River, to 130th Street at the Hudson, with "all the soils, creeks, quarries, woods, meadows, pastures, marshes, waters, lakes, fishing, hawking, hunting, and fowling . . . . and freedom of commonage for range and feed of cattle and horses further west into the woods, upon this Island as well without as within their bounds and limits."

This charter further empowered the town to establish a ferry, at 125th Street, to the Bronx, and authority was later given, in order to divert the traffic to the ferry, that the road to Spuyten Duyvil should be stopped up. This course was pursued, and fences were built for the purpose, but the growing number of travelers to and from the Westchester side, found the tolls of the ferry excessive, and continued to drive their cattle and horses through the "wading place" at Kingsbridge, a shallow place still traceable at 230th Street. So persistent was the public in preferring its own line of travel, that in 1668, a change of policy was decided upon, and preparations were made for removing the ferry to Kingsbridge. Johannes Verveelen, the ferry-man, was, in 1669, authorized to establish the ferry there, and was further given a grant of all or great part of Papparinemin (Marble Hill) and of land on the Kingsbridge side, on the latter of which he proceeded to erect a habitation for himself, and for the accommodation of travellers, probably on the site of the later hostelry, which occupied the site of the Macomb house, still standing at 230th Street, and in 1670, he commenced, as part of his agreements required, the making of a bridge, "over the marsh between Papparinemin and Fordham."

At the latter locality, an enterprising proprietor, John Arcer (later known as Archer) had established a community of settlers.

The Wick-quas-keeks, though many of them had been "beaten off by the Maques," from their resort at Inwood and Westchester County, and were mostly at this time, in hiding in the wild forests of the Ramapo, still from time to time, reasserted their rights to the Harlem lands. Rechewack, the sachem who in 1639, had been party to the sale of Morrisania to Bronck, was still insistent on his claim to the old haunt of his particular clan, upon Rechwa's or Montagnes' point, and in order to quiet this claim, Jan la Montagne made a bargain with him, by which, for some consideration not stated, he secured the acknowledgment of its sale to him, as follows: —

1669.

"On this date, 20th August, old style, the underwritten Indians (willden) have sold to me, Jan la Montagne, the Point named Rechwanis, bounded between two creeks and hills, and behind, a stream which runs to Montagne's Flat, with the meadows from the bend of the Helle-gat to Konaande Kongh

| Sellers of the Point | { Rechkewacken
Achwaarowes
Sacharoch
Pasach keeginc
Niepenchan
Kouhamwen
Kottaren } | Tappan |

This was by no means all of the Indian claim. On April 9, 1670, when several Sachems were concluding a deal with Governor Lovelace, for the sale of Staten Island, "some of the Indians present laid claim to the land by Harlem," and repudiated, when it was exhibited to them, the deed, of 1626, or its effect. Some of those who signed Montagne's deed, just recited, also became parties to another sale of lands along the east shore of the Harlem, as far as "Bronxland," by which their proprietorship in that borough was recognized to have been still existent.

In 1673, the Dutch re-captured New York, a short-lived triumph for in 1674, Sir Edmund Andros arrived with the news of the cession of the Colony to England, and the Harlem township settled down under British rule which continued until the end of the Revolution.

In 1675, the disquieting news arrived of the great outbreak of the Narragansett Indians, under King Philip, and as a precaution, some of our local Sachems were invited to an interview for the purpose of securing the continuance of their friendship and neutrality. As a further precautionary measure, in the fall of that year, orders were issued that the canoes of Indians along the Westchester shores of the Sound, should be laid up where they could not be used, and the Wick-quas-keeks at their summer haunt on Pelham Neck, then known as Ann's hook, were directed "to remove within a fortnight to their usual winter quarters within Hellgate upon this island."

"This winter retreat," says Riker, "was either the woodlands between Harlem Plains and Kingsbridge at that date still claimed by these Indians as hunting grounds, or Rechewanes on the Bay of Hellgate."

We have seen, however, that they had already definitely parted with Rechewane's point.

Thus, the winter retreat, of which we now know more particularly, was no doubt the Inwood resort, and the rock-shelters in Cold Spring Hollow. That this was the case, seems also to follow from the action of the Indians referred to, who in obedience to this order and their usual habits, attempted to pass up the Harlem River in their canoes, stating that they were going to "Wickers Creek." They were stopped by the local force of watchmen or militia, under the direction of Town-constable Demarest, who, in reporting his action to the Governor, received from him a reply as follows:

"Mr. Constable:

I have just now seen, by your of this day sent express by Wm. Palmer, of your having stopt 10 or 12 Indian canoes, with women, children, corn and baggage, coming as they say from Westchester, and going to Wickers-creek, but not any Pass mentioned; So that you have done very well in stopping the said Indians and giving notice thereof.

There are now to order all the said Indians to stay in your Town, and that you send some of the chiefest of them to me early to-morrow, and one of your overseers for further orders; and that it may be better effected, you are to order them some convenient house or barn to be in, and draw up their canoes until the return of them you shall send; and that you double your watch.

Your loving Friend,

E. Andros.

N. York, October the 21, 1675.

These unwelcome guests were soon permitted to pass on, but the distrust of their actions continued, and a close watch appears to have been kept upon their movements.

On Jan. 7, 1676, however, some eighteen members of the tribe, headed by one known as "Claes, the Indian,"[1] voluntarily visited the Governor, assuring him of their friendship, by word of mouth, confirmed by a present of venison and deer skins, and asking for protection against their fellow redskins. The Governor promised them all the help in his power, and offered them a present of "coates, but they desired drink, which is ordered for them." The natives thereupon shrewdly seized the opportunity to demand official permission for cultivating their old maize lands on Manhattan Island, which they would have to leave again the next spring if they were compelled then to remove to their summer haunts at Ann-hook, and their request being brought formally before the Council, it was: —

---

[1] Claes or Claus De Wilt (Willden Indians) was also described as Longe Clause or Claes, and as a "native Indian." With a squaw, named Kara-capa-co-mont, he entered into a deed in 1707, confirming the title to the Van Cortlandt lands at Kingsbridge.

"*Resolved*, That the Wickers-creek Indians, if they desire it, be admitted with their wives and children, to plant upon this Island, but nowhere else, if they remove, and that it be upon the north point of the Island near Spuyten Duyvil."

This must have referred to the planting field, to which reference has been made, at Seaman Avenue and Isham Avenue, and the grudging permission evidently conceded to some extent, the Indian's claim to that locality.

The tribe proved the sincerity of their profession of friendship, and the defeat of King Philip and his warriors in August of 1676, brought greater sense of security to the colony, and evidently a less regard for the Indians and their claims, so that in 1677, the free-holders of New Haerlem began to divide up between themselves available common lands included in the wide terms of their Charter.

First they surveyed, and then divided up Marble Hill and the remainder of the Matthys Jansen property down to the line of 211th Street, staking the property off in five allotments, which were "given out by lot." These fell to Vermilje, Boch, Nagel, and Dyckman, the two latter of whom purchased the shares of the others, and thus formed the tract which afterwards became the Nagel farm.

Of this property they made a lease to Hendrick Kiersen and Michael Bastidensen, conditioned upon their planting sundry apple and pear trees yearly, and for the first seven years as an acknowledgment of title, a quit rent of "each one hen every year." The same two owners subsequently acquired the Jansen and Aertsen tract, or Round Meadow, being all lands between 211th Street and Dyckman Street, and east of the present Broadway to the Harlem River, with the exception of some patches of meadow land, already granted to other owners, Myndert Iouriaen, and Pierre Cresson.

October 26, 1677, the long-abandoned home of Tobias Teunissen, was thus again the scene of the White man's husbandry, and the natives again found their home locality invaded by the White settler. No attempt has been made, however, so far, to till or to allot lands lying around Inwood hill, nor in the wild woods of Washington Heights, which the wolves and other wild creatures still infested.

By official command, Aug. 1, 1685, Governor Dongan, granted "liberty and licence" to any of the inhabitants "to hunt and destroy the said wolves," and a general foray resulted in wiping out the dangerous creatures, which had shared with the Red Man the actual possession of Washington Heights.

The desire to increase the town revenues, and to extend the area of available cultivable lands, led the township authorities to appropriate the Indian clearing known as the great Maize Land, south of 181st Street, lying, probably, west of the trail, which is now the course of Broadway.

Jan Kiersen, who may have vacated the rather dangerous lease of Nagel's lands at 211th Street, undertook the task with his father-in-law, Captain Jan Gerritsen Van Dalsen, and the town entered, March 30, 1686, into a lease of "The great Maize Land, belonging under the jurisdiction of New Haerlem," for a period of twelve years, the first seven, at the rent of a fat capon yearly, and the last five, at two hundred guilders in good wheat, rye, peas, or barley, at the market price; "from each parcel the just fourth to be given to God the Lord."

The lease, rather than the partition or the sale, of this Indian planting ground, may have been due to a recognition of the lack of moral if not of actual warrant for its appropriation from its original owners, who, now that their right of planting was restricted to the north end of the island, were no longer able to continue the use of the 181st Street tract.

James, Duke of York, and proprietor of Manhattan, became James II., king, in 1685, and his representative, Governor Dongan, looking out for an increase in the emoluments of the Colony, now asserted his intention to appropriate all common lands not yet purchased of the Indians, which could be construed as belonging to the King, who was not to be regarded as bounden by his own acts as Duke.

A new Charter was therefore solicited by the Harlem settlers, and was issued on March 7, 1686, under terms of a new quit rent. Once again, then, was confirmed to the free-holders of New Harlem, their heirs, and assigns, all lands included in the original area, without any reference to, or regard for, the claims or unextinguished title of the aborigines.

The woodlands of Washington Heights were as yet unbroken from Manhattanville to the Creek, except by the road which wound its way up the line of the old Kings Bridge road, now St. Nicholas Avenue, and of Broadway to the Inwood flat-lands, on which the Nagel and Dyckman meadows were partly opened to cultivation.

The time, however, had come when the townspeople realized that a final adjustment must be made with the Indians, or their charter rights would stand a good chance of being affected, so on February 28, 1688, Colonel Stephen Van Cortlandt, acting on behalf of the town of New Harlem, delivered to the representatives of the Wick-quas-keeks, "Sundries" in exchange for their surrender of their entire claims, with a cash or "Sundry" balance to be paid to them later. This full settlement was not effected, by reason of the negligence or poverty of the townspeople, until March 1, 1715, when a special tax was levied for the purpose, and the amount thus raised, we must suppose, was paid to the dwindling remnant of the tribe.

Thus passed away the native ownership of Washington Heights, and their occupation of the primeval homes, fields and fisheries of the Red Man on our Island. Scattered over their one-time busy village sites, and around the wide mounds of shells, the traces of many a generation of occupancy lay abandoned, till the plough of their supplanters, or the veil of growing vegetation hid them from sight. Below the sods of the Nagel farm and along the bank of the Harlem, the remains of tribal ceremonies and the treasured pottery of the squaws, lay concealed. Over these grazed the cattle of the Colonial farmers, and among them were buried the dead of the colonists and of their slaves. The tide of Revolutionary warfare swept over the scene, and for seven long years thereafter, the armies of Britain and Hesse-Cassel camped around and upon the vestiges of neolithic man, yet failed to discover or disturb them, and thus two hundred years elapsed before the inquisitive antiquarian, prying into the shell heaps, and among the rocks of Inwood, re-discovered the home and unearthed the bones, the débris, the pottery and implements of the long-forgotten Wick-quas-keek.

ARCHAEOLOGY OF MANHATTAN ISLAND.

BY

ALANSON SKINNER.

Owing to the fact that a large part of the original surface in Manhattan has been destroyed, the statements and deductions here given are based on the remains obtained from but a few sites, notably those mentioned by Messrs. Bolton and Finch in their parts of this volume and from one site excavated by Mr. J. A. James at Van Cortlandt Park. Fortunately, these collections are comprehensive enough to give us a fair view of the prehistoric culture of the Island. The remains may be divided into three classes: objects of stone, objects of clay, and objects of bone and antler; varying in abundance in the order named.

Of the stone material, by far the most abundant here, as elsewhere, are the chipped arrow points, knives, drills, and scrapers. Arrow points of two general types, the triangular and notched, or stemmed forms, occur. They are made from a variety of materials mostly obtained in the immediate vicinity, an impure white quartz, red jasper, and a black or bluish flint, or chert. The latter is the most frequent. A few stones of exotic origin occur, and points made of the typical purple Trenton argillite are not infrequent. The notched and stemmed points seem to be more common than the triangular variety, a fact which may go to bear out the idea that the latter were used for warlike purposes in the coastal Algonkin region of New York, although in this instance none of them have been found (as in the case of Staten Island

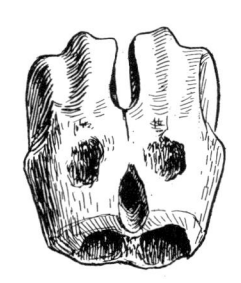

Fig. 11 (1–3940). Piece of Worked Bone. Van Cortlandt Park. Length, 3.8 cm.

where triangular flint points were found in and among the bones of three human skeletons at Burial Ridge, Tottenville) to prove the certainty of this supposition. Antler arrow points have been found on Manhattan Island. Fig. 7d shows one obtained by W. L. Calver in a shell heap at Spuyten Duyvil. Notched and stemmed arrow points with notched or bifurcated bases are not at all a common form hereabouts, although they occur sparingly in most regions. The projectile points from Manhattan Island are precisely similar to those shown on Plate XII.

Notched pebbles, probably used as weights or sinkers for nets are very frequent. They are of several varieties, those notched on the opposite sides of the long axis, which are the least common of this type, and those notched across the short axis. Figs. 10 and 11, Plate v, show both types. Net-sinkers pitted and used secondarily as a hammerstone, or vice versa, are occasionally found.

Figs. 8 and 9 Plate v, show the rarer grooved form of the net-sinkers. They are grooved either across the short or the round axis. These are found sparingly in this section.

Agricultural implements, or articles used in preparing vegetable food are few in number. The collection contains a rudely chipped hoe, polished slightly on the blade from use, from Van Cortlandt Park. Fig. 12, a large chipped implement also from Van Cortlandt Park, may have had a similar use.

The long stone pestle has been found in this region. Stone mortars, slabs slightly hollowed out on one side, in which corn may have been ground with small round flat stone, are found. The long stone pestle seems to have been used with the wooden mortar.

Shell, bone, and wooden hoes, may have been used by the Manhattan,

Fig. 12 (1–4090). Stone Implement. Van Cortlandt Park. Length, 38 cm.

but none have survived to the present day. Fragments of clay pipes, and one or two stone pipes that have been found in this region, suggest the cultivation of tobacco, which the early contemporary writers mention as having been raised in this vicinity. Fig. 4, Plate xvii shows a steatite pipe with a crude incised human face on the front of the bowl, collected by Bolton and Calver.

Two forms of the grooved axe occur in Manhattan territory. The first is grooved on three sides and the fourth side is flat. Fig. 11 Plate xvii represents the other type which is grooved entirely around the butt, and is in the Bolton and Calver Collection. Fig. 13 Plate xvii represents an unusual form of the notched axe of better finish than most specimens of this class, and with the notches worn until they appear as grooves on the opposite sides of the butt. This specimen is from Inwood.

Specimens of the ungrooved axe or celt occur on Manhattan Island and are similar to those shown in Figs. 8–17 Plate v. In case of the grooved axe, the haft was split for the reception of the blade which was fitted in the groove and bound above and below, but the celt was set in a hole at one end of the handle, with the larger forms, the butt protruded from the upper side; but with the smaller kind, the blade was merely set in like a spike.

Some celts in process of manufacture by means of chipping have been found, showing, as do all the finished implements at hand, that some care was bestowed in their making. In many parts of this locality, selected pebbles were merely grooved or sharpened to serve as axes and celts.

Several rude chipped objects collected may have been crude chopping tools or skin fleshers, but are probably unfinished implements or rejects. Figs. 11 to 25 Plate VI show chipped drills very similar to those from Manhattan Island. Such drills were used in perforating stone, wood, bone or pottery. In the latter case, a series of parallel holes was made on either

Fig. 13 *a* (20–6546), *b* (20–3533), *c* (1–4008), *d* (6546). Incised Designs from Iroquoian Vessels. Manhattan Island.

side of the injury on a cracked or broken vessel and the sides were tightly laced together by means of thongs or cord.

Knives of chipped stone, as shown in Figs. 1 to 15 Plate VII occur in several forms. Some are like exaggerated arrow points, others are leaf shaped. So far as known, no specimens of the slate semilunar knife have been found in this region. Pitted, so-called "hammerstones," are abundant. Fig. 8 Plate XVII illustrates one of these. The usual form has two pits, one on either side, perhaps to facilitate gripping with the thumb or fore-finger. This specimen has three such finger pits. Many of these specimens have worn and battered edges but others have the edges perfectly smooth and apparently unused.

A single double-holed "gorget" Fig. 2 Plate XVII is in our collection from Manhattan territory. This form is still used by the Lenapé Indians of Canada as a hair ornament.[1] The single-holed pendant type was doubtless once common as it occurs all about this region.

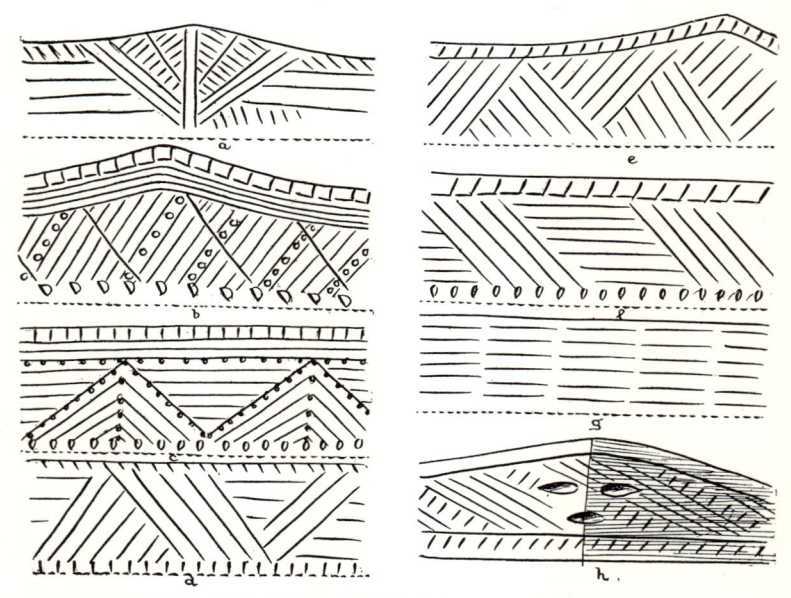

Fig. 14 a (20–3498), b (20–3463(, c (1–4006), d (1–4018), e (20–3495) g (20–6580), h (20–3533). Incised Designs from Iroquoian Vessels. Manhattan Island (a, b, e, g, h) and Van Cortlandt Park (c, d).

Fig. 15 a (20–2557), b (1–4039). Incised Designs from Iroquoian Pottery Vessels, Showing Conventional Faces. Kingsbridge (a) and Van Cortlandt Park (b).

The interesting and little known class of polished stone articles known as "banner stones" is represented by a fine specimen of the perforated

---

[1] See M. R. Harrington, American Anthropologist, Vol. 10, p. 414, 1908.

type from the Bolton and Calver Collection and is shown in Fig. 6 Plate XVII. One "wing" of this specimen is broken and perforations have been made near the point of fracture for mending it by lacing the parts together. There are also rude incised lines upon it which may have had ornamental or other significance. No specimen of the notched form is at hand, though perhaps such specimens have occurred. Fig. 4 Plate XVII is a rude banner

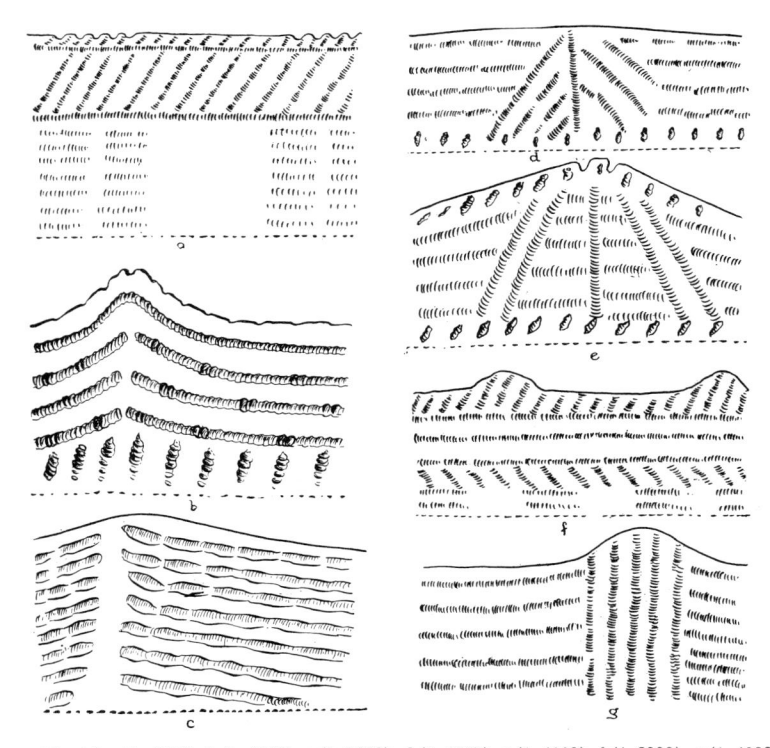

Fig. 16 a (1–4019), b (1–4000), c (1–3998), d (1–4007), e (1–4009), f (1–3999), g (1–4028). Stamped Designs from the Intermediate Type of Vessels. Van Cortlandt Park.

stone grooved only on one side, an unusual, though not unknown feature in this general region.

A fragment of limonite used to obtain pigment for red paint and showing the marks of scraping implements upon it, has been found at Inwood. Such paint stones are not uncommon throughout the New York coastal Algonkin region. In some cases simple water worn pebbles have been picked up by the Indians and used as they were found.

Bone and antler implements, nowhere abundant among the New York coastal Algonkin as compared to the Iroquois tribes of the interior, are but sparsely represented. Fig. 7a represents a bone used as an awl, from the Inwood rock-shelters. There is none of the finish about this specimen which characterizes many of the bone and antler implements found even in immediately contingent areas. Fig. 7b represents a carefully made polished bone awl from Van Cortlandt Park. This specimen has been worked all over

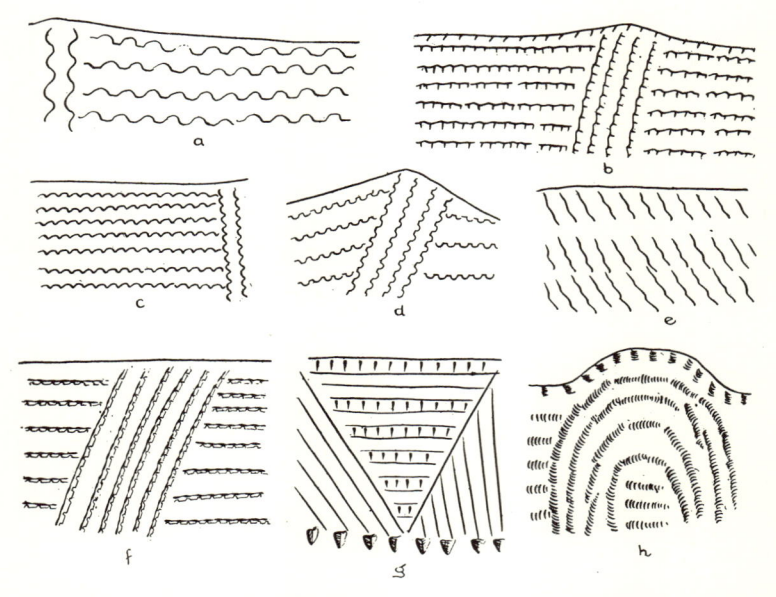

Fig. 17 a (20-3497), b (1-4029), c (1-4013), d (20-6546), e (1-4041), f (1-4017), g (T-24508), h (1-4033). Stamped and Incised. Design from Intermediate and Iroquoian Types. Van Cortlandt Park.

and shows that far more pains were taken in its manufacture than in the preceding three from Inwood.

Fig. 7c represents another awl or needle in the Bolton and Calver Collection which is also well made. It is perforated near the blunt end or butt. Fig. 11 shows the end of a bone sawed off and partially perforated in five places (two at the base and three in front) perhaps for use as a "cup" in the cup and ball game, for which, by the way, the northern, or more properly the eastern Cree of the James Bay Region of Canada use a typical "bone awl" as a striking pin. This specimen like all the following bone and antler objects comes from Van Cortlandt Park.

Several fragments of cups or dishes made from the bony carapace of the box tortoise (*Tranene Carolina*) have been gathered. These show that in finishing the utensil, the inner ribs have been cut and scraped, presenting a smooth surface.

Fragments of antler prongs, slightly worked on one end, perhaps used as pitching tools, or flakers, in the manufacture of stone arrow points, and tips of an antler prong also showing signs of wear, occur in the shell heaps, as well as antler prongs broken from the shaft by percussion and

Fig. 18 *a* (20–3520), *b* (20–3519), *c* (20–3498), *d* (20–6580), *e* (20–6500), *f* (20–3508). Incised Designs from Algonkin Pottery Vessels. Manhattan Island.

from which the tips have been cut, or rather sawed, with a stone knife. In cutting bone and antler with a stone knife, the Indian sawed part way through on all sides and then broke off the portion desired.

Tips from antler prongs were often hollowed and sharpened in this way, and used as arrow points. Mr. W. L. Calver has such an arrow point, ornamented by incised cross hatching which he obtained in a shell heap at Spuyten Duyvil. This is shown in Fig. 7d.

Unless we admit that the triangular arrow point was an object of warlike use in this neighborhood, the only object positively used for this purpose is a wooden war club in the Leiden Museum.[1] It was evidently taken back from New Amsterdam, as it was the type of weapon used by the Iroquois and western Algonkian tribes. It is made of maple, turned dark with age and highly polished from use. The dimensions are: extreme length, 555 mm.; greatest diameter, 102 mm.; thickness of the handle, 30 mm. As shown in the illustration, there is a perforation above the handle or grip, while on the outer edge, near the perforation, are twelve small notches. The weapon is not decorated, but in form it closely resembles a highly decorated example in the Ashmolean Museum, Oxford.

As to the pottery of this region, so much regarding its manufacture and general characteristics has been stated in our preceding paper that a general statement will suffice. Pottery, considering the few Manhattan sites examined, is exceedingly abundant, and the Iroquoian type is unusually

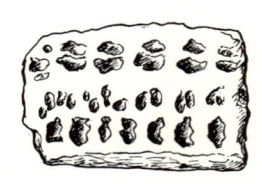

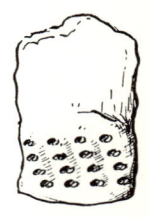

Fig. 19 a (1–4056) b (20–6546). Potsherds of the Intermediate Type Showing Odd Designs.

common. Not so many varieties in shape are to be observed as on Staten Island, only three general types occurring; the typical pointed bottom Algonkin form, an intermediate between Iroquoian and Algonkin, and the Iroquoian.

Two methods of design, rare or unknown elsewhere, are noted; one (Fig. 9) in stamped ornamentation in curved lines; the other, as in Fig. 18f consists in stamping the damp clay with the cut end of a straw or quill presenting a round depression with a little point or nipple in the centre, these two are on fragments of the Algonkin type. Fig. 13b is perhaps marked along the edge of the angle by impressions of the thumb nail, and is Iroquoian, as are Figs. 14h and 15a–b where the human face is conventionally incised after the manner of specimens not infrequently seen from village sites of the Iroquois proper. All these unusual types are from Manhattan Island. Fig. 18f shows a design from a typically Algonkin

---

[1] Illustrated in the American Anthropologist for April–June 1908, Vol. 10, p. 333, by Mr. David I. Bushnell, Jr.

vessel made by incised lines and pressing some object, perhaps a bird's quill in the damp clay, leaving a circular depression with a tiny nipple in the centre.

Plate XV represents a splendid and nearly perfect Iroquoian vessel of great size found on 214th Street near East River by Mr. W. L. Calver in October, 1906. It has a hole half way down one side, apparently made with a stone perforator, perhaps for the purpose of "killing" the pots as done in mortuary pottery from the southeast, that its spirit may accompany the owner to the hereafter. The pot was found in a deposit of stained sand where a skeleton may have lain, but no traces of human remains were seen (p. 88).

Traces of grease and soot from cooking are often seen on Manhattan pottery as from most of the neighboring sites. Broken vessels, here as elsewhere were mended by boring holes on either side of the break in parallel order and then lacing together with sinew. No steatite is reported although it may have been used.

THE ROCK-SHELTERS OF ARMONK, NEW YORK.

BY

M. R. HARRINGTON.

INTRODUCTION.

The vicinity of Armonk, Westchester County, New York, is a country of rocky ledges running north and south, with valleys, between, some of which contain streams. Great glacial boulders may be seen upon the hilltops, while small patches of drift lie at the junction of the valleys, probably representing the sand bars of the post-glacial torrents running bank full down the narrow valleys through which the tiny brooks of to-day wind their peaceful course. The bed rock forming the ledges is mainly gneissic, with a few outcrops of dolomite limestone, known as "Tuckahoe Marble." The strata, as a rule, tip up to the east. Here and there, in the sheltered valleys, along some running brook, the plow turns up the stone chips and charcoal of an ancient village or encampment, from which many specimens illustrating the life of the aborigines have been picked up by local collectors. Back among the rocks from these village sites, yet usually near them, in places where the outcropping strata overhang in the form of a rock-shelter, may sometimes be found other traces of primitive man.

FINCH'S ROCK HOUSE.

By far the largest of these rock-shelters is known as Finch's Rock House. It lies a little less than 2½ miles northeast of the village of Armonk (three miles by road) on the property of George Sniffen. The shelter has been formed by the falling of a huge mass of rock from the face of the ledge, leaving a cave 23 feet long, 10 feet wide and 11 feet high in front. The great slab did not fall away from the ledge, but remained so as to practically block the mouth of the cave and shelter it on the fourth side, though leaving an entrance at each end (Plate XVIII).

Although the cave has long been a favorite place of resort for the country people, no one ever suspected its contents, until the writer thrust his spade into the black earth of the floor and turned up split deer bones and charcoal, revealing the character of the place beyond a doubt. On the surface, little was apparent, except a fan-shaped dump of earth at the north entrance the "sweepings" of the ancient dwellers. At the bottom of this dump, 24 feet from the north entrance, digging was begun, covering the whole slope up to the mouth of the shelter in five transverse sections.

The soil of the dump was stony and the Indian deposit shallow, only 18 inches deep at the cave mouth, the deepest point. In this dump were found charcoal, split and broken animal bones, shells of marine and fresh water species, potsherds, chips and fragments of quartz and chert, nine chipped implements (mostly arrow points), a very rude celt and three pieces of the stems of Indian terra cotta pipes, together with three fragments of English clay trade pipes, stamped R. T. on the back and R. Tippet on the front. The stone objects lay near the bottom of the dump, while the pottery and bones were well scattered, though more numerous on the side nearest the fallen rock.

The cave was then excavated by means of three transverse trenches,

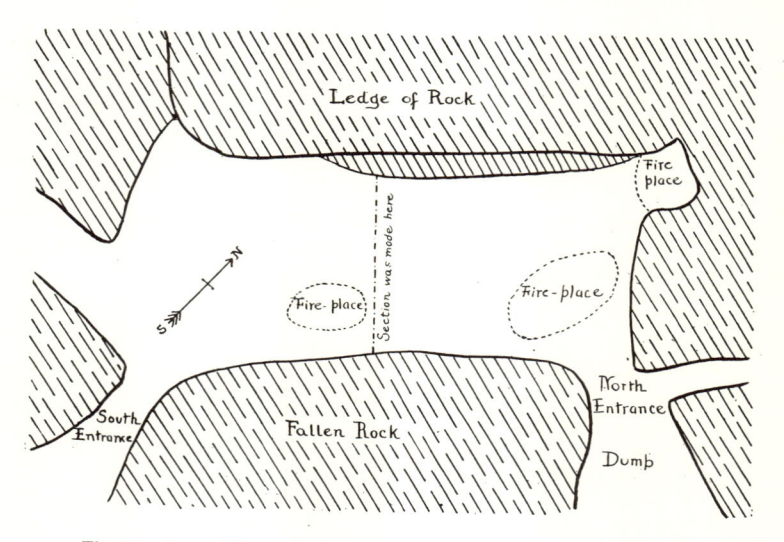

Fig. 20. Ground Plan of "Finch's Rock House." Scale — 1 inch = 8 ft.

10 feet long by 5 feet broad, and one 10 feet long by 3 feet broad — four trenches in all. It was soon found that the deposit forming the floor of the cave consisted of three layers: — a top layer of relic-bearing black earth, thickest and richest near the northern entrance; an intermediate layer of yellowish sand, varying in thickness and containing no relics; and finally, a bottom layer of black earth, thickest near the southern entrance, and containing relics (Figs. 20, 21, and 22). The first trench contained many split deer bones, scattered in patches. This trench was begun at the north entrance, and here the bones lay thickest. Several hearths and ash beds were observed, one of the former being in a natural niche in the northern

corner of the cave. Two triangular arrow points of sheet copper or brass, two gun-flints (one of these of European stone) eleven whole and broken chipped points, nine pieces of early clay trade pipes, three bone awls and two cut bones, besides the usual split deer bones, shells, burnt stones and potsherds were found in the top layer, which was about one foot deep. The bottom layer, divided from the top layer at this point by only a narrow band of yellow sand and ashes, was from 6 to 14 inches deep and contained rude and partly chipped pieces of quartz, a rude quartz blade, a broken arrow point, a scraper polished by use, and shells, bones, and charcoal.

The second trench revealed, in the top layer, a bone awl, two pieces of terra cotta pipe stem, one of which shows the toothmarks of the user, two pieces of trade pipes, a piece of clam shell showing marks of use as sinew-dresser (?), and the common potsherds, bones, shells and bits of quartz. The bottom layer contained five rude implements and rejects of quartz, a piece of cut unio shell, and a very rude arrow point of slaty stone with the notches scratched in, instead of chipped. A hammerstone was also found, together with the common chips, shells and bones, but no pottery. A large hearth was in this layer, at the eastern end of the trench (Fig. 21).

The third trench contained in the top layer a trade pipe marked "T. Grant," an arrow-head, a few hammerstones, and the usual material. The contents of the bottom layer of this trench were as follows: —

Piece of cut antler, 4 feet from surface.
Small quartz triangular point, 4 feet.
Large, celt-like chipped implement, 3½ feet.
Oval blade of quartz and small arrow point, 3 feet.
Quartz reject, 3 feet.
Leaf-shaped blade of quartz, and 2 arrow points, 2 feet.
Point of large quartzite blade, 2 feet.
Portion of poll of grooved ax.
3 hammerstones, one of them with pits.

Pieces of quartz, animal bones and pottery were common. The points were found in patches, while most of the bones, shells and chips were in the east end.

The fourth trench was larger than the others, being 8 feet instead of 5 feet wide. Here, however, the top layer disappeared, after yielding a few of the common objects and a grooved stone upon which bone awls had been sharpened, the yellow layer became very deep, and the bottom layer finally came to an end at a depth of over 4 feet after yielding the following objects: —

Broken hammerstone with scratched notches, 2½ feet deep.
Thick quartz spear point, 2 feet.

Very crude slate point, chipped, 2 feet.
Quartz reject, rude, 4 feet.
Black triangular point, rude point and 2 rude objects, 3 feet.
2 pieces of antler, one gnawed.
Chips, shells and bones.

This finished the work in the cave. Two very shallow and heavy mortars, or anvil stones, were noticed in digging, but their great weight and the consequent difficulty of transportation made it unprofitable to remove them. Below the southern entrance of the cave some crevices in the rocks contained refuse such as bones, chips, etc. In one crevice 22 feet from the southern entrance, a number of pieces of well-decorated pot rims were found. A number of bones of domestic animals in a good state of preservation were found in some of the crevices; but these were probably dragged to the site by foxes, numerous at the present day in this region.

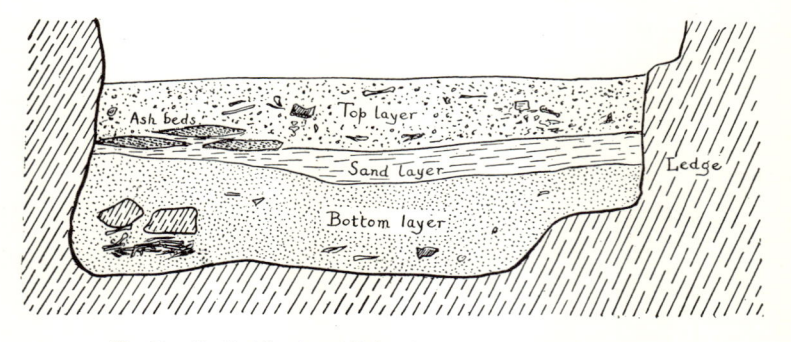

Fig. 21. Vertical Section of Refuse in Finch's Rock House, Trench 2.
Scale — 1 inch = 4ft.

When the exploration described above had been completed, it was thought that everything of value had been found and removed from the cave; but on further deliberation, taking into consideration the darkness of the cave and the blackness and stickiness of the cave dirt, it was thought best to sift the entire contents. The results were surprising. The earth had all been carefully trowelled over, then thrown with a shovel so that it could be watched — but a great number of things had been overlooked, as the subsequent sifting showed. Of course all data as to depth and position have been lost, yet the specimens are valuable as having come from the cave. They are as follows: —

Perforated arrow point of sheet brass or copper.
3 more or less perfect stone drills.

95 perfect or nearly perfect arrow points.
5 small scrapers.
A rude celt with edge broken.
Portion of a banner stone.
Portion of a terra cotta pipe.
Cut and drilled bone of deer, used in game.
Portion of a bird bone bead.
10 worked bones.

There were many other objects of minor importance. The arrow points varied from some of the finest to some of the rudest local specimens the writer has ever seen.

The foods used by the Indians living in this Rock House as shown by

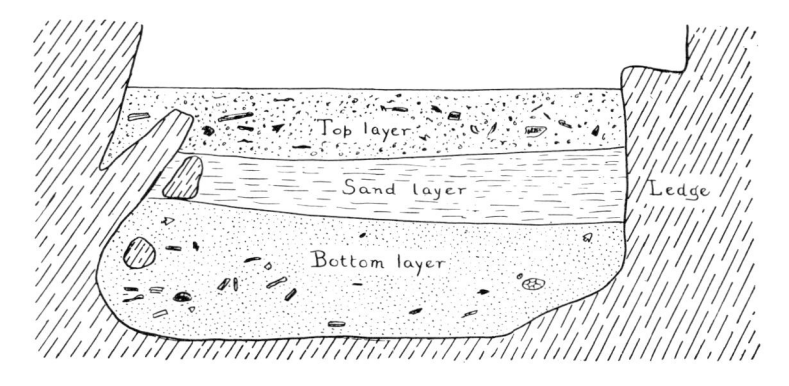

Fig. 22. Vertical Section of Refuse in Finch's Rock House, about midway of the Cave, Fig. 21.
Scale — 1 inch = 4 ft.

the refuse examined, were as follows: deer, bear, raccoon, woodchuck, squirrel, small animals and birds not identified, snapping turtle, land turtle, oyster (*ostrea edulis* Linn.), quahog (*mercenaria mercenaria* Linn.), soft clam (*mya arenaria* Linn.), scallop (*pecten concentricus* Say), mussel (*modiola plicatula* Lamk.), black mussel (*mytilus edulis* Linn.), brook mussel (*unio complanatus* Sol.), land snail (*helix abolabris* Say, *helix alternata*), limpet (*crepidula formista* Lamk.), and "jingle shells" (*anomia glabra* Verrill).

This Rock House must have been a favorite place of resort in the old days. So hidden was it, that marauding war-parties could pass through the valley of the Mianus, but a short distance away, and never suspect its existence. Water was near at hand, both in a "pond hole" about 50 feet from the cave, and in a small stream a few rods away. When the cold winds of winter came whistling over the snowy hills, a few poles and mats leaned against the ledge from the great rock in front, and made fast with a few stones, would make as warm and comfortable a house as any Indian could wish. The smoke of the fires could escape through crevices in the rocks. Nature had even provided a shelf of stone upon which the Indian could lay his possessions. In fact, the conditions were so good that the place was occupied soon after the great stone had fallen from the ledge. This is shown by the presence of implements on the original rock bottom of the cave. Then followed a long period of habitation, enough to build up refuse to the depth of two feet in favorable places.

Very fine arrow points were made at this time, but the other stone tools were rude, and there was no pottery. The culture had reached the grooved ax and notched banner stone stage, however. Chips and rejects attest the manufacture of implements, while beds of ashes and charcoal tell of bygone fires. The deer was hunted, his meat cooked and his bones split for the marrow. Clams, oysters and scallops were brought from Long Island Sound about 15 miles away, and even the brook mussels (unio) were gathered. Well worn scrapers and battered hammerstones tell the story of toil — the story as old as man. These people lived and died; then came a period when the Rock House stood without a tenant, and the yellow sand sifted in and washed down over the deserted hearths. How long this period was, no man can say, but when the Indians came back they had pottery, well-made decorated pottery. Then life began again, much as before; the deer was still hunted, the shell-fish still brought from the distant Sound and the neighboring brooks, the refuse accumulated and was swept from the cave, but the people had the pottery which marks a great step in the advancement of a race. This pottery is mainly of the Iroquoian type, as is much of ancient Westchester County pottery in contrast to the typically Algonkin pottery of Long Island, where Iroquois forms are very rare. The people of the upper layer were, however, probably Algonkins, either of the Siwanoy or Tankiteke tribes, which history and tradition assign to the locality. These people saw the first coming of the White man — accepted his wonderful gifts, his guns, his unbreakable shining arrow points of brass, his beautiful white clay pipes — all very good and useful in their way, even if the gun did scare away more deer than it killed. Then came the final gifts of civilization to the Indian, whiskey, smallpox, and death. So the book was closed, the story written, the fox and the woodchuck took possession.

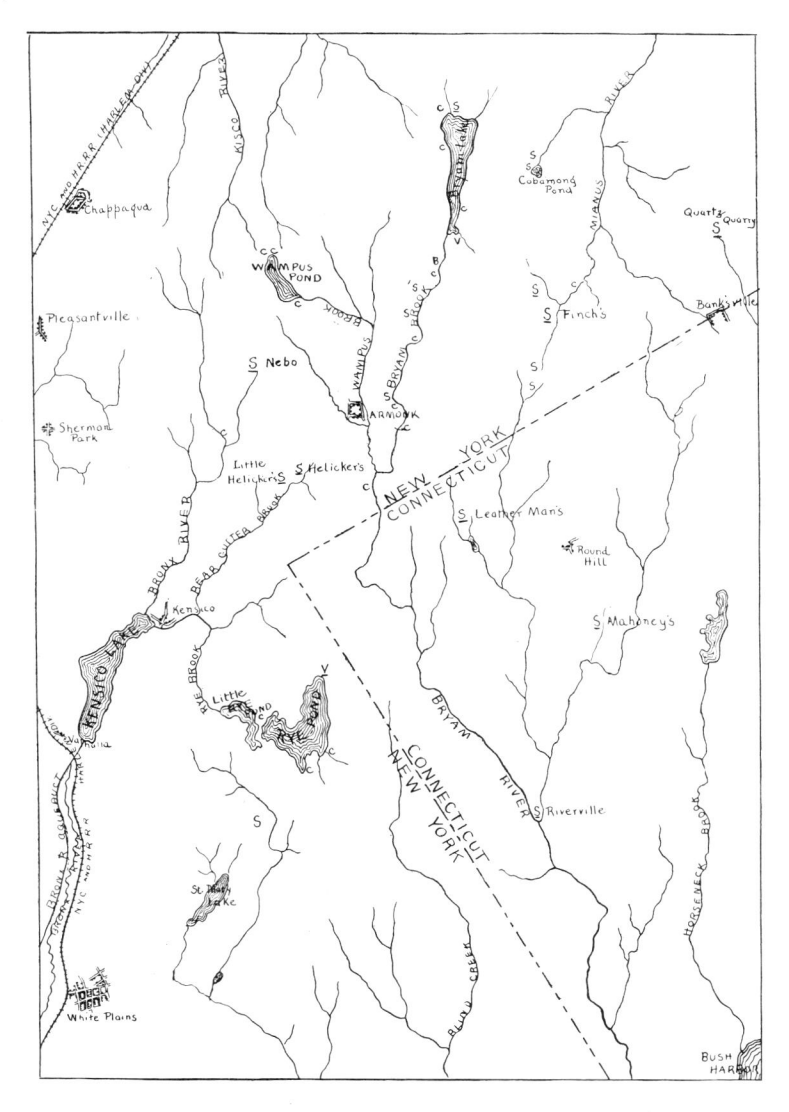

Fig. 23. Rock-shelter Region of Westchester Co., N. Y. and Fairfield Co., Conn.
Scale — 1 inch = 1 mile.

B   Burial Ground.
C   Camp Site.
S   Rock-shelter.
V   Village Site.

— Explored by the Writer.

Nebo Rocks.

This rock-shelter is situated about 1½ miles west northwest of Armonk, on the west bank of a little brook, one of the tributaries of the Bronx River (Fig. 23). It consists of a ledge of rock overhanging to the east, forming a shelter 26 feet long, 14 feet high in front, and 10 feet wide at the widest part. The ground was covered with chips and fragments of quartz and flint, while a large pitted stone, weighing perhaps 50 pounds, lay in full view. This was not disturbed because of its weight. Excavations revealed only an arrow point and a reject near the back of the shelter, and the common chips and bits of quartz. This place had been thoroughly dug over by local collectors, hence it was not surprising that so little was found. Arrowheads only, however, were found by previous collectors, but neither bones nor pottery.

Another shelter, very small, was discovered at the north end of Byram Lake, near a camp site. Nothing of importance was found.

Helicker's Cave.

About one mile southwest of Armonk, near the headwater of Bear Gutter Brook and but a few hundred yards west of the road to Kensico, is "Bet Helicker's Cave," its gaping mouth facing southeast (Fig. 23). It more nearly approaches a true cave in form than any of the others seen by the writer; but instead of opening out inside it becomes smaller and smaller, finally making a sharp turn to the left (Plate XVIII and Fig. 24). At this point the width is about 6 feet and the height 3 feet, in contrast to the mouth measurements:— width, 15 feet, height 12 feet. The turn is 25 feet from the mouth, beyond that, the cave becomes so low that further progress is impossible and the explorer backs out as best he can, gladly leaving the far end of the passage to the foxes and copper-head snakes which haunt the place.

The remains of a rude wall of irregular fragments of rock were observed across the southern side of the cave mouth, but whether the structure was the work of Indians or more modern campers is impossible to say. The wall, when complete, together with a fallen stone which blocks the northern side of the entrance would have effectually protected the cave. On and near the surface within the cave were clay pipes and broken crockery of the Revolutionary period, also a White man's fireplace with bones of domestic animals bearing saw marks. The crockery is very similar to that found by Mr. Calver in the ash heap of the "Blue Bell Tavern" a Revolutionary hostlery at 181st Street, Manhattan. In addition to these objects of European manufacture, were found a bone awl, a copper stained bone, and a number of animal bones and teeth, most, if not all of which are of undoubted Indian origin. Two Indian fireplaces were also found, one of them near the fallen rock, the other further back. The former consisted of an angular cavity in the rock floor, 18 inches wide by 2 feet long and 18 inches deep. Ashes, charcoal, charred bones and teeth of animals, two potsherds, a broken

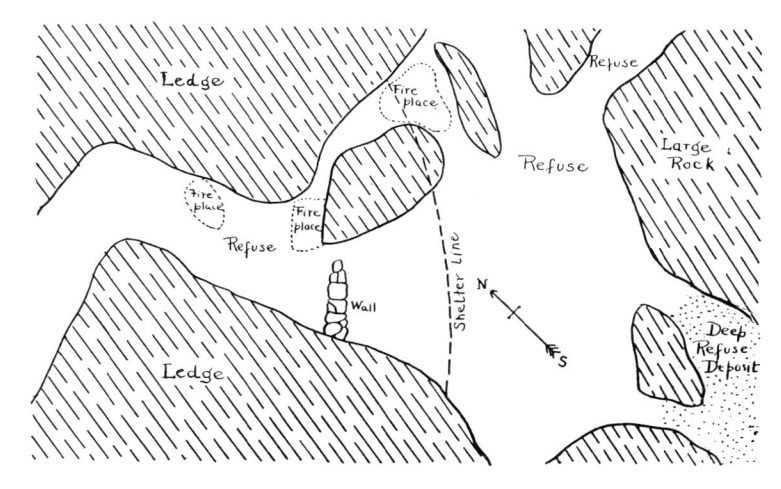

Fig. 24. Ground Plan of Helicker's Cave.
Scale — 1 inch = 12 ft.

English trade pipe, shells of marine and fresh water species, rejects and chips were found in the cavity. Bones, potsherds, rejects and chips were found in the earth of the cave floor, some of them as much as 10 inches deep. The Indian layer became thinner as the work progressed, until it disappeared altogether at the first turn of the passage.

To the north of the entrance, just outside the line of shelter was another "pocket" in the rocks possibly used as a fireplace. It contained a few broken arrow points, a quantity of animal bones, a few potsherds and a number of shells, rejects, etc. In the refuse in the vicinity of this fireplace, were found, among the more common materials a scraper made of oyster shell, and much pottery, some decorated.

Down the bluff, about 15 feet from the entrance and to the southeast of it was another deposit of refuse, 3 feet deep in places. Here were found a celt-like implement of chipped quartzite, arrow-heads, chips, rejects, potsherds, bones, charcoal, and an English trade pipe stamped R. T. on the right side. All through the refuse deposits were found scattered shells of unio, oysters, quahog, soft clam, mussel and scallop. Salt water is nearly 15 miles from this cave, hence the shells must have been transported that distance.

The impression conveyed by the results of this exploration was that the site had been occupied subsequent to the coming of the White man. This impression was strengthened by the finding of many sheep bones in the cave, as well as the bones of deer. The name of the cave, "Bet Helicker's Rocks" was given on account of an old woman of that name whose hut had once stood in the woods near by.

A large overhanging rock just north of the cave showed no signs of use as a shelter.

Leather Man's Shelter.

On Quaker Ridge, just across the State line into Connecticut and 2½ miles southeast of Armonk, is Leather Man's Rock-shelter (Plate XIX). The name of "Leather Man" a solitary wanderer dressed from head to foot in leather clothing of his own manufacture, is well known to this day throughout the northern part of Westchester County, although the strange old man died in 1888. The shelter above mentioned was one of the many caves and stopping places used by the hermit in his wanderings, thus getting its name. The shelter was rather small, overhanging but 3½ feet; the length was 20 feet, facing east. Scraps and thongs of leather abounded on the surface while beneath was an Indian layer, in places 8 inches deep. No bones were found here, only chips, broken points and last, but not least, a large part of the rim of the most ornate local pot of the Iroquois type the writer has ever seen.

Little Helicker's.

Not far southwest of Helicker's Cave (previously described) was found a small shelter containing a spring. Here were found a few potsherds, chips and broken arrow-heads — nothing more.

A small shelter just north of Finch's Rock House contained a number of fragments of a single jar, but nothing else.

Mahoney Shelter.

This is a small shelter situated on one of the branches of the east fork of the Byram River, about two miles north by east of Riverville, Connecticut and four miles southeast of Armonk. It is in Fairfield County, Connecticut on the property of Philip Mahoney. The Indian layer ran to the depth of 8 inches in places, and contained many marine shells, a few animal bones and chips, a pitted stone and three first rate arrow points. This was probably a temporary stopping place (Plate xx).

QUARTZ QUARRY ROCK-SHELTER.

Five miles northeast by east of Armonk, north of Banksville and southwest of East Middle Patent lies a great stretch of woods, very nearly in its primitive condition. The few farms which border the unfrequented, rocky and tortuous roads are for the most part deserted, their fields overgrown with briers and saplings, their houses fallen in ruin. In the middle of this wooded area is a large tract of swampy ground, furnishing water to a number of tributaries of the Mianus River. A great ledge of quartz towers among the trees at the source of one of these streams, overhanging at one point in

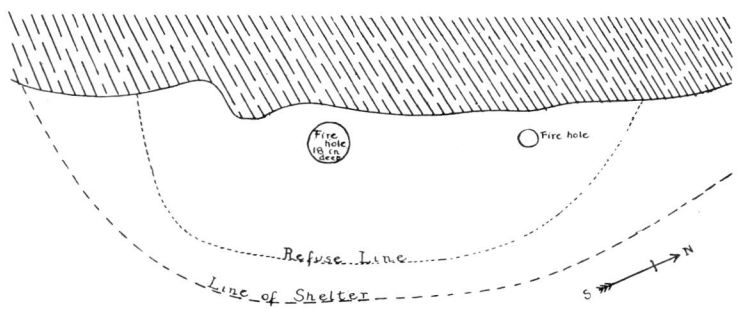

Fig. 25. Ground Plan of Quartz Quarry Rock-shelter.
Scale — 1 inch = 10 ft.

the form of a rock-shelter. Most of the quartz in the vicinity is very impure but wherever there is a vein of good stone, the ground is full of broken fragments and chips. For lack of time no attention was paid to the quarry. The shelter however, was examined. It proved to be forty feet long and nine feet deep, the cliff being thirty feet high (Plate xx). The refuse beneath the shelter was limited in extent, varying from four to eight inches in depth. Two fire pits were found, one of them 18 inches deep. The following is a list of the material found: —

Stemmed arrow point of quartz, 6 inches below the surface.
Stemmed arrow point of quartz, small, 10 inches below.

Large reject of quartz, 12 inches below.
17 more or less perfect points of different materials, rejects, etc., also 2 pieces of mica.
Small bone awl, weathered.
Piece of cut bone.
Prong of deer antler, 2 raccoon jaws, 1 mink jaw.
29 small potsherds, some decorated.
5 hammerstones, 3 of them quartz.
75 more or less chipped pieces of quartz, also flint.
One lot of shells, mainly marine, and 100 split deer bones.

It is probable that the Indians camped here while mining quartz.

Riverville Shelter.

The two principal forks of the Byram River, one taking its rise in Wampus and Byram Lakes, the other near the source of the Mianus River, join their waters at Riverville, Fairfield County, Connecticut, and begin their final journey to Long Island Sound. At the very forks where the valleys meet, the last intervening ridge ends in a rocky ledge — a ledge which overhangs slightly, forming a rock-shelter, withal a very poor one (Plate xix). However, the very favorable location, at the junction of two valleys and hence two lines of travel, caused it to be such a desirable stopping place — no one could miss it — that the traces left behind are second only to those found in Finch's Rock House, which latter was doubtless a more or less permanent dwelling place. Although the shelter lay at the forks of two roads as well as of two streams, no one had ever suspected that Indian relics lay within. Three whitened, split deer bones, a few bits of shell and quartz, and a weather beaten fragment of decorated pottery, all lying on the surface, told the story.

The shelter, which is slightly curved in form, faces southwest and south and is 65 feet long over all. Of this, only about 45 feet had been occupied — the portion facing southwest. Eight feet is the greatest width, the average width being less than that, so it is probable that poles were leaned up against the shelter to make it habitable. At the western end a number of large stones had fallen from the ledge, and among these, the deepest refuse deposit lay, 2½ feet deep. The earth of this large hole was intensely black, containing split bones, arrow-heads, pottery, etc. (Fig. 26). Near the bottom of this cavity, which was seven or eight feet in diameter, were a number of slabs which had fallen from the ledge above; but the black earth continued beneath them. In the dump just outside of this cavity, a number of water-worn pebbles were noticed, as well as the usual relics. A terrace of black refuse dirt continued eastward under the shelter for 30 feet, where the black faded into brown and yellow earth containing no relics. This terrace was richest near the back of the shelter, arrow-heads, rejects, etc., being plentiful, while pottery was scarce. Most of the material lay near the surface, very

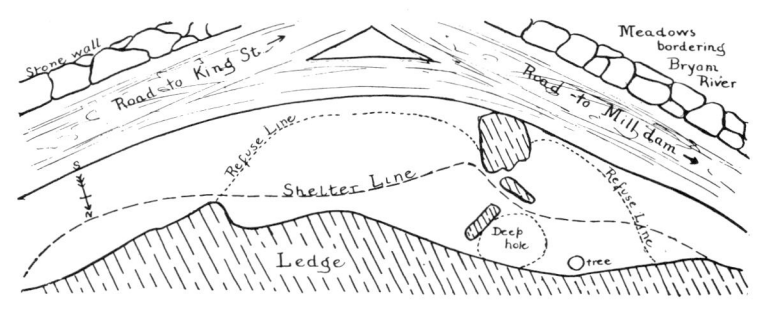

Fig. 26. Plan of Riverville Rock-shelter.
Scale — 1 inch = 20 ft.

little of it being 30 inches deep. The most important objects found, are embraced in the following list: —

Large spear or knife point of red jasper.
Small triangular flint point, resharpened.
Quartz point, stemmed, much worn by use as a drill.
23 arrow points, etc., different materials.
Deeply scored red paintstone.
Rejects, rude blades, etc.
About 75 potsherds, some decorated.
Split animal bones, mostly of deer.
Bones of raccoon and turtle.
7 worked bones and broken bone implements.
9 crude hammerstones.
Broken pestle.
48 broken points and rejects, one slightly pitted stone.
Chips, flakes, and pieces of flint and quartz.
1 human tooth.
Shells of marine species.

Nothing of European manufacture was discovered, and this fact, together with the scarcity of pottery, seems to give an early date to this site. It was probably merely a stopping place, a sort of primitive "road house" for the travellers en route from the woods to the Sound or from the Sound to the woods.

The explorations upon which this paper is based were conducted by the writer for the Museum in 1900 and 1901 and the collections, together with other data are in the possession of this institution.

It is only fair to say, before closing this paper, that the purposes of the Museum were greatly facilitated by Mr. J. Howard Quinby of Armonk, who acted as guide and general assistant, and who assisted the writer in every way possible. Mr. Quinby has been a collector of surface material for many years, has explored several small shelters on his own account, and has thus accumulated a large and interesting collection.

INDIAN ROCK-SHELTERS IN NORTHERN NEW JERSEY AND SOUTHERN NEW YORK.

BY
MAX SCHRABISCH.

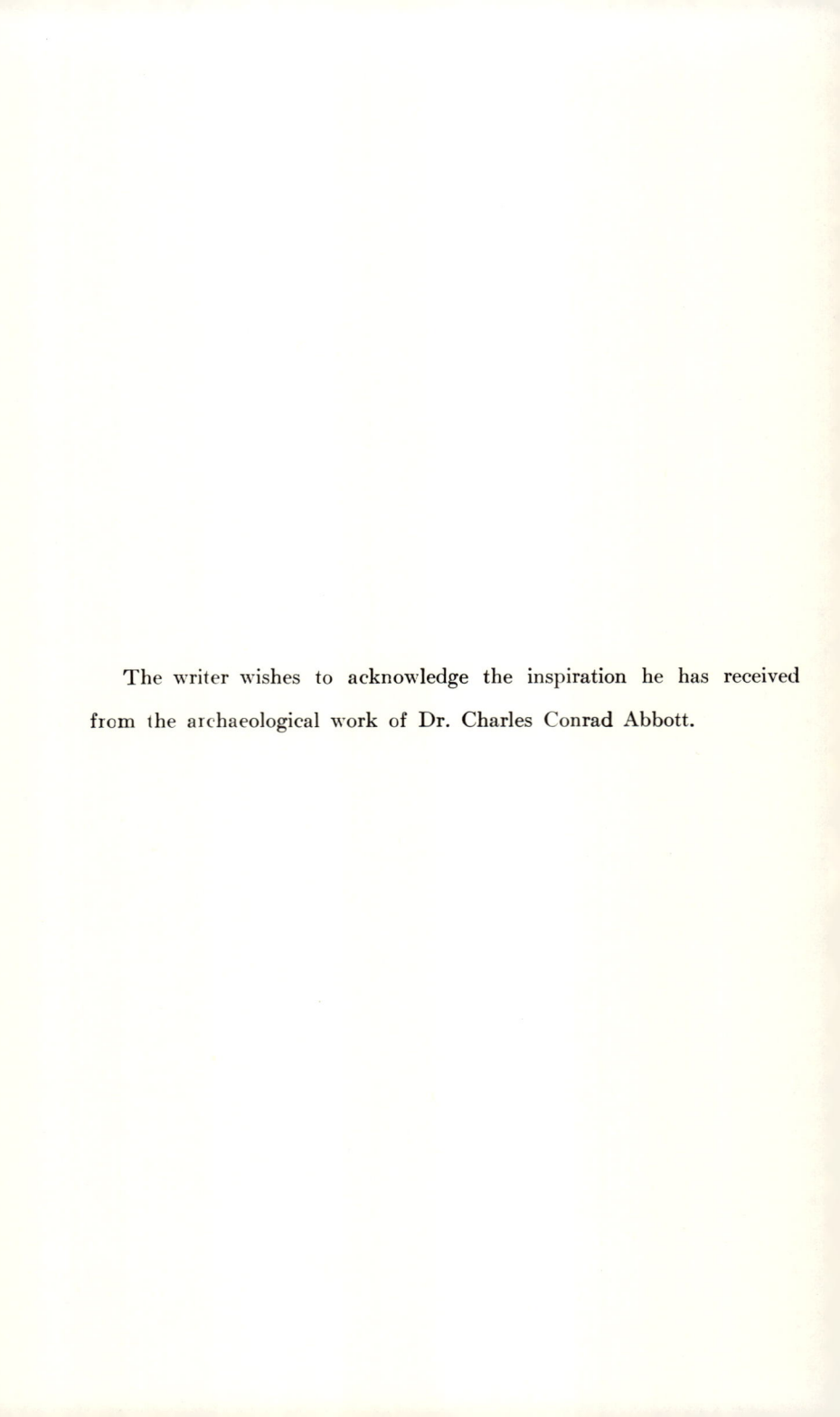

The writer wishes to acknowledge the inspiration he has received from the archaeological work of Dr. Charles Conrad Abbott.

PASSAIC COUNTY, NEW JERSEY.

Upper Preakness. During the last eight years, i. e. since 1900, the writer has discovered altogether seventeen Indian rock-shelters, that is to say, such as give unmistakable evidence of ancient occupation. Nine of them have been located in the State of New Jersey; viz., three in Passaic County and six in Morris County. The remaining eight are in the State of New York, Rockland County figuring with five, Orange County with three. It was in the early part of the summer of 1900 that I came across the first of the seventeen shelters. It is at Upper Preakness, in the County of Passaic, six miles north of Paterson, in a section of country which is thickly wooded and little frequented by human beings. A striking feature of this region is the large number of gullies or ravines, intersecting it in all directions. One of these, locally known as the Clove, is particularly interesting because of its wildness and scenic charms. It occupies a central portion in this labyrinth of woodland, is perfectly straight for nearly a mile and runs north due south from Franklin Lake, a sheet of water which the aborigines in their flowery language called Crystal Eye, towards the road connecting the Pompton turnpike with Oakland. On the western side of the Clove, not far from its southern extremity, a series of overhanging rocks will be noticed which attracted the writer's attention by reason of the ancient smoke marks, displayed on the walls of the ledge. Later investigations established the fact that this locality had, at some remote time, served for human habitation. There are in all, four cave-like compartments at the base of the precipitous rock, which is about twenty feet high and three hundred feet long. Some time during the winter of 1907–1908 the roof of the northernmost compartment had tumbled down, heaved by frost, its fragments, some of them very large, being deposited along the base of the cliff. About four hundred meters up the Clove, the Singac brook takes its rise and in its course down the ravine it flows past the shelters, spreading its waters over a rock-girt swamp a short distance below.

When the writer began his investigations, he had to remove from under the ledge a layer of decayed leaves and other vegetable matter, more than two feet thick, which deposit represented the accumulation of at least two hundred years. Under this he found, right on the surface of the soil thus exposed, hundreds of pieces of broken pottery, with and without ornamentation, the largest fragments being of the size of a man's palm. The ornamented pieces were either cord-marked or they showed such conventional designs as dotted and incised lines. The last-named design displayed two patterns, viz., parallel and zigzag lines. One of the fragments, evidently belonging to the brim of a pot, was deeply notched or serrated along the edge, the number of indentations being four to an inch. While all of the potsherds were found either on the surface or at a depth not exceeding two inches, none of the other objects was a surface find. Altogether, I unearthed twenty-nine arrow-heads, seven spear-points, several stone hammers, flint knives, scrapers, drills, sinew dressers and one rubbing stone. Needless to say that there was a profusion of flakes scattered all through the subsoil, a fact which demonstrates that the occupants of this spot were busy fashioning their implements under these very rocks. Some of the arrow points were made of flint, others of slate, argillite, quartz, bluestone and chert. One exceptionally fine spear-head was made of jasper. The stone hammers were simply water-worn pebbles, such as are used for cracking nuts, etc., oval in shape, with a depression on the upper and lower surface, and of the kind designated as pitted hand-hammers. Furthermore, the remains of six fireplaces were laid bare, as indicated by flat stones arranged in a square. Considerable quantities of charcoal were here mixed with the soil, imparting to it a black color. Imbedded in these various layers many bones were found, most of them cracked and charred by the heat. With the brook in close proximity and the front of the ledge facing the sun, this locality no doubt proved very attractive to the sons of the forest, especially when the inclemency of winter called for additional protection. Indeed, the presence of all these objects seems to justify the assumption that this spot was much frequented and often for long periods. At all events, we may be certain that it was regularly occupied during the winter months.

Special stress must be laid on the fact that the pottery occurred only in the upper layer of debris. More than two inches below there was none to be found.

The location of this shelter at the very entrance to the Clove and near a brook which does not dry up even during the hottest season, must have been ideal from the Indian's viewpoint. Moreover, the Clove forms a natural pass across this rough and broken section, and on the strength of other evidence we may feel confident that through it ran one of their trails, over which they travelled to Franklin Lake. Collectively taken, all these data must, we think, be interpreted as meaning that this shelter was in great demand at the time when this land had not yet been trodden by the foot of a White man, and that it was widely known to the tribes roving over this section.

Almost simultaneously with this, my first discovery of an Indian rockshelter, I chanced to find a second one. Seen from a distance, it had the appearance of a small cave, but on coming a little nearer I recognized it as an ordinary shelter. To establish its archæological significance required two days' hard digging and even then, after much physical exertion, the results obtained were practically nil. The elevation is about the same as that of the Clove shelter, i. e., 500 feet above the sea level, and both look nearly south. Here also a brook flows past; but, owing to the peculiar topographical conditions, it contains water only during the wet season. In point of size they differ greatly, the Clove shelter being at least four times as spacious. On the other hand, the second one projects fully two feet more, and its roof, instead of sloping towards the background, as in the first, is perfectly level and smooth, enabling one to stand upright close to the wall. As stated above, the finds made here are hardly worth mentioning, consisting of a score of chips, the base of a spear-point, a crude polishing stone and a few bones. However, I must confess that I have excavated only about one-half of the space going to a depth of two feet; the rest I left undisturbed on account of having been disappointed in my expectations during the initial work and not caring to waste any more time and energy.

Pompton Junction. The third and last rock-shelter in Passaic County which has come to my notice is west of Pompton Junction, that is to say, within five hundred meters from the intersection of the Greenwood Lake branch of the Erie with the Susquehanna Railway. Its distance from the Clove by highway is eight miles; but in a straight line drawn from the latter place in a direction W. N. W., it is but five miles distant. Within the angle formed by the two railway lines there rises a hill, locally known as Federal Hill, and composed entirely of granite. The Erie skirts along its eastern base, the Susquehanna along its southern. The height of this hill is a little over six hundred feet, but as it overlooks a level country, the so-called Pompton Plains, the average elevation of which is but two hundred feet, it forms a striking feature of the landscape, appearing almost like a promontory jutting out into the adjacent plains. Being on the very outskirts of what are known as the Jersey Highlands and especially at the entrance to the Butler Valley, through which the Pequannock River pursues its meandering course, this hill may safely be assumed to have been a famous landmark at the time of the redskins. By what name it was known among the aborigines we shall never learn. Its modern appellation, Federal Hill, is, if we may believe the voice of tradition, accounted for by the fact that from its top the ubiquitous George Washington scanned the surrounding lowlands for traces of the English.

Viewing its southern extremity from the banks of the Pequannock River,

Federal Hill looms dark and grim, a tumbled and broken region, stimulating in its wildness. Perpendicular cliffs, torn and cleft by the upheavals of Nature, tower above the lower portion of the hill, which in turn is bestrewn with cyclopean boulders and covered with a tangled growth of underbrush. The jagged hillside abounds in crags and fissures and gigantic rocks are piled up on top of each other, as if placed there by beings gifted with inconceivable strength. One of these cavernous recesses close to the bottom of the cliff attracted my particular attention and crawling into it, I began a thorough search. It is a place which resembles a real cave more closely than any others I have thus far come across. But unlike most caves it has two entrances opposite each other, to the north and south respectively. This singularity of structure is due to the fact that a huge rock leans lengthwise against the side of the steep cliff at an angle of about seventy degrees. Its top is well covered over by other boulders, so as to keep out wind and rain. In addition, both openings are partially protected by large rocks so that, all in all, the place was as little exposed to the severity of the elements as its tenants might reasonably expect. Its inside dimensions show a uniform width of six feet, a length of twelve and an average height of seven feet. The floor was covered with rich soil or humus about two feet thick, and there were comparatively few stones imbedded in it. Removing the leaves which the wind had blown in, I discovered right on the surface a large arrow point, made of chert, and nearly four inches long. Nearby, I found several others of smaller size, all of flint, among them a beautifully shaped triangular point, and the base of an argillite spear-head, deeply notched and with both auricles intact. Close to one of the walls and opposite the centre, the soil was almost black, owing to the presence of charcoal, and here I picked up a large number of potsherds together with many bones, obviously the refuse of aboriginal repasts. This, then, was evidently the old fireplace and, as if to dispel all doubts about it, further proof was forthcoming in the shape of fire-cracked pebbles or heat-stones and pieces of flat rock used in its construction. None of the pottery was ornamented save two small fragments, and these were cord-marked. Here, too, all the pottery occurred on the surface only, while most of the other objects were nearer the base.

From the absence of water in the immediate vicinity, we may infer that this spot was but rarely occupied, and this conclusion deductively arrived at, is borne out inductively, by the small number of relics. The *à priori* argument may be controverted, though, on the ground that the natural conditions have been changed by the cutting of the timber, resulting in the complete drying up of springs; so that where there is now hopeless aridity, there may once have been plenty of water. However, the validity of the *à posteriori* argument can hardly be questioned, inasmuch as, most naturally, paucity of relics is to be interpreted as betokening infrequent occupancy, rather than the contrary. Nor was the Pequannock River, laving the base of the hill, near enough to furnish water for the Indian troglodyte two hundred feet up its side. Obviously, this drawback detracted from the otherwise striking advantages of the place and made it appear less desirable from the Indian's viewpoint.

It must not be surmised that the three rock-shelters just spoken of are the only ones to be found in the County of Passaic. In so far as they are in a section which, though hilly and broken, is yet quite tame, we may accept it as a foregone conclusion that the northern portion of the County contains many more of them, by reason of its being vastly more rugged and wild. With the exception of a narrow strip of level land, the Wanaque Valley, all of this territory is decidedly mountainous, covered as it is by several chains of hills, i. e., the southernmost portion of the Ramapo range in the east, the Kanouse and Bearfort Mountains in the west. Indeed, on interrogating some of the natives and others acquainted with this region, we received information, more or less vague, as to the whereabouts of various rock-shelters which happened to attract their attention. To explore these mountains and determine the site of aboriginal rock-houses will be our aim in the future.

MORRIS COUNTY, NEW JERSEY.

We shall now leave Passaic County and turn our attention to some of the rock-dwellings situated in the County of Morris. How many there are in the whole county no one knows, nor can their exact number ever be determined except by a systematic search of the area in question. At any rate, I have succeeded, as already stated, in discovering six of them in three different parts of the county. Three of these rock-shelters, all close together, are situated in the hills, two miles west of Pompton Plains, and we may refer to them as the Pompton Plains shelters. Another one, still farther west, is known by the name of Bear Rock; and the last two, also close together, lie in the Towakhow or Hook Mountains, and these we may designate as the Towakhow shelters.

Pompton Plains. The Pompton Plains shelters were discovered first. A most thorough-going search of the hills west of Pompton Plains has disclosed the presence of three aboriginal rock-shelters, all of them on the eastern slope. This particular section is remarkable for the extraordinary number of gullies extending down the hillside. They are nearly all parallel and a brook flows through most of them. While spending the summer of 1902 in that charming section of the country, I used to take long walks into the neighboring hills, bordering the village to the west. On one of those jaunts, stumbling through a rocky ravine, I noticed a deep hole on the face of a ledge, dark and uninviting, and screened from the outside by a luxuriant growth of underbrush and small trees. At that time my experience with Indian rock-shelters was still confined to those in the Upper Preakness Clove, and I had almost come to regard them as being without duplicates hereabouts. Thus, with little or no thought of its archæological significance and not a bit sanguine as to possible finds, I began sweeping out the leaves preparatory to further investigation. Half-heartedly I started to dig, but how quickly was the lie given to initial diffidence when, on upsetting a boulder, I found under it a neatly fashioned leaf-shaped flint arrow point. Of course, such a discovery at once invested this place, to me at least, with a charm which only those can know whose mind is of a similar bent. That same day I carried off four arrow points and some potsherds, none of these articles being more than three inches below the surface. On subsequent visits I dug out many more specimens, penetrating to a depth of from twelve to twenty inches, when the base of the floor was reached. I could plainly discern three fireplaces as indicated by the presence of charcoal and smoke-stained slabs, arranged in squares. The total yield of this spot amounted to twenty-four arrow-heads, four spear-heads, over a hundred fragments of pottery, three pitted hand-hammers, one rubbing stone, several heat stones, some bones, a large quantity of flakes and a few nodules, such as furnish the material in the manufacture of various implements. Again the potsherds were either on the surface or a few inches below, a condition disclosing, as before, two distinct horizons of culture; the lower or older layers pointing to a cruder stage of material culture, by reason of the absence of pottery.

If the number of objects left at this shelter by its ancient occupants demonstrates anything at all, it must be in favor of the supposition that it was greatly frequented. Aside from this consideration there are factors of an *à priori* character which tend to prove that such was the case. In the first place, its shape and size leave little to be desired. Carved deep into the rock, much like the entrance to a modern mine, with well-defined sidewalls and a roof hanging over fully fifteen feet, it is shaped almost like a cave. The roof slants towards the background, its forward part being about twelve feet above the floor, while in the rear it is no more than five feet high. The ravine itself rises with a gradual slope from east to west, and is well protected from boreal blasts. Moreover, the shelter is exposed to the sun from morning to night. Thus, the genial warmth, may have conduced considerably to its attractiveness. Yet, notwithstanding all these advantages, the place would have been worthless from the Indian's point of view, had it not been for the presence of water. Of this, too, there is an abundance. Nature has here provided a twofold water supply, namely, a brook and a spring; the brook flowing down the ravine almost within reach of the shelter, the spring, also conveniently near, bubbling up on the opposite side of the cliff, where it stretches northward in a gentle slope. A conjunction of favorable circumstances such as these could, of course, not have escaped the keen senses of the savage, in quest of shelter, and it accounts for the large number of implements left under that rock.

However there are other ancient rock-dwellings almost within hailing distance of the one just discussed. We refer, of course, to the two remaining ones, classified as Pompton Plains shelters. They are less than two hundred meters to the north in one of the largest ravines hereabouts. The surrounding cliffs are steep and jagged, cleft in many places and rising to a height of fifty feet above the bed of the ravine. Boulders are scattered all over in picturesque disorder, seemingly impeding the flow of the brook which lazily wends its way through this rocky labyrinth. Amid these circean environments, appealing to all who love Nature in her primitive and untamed state, I found two of the former abodes of the redskin, less than fifty meters apart. Both face south, by reason of being on the north side of the ravine which runs west by east. The first to be examined was the westerly one. Its floor is on a level with that of the ravine, and what little protection there is, is due to a flat and smooth ledge, inclining or leaning over at an angle of, say, sixty degrees. This ledge is nearly fifteen feet long, measured from base to top, twelve feet high at the outermost point and projects no less than ten feet, thus affording cover for a dozen or more people. As there are no rocks enclosing it laterally, it is open on all sides save on the north. Adjoining it there is another and smaller compartment with a roof jutting out a few feet. To get the investigation under way proved to be a laborious task, as the floor was covered with many rocks of all sizes, the heaviest ones weighing at least a hundred pounds. These removed, digging became quite easy and one by one I brought to light specimens of the red man's handiwork. All told, I found fourteen arrow-heads, mostly of flint, two scrapers, one hand-hammer, one rubbing stone, some heat stones, two bones, a large quantity of flakes and eighty odd fragments of pottery. Some of the potsherds were decorated with dots and zigzag lines, others were cord-marked. In complete analogy with previous experience all of the pottery was on top of the debris, a fact demonstrating, as formerly, relatively recent introduction. In addition, I laid bare two ancient hearths, indicated by smoke-stained slabs, fire-cracked pebbles and soil blackened by an admixture of charcoal.

As regards the other shelter, it is a little farther down the gully, at a point where the rock formations attain their greatest height. Nestling among a pile of rocks at the foot of the cliff, the spot looks gloomy and forbidding, suggesting the lair of some wild animal, and, as if to lend some color to this conception, a hole, six feet deep and large enough for a bear to crawl in, enters into the solid rock at one end of the shelter. Its floor is about five feet above the bed of the ravine, and the sand composing it is coarse and full of small mineral particles, the products of an erosive process which has been going on for an immeasurable epoch. Five feet from the ledge and parallel to it, an oblong boulder extends rampart-like the whole length of shelter, marking off its elevated floor from the lower level of the ravine. In spite of the most diligent search which seemed to be warranted by the promising character of the locality, it yielded amazingly few objects of Indian workmanship. Apart from a finely chipped chert spearpoint nothing was found but the base of a small arrow point and a quantity of flakes. On leaving the place, I almost felt tempted, after so much toil and little success, to apply to it the words of the Italian poet, who exclaimed, "Lasciate ogni speranza o voi che entrate."

Special significance attaches to the above rock-shelters from the fact that within a mile of them there was situated on Pompton Plains, quite near the foot of the hills, an Indian village of considerable size. It is, therefore, more than probable that the occupants, of the shelters were tribesmen of the Pompton Indians who, indeed, spent most of their time in the village below and roamed over the hilly section only when the exigencies of existence compelled them to do so; for they, like all other creatures, yielded to necessity. In other words, the dusky sons of the forest camped at these places while on the hunt. Not using them as permanent abodes, they came and went, lodging there over night, to make room for others the next morning, as the case might be. While all this may legitimately be inferred from the evidence extant, there is one fact, however, which it will be difficult to explain and regarding which different theories may be advanced. We refer to the incongruity obtaining between the abundance of pottery on the one hand and the absence of bones on the other. At all the shelters hitherto investigated, potsherds and fireplaces were invariably associated with considerable quantities of bones, and this rule held good so unfailingly as to point to a casual relation between the two. But here we find it infringed. As none of the Pompton Plains shelters had in the least been disturbed by White intruders, we found them in the very condition which obtained at the time of the Indian's final departure. Thus, the absence of bones cannot be attributed to the agency of the Whites. Not caring to proffer any explanation, fanciful as it must be, we are here confronted by one of the many enigmas, which it is obviously beyond the range of human ken to unravel.

Bear Rock. On a fine summer morning, in the month of August, 1903, I started out from Pompton Plains bound on an errand which, if uncertain as to its outcome, still held out some hope of its ultimate success. The goal of my pilgrimage was a place known as Bear Rock, six miles southwest of Butler, five miles northeast of Boonton and six miles west of Pompton Plains. Bear Rock is a granite boulder of enormous size deposited here during the glacial period. Its dimensions are fifty feet long, eighteen feet wide and thirty-five feet high. In point of size it has no equal in the State of New Jersey, but it is also unique for the reason that it hangs over on two opposite sides, the result being a double rock-shelter, facing east and west respectively. A brook, which has never been known to dry up, flows down the valley in front and within a few feet of the eastern shelter; while opposite the other one there is a hollow, always swampy and often full of water. I had scarcely scratched the surface layer, when I detected an Indian chip. This augured well of the future and with anticipations thus stimulated, I redoubled my efforts, removing leaves and throwing out stones. But imagine my surprise when on lifting a heavy boulder I found underneath it a large copper cent, bearing the date, 1838. An interesting rock, indeed, well worthy of a tramp of nine miles, for apart from Indian relics it yielded modern treasures to boot! However, this coin was destined to remain the only trace of the presence of White men, as all other objects were genuine specimens of primitive culture.

Examining the surface more closely, I observed many flakes and broken bones distributed over the floor of the shelter. As its roof slopes towards the rear I could not enter far save by crawling on my hands and knees. This I did and I was amply repaid for the slight inconvenience, for on looking around I saw two small triangular flint heads and a large one, exquisitely formed with serrated edges. After this rather thorough examination of the top layer, I set myself to dig up the subsoil underneath the roof, beginning at one end and advancing to the other. In order to reach the rock bottom it became necessary to go to a depth of nearly two feet. During this process many stones had to be thrown out, some of them weighing over a hundred pounds; but my work was not in vain, for in every cubic foot of debris I detected traces of the Indian's former presence, such as chips, potsherds, rejects, arrow-heads, heat stones, hammers and vast quantities of bones. A rich archæological harvest it was, the arrow-heads alone numbering thirty-two, counting only the more perfect ones. A majority of the points consisted of flint, a few others of quartz and jasper. Nodules and flakes of various material were scattered all through the soil, their number aggregating close to one thousand. Most plentiful of all were the bones and every thrust of the trowel fetched one or more. About half their number were blackened and charred, while others displayed a reddish brown color. All had been cracked open, no doubt with a view to extracting the marrow. A perforated bear tooth, once part of a necklace, proved no doubt the most interesting of all the objects left there. Relics of this kind, known as tooth-pendants, are of rare occurrence in this part of the country, but much more common in the West. Potsherds alone were scarce and their number did not exceed an even dozen, the largest the size of a silver dollar. Some of the fragments were decorated with straight parallel lines.

We shall now proceed to discuss the shelter on the opposite side of the rock. Although much more spacious, it contained comparatively few Indian implements. Its roof is at least ten feet above the floor and a large rock in front protects it from the outside, concealing the interior. The floor is hard and gravelly and in places the rock bottom crops out. In one of the corners there was an ancient fireplace with plenty of charcoal and fire-cracked pebbles. Here I found also quite a number of potsherds and chips, together with three arrow points, of which only one was perfect. Bones, too, occurred in considerable quantities, most of them, as usual, cracked and fire-stained. Although, on the whole, this shelter did not compare with the other, both as to the number and variety of the objects left, it proved far more prolific in potsherds. In both these shelters, as in all the preceding ones, the pottery lay either on top of the débris or a little below; but nowhere near the base.

In view of the abundance of relics met with in the eastern shelter, as compared with their relative scarcity in the western, we may take it for granted that the former was held in greater favor than the latter. Inquiring into the reasons for this preference, we find that they resolve themselves into a question of heliotropism; in other words, the first was exposed to the sun the greater part of the day, i. e., from the early morning till about two o'clock in the afternoon. This supposition is, in the present case, supported by the circumstance that the other shelter is really superior in size as well as shape.

Towakhow. The last two Indian rock-dwellings in Morris County, known to me, are situated in the Towakhow, or Hook Mountains. This range of hills consists of two arms, each about five miles long, forming a right angle, the apex of which is near White Hall, a station on the Delaware, Lackawanna and Western railway. One arm extends almost exactly due east from White Hall to Mountain View, the other almost exactly due south from White Hall to Pine Brook, the highest altitude, 442 feet, being about half-way between the two latter places. Within the angle thus composed there lies an extensive tract of marshy land, known as the Great Piece Meadows, through which the Passaic River flows in a tortuous course. Not far from the apex or corner of this angle a strip of elevated land stretches forth into the swampy meadows, not unlike a small promontory. It is called Tom's Point. On this high ground, surrounded on three sides by bogs, the redskins had a settlement, a fact borne out by the countless objects they left behind.

The two rock-dwellings above referred to are in the very corner of the Hook Mountains, a little way up the side of the hill. Both face south and they are less than a hundred meters apart. The map shows them to be a little over five miles southeast of Bear Rock, five miles southwest of Pompton Plains and four miles west of Mountain View. Besides, they are less than half a mile from Tom's Point and less than a mile from White Hall. In appearance they differ much from the seven preceding shelters. These, we remember, were simply overhanging rocks, with the exception of the one on Federal Hill which partook of the nature of a cavern. The Towakhow shelters, on the other hand, represent a different type of structure, characterized by rifts or clefts extending from six to eight feet into the rock. There exists between them a striking similarity as to general conformation. Apart from the fissure peculiar to both, they have other features in common, such as the same elevation above sea level, which is 300 feet. Both are on the southern slope of the chain which bounds the Great Piece Meadows to the north and runs eastward from White Hall. Again, at either shelter a huge rocky mass stands out prominently from the cliff crowning the lower and gentler slope of the hill. These rocks protrude perpendicularly to the ledge and from the corner thus formed a rift extends into the interior. In front of either there is a level triangular space, bounded north and west by the ledges just described. Water may be found a short distance down the declivity, bubbling up from amid the rocks and flowing in a tiny stream to the marshlands below.

Investigation of both places was begun in the summer of 1904. The westerly one received my first attention. No sooner had I swept out the leaves than I found the surface soil littered with numerous potsherds. Alongside the ledge, in particular, some large fragments were projecting above the débris and here a deep hole was dug. It happened to be the location of a fireplace, built of slabs after the conventional fashion, all of them *in situ*. At the foot of the opposite ledge another fireplace was laid bare, full of charcoal, chips, potsherds and bones. It may seem somewhat strange that a most painstaking examination of the cleft did not reveal anything in the line of antiquities save a few flint flakes; but considering that this cleft amounts to no more than a narrow passage-way, barely wide enough for a man to crawl into, we understand why the redskins should have regarded it as a rather useless adjunct. The space between the two hearths in front of the crevice, proved to be most prolific in Indian artifacts, some near the surface, others more than twelve inches deep. Along with numerous chips, potsherds and bones, the harvest included three notched arrowpoints, one scraper, one pitted hand-hammer, one chipped knife and a broken steatite bead. The bones were mostly those of deer, but among them were also the upper jawbone of a raccoon with some teeth attached, the femur of an opossum and, *mirabile dictu*, a couple of oyster shells. Most of the pottery was plain; the ornamented pieces were either cord-marked or incised, the zigzag design predominating.

Little remains to be said of the other place. In contour and general structure, it is almost analogous to the first, though considerably smaller. A careful investigation revealed the presence of some few potsherds and chips, together with one argillite spear-point and a straight stem arrow point, made of slaty material. A fireplace was wanting; at any rate, digging all along the ledge did not furnish any indications whatsoever of such an one. Still, there was one redeeming feature about this spot, a feature more than sufficient to counterbalance its inanition in other respects, a relic of rare occurrence. This pièce de·résistance, the princely reward for my toil, was a gorget, made of steatite and elaborately carved. It is about four inches long, elliptical in shape and perforated at both ends. It was while excavating the fissure, which was filled with sand two feet above the level of the outside space, that it dropped out of the escarpment, where it was imbedded three inches below the top. A find of such a character appears doubly precious in a place where little is expected, and it would, in fact, be appreciated even in localities where relics of the finer sort abound. In conformity with previous observations, the position of the pottery in either locality gives positive evidence of a succession of culture-horizons.

Doubtless, the Indians who inhabited these rocks were identical with those who lived on Tom's Point or thereabouts. The latter place was, as already stated, the site of an Indian village, and almost within earshot of the shelters. Being thus within easy reach, it goes without saying that these rocks were often visited and, moreover, that their tenants frequently changed. Unless all the evidence extant deceives us, the knolls and elevated land, contiguous to the Great Piece Meadows, were once much frequented by the aborigines, a fact attested by the numberless remains of their primitive industry. Again, it is patent that these various settlements were connected by trails, and as regards their probable site, the topographical character of the land shows conclusively that they must have skirted along the base of the Towakhow Mountains, viz., from Mountain View westward to Tom's Point, thence southward to Pine Brook.

Our account of the above rock-dwellings would not be complete without presenting a brief recapitulation or summary of the results obtained, together with a few general observations. For completeness' sake, it will be appropriate to make a few statements as to the racial relations of these Indian rock-dwellers. Who, then, were the occupants of these shelters, and to what tribe did they belong? To begin with, the Indians who inhabited the State of New Jersey were Delawares, or, to use their own appellation, Lenni Lenapé. As such, they belonged to the Algonkin family. Roughly speaking, their distribution was conterminous with the State of New Jersey and they were divided into three sub-tribes or gentes, as follows: — the Unalachtigo or Turkey clan, inhabiting the southern portion of the State; the Unami or Turtle clan, living north of them; and the Minsi or Wolf clan, occupying the section in which we are here interested. Thus, the Minsi must be regarded as the erstwhile occupants of the shelters, of which we have presented a brief account.

It is manifest that prehistoric rock-shelters can occur only in those parts of the State that are by nature rocky and mountainous. Accordingly, they are quite plentiful in Northern New Jersey. All we have examined had two important features in common. In the first place, they invariably faced more or less southward; in other words, those with a northern exposure showed few signs of former occupation. Secondly, all of them were situated near some water, whether it be a spring, a brook or a swamp. Sunshine and water were, then, essential factors in determining the choice of a shelter. Although we found this combination of favorable circumstances realized at all the seventeen rock-dwellings, examined by us heretofore, including the eight New York shelters, we do not imagine for a moment that it exists at all shelters at one time inhabited by the red men. There may, indeed, be many a rock-dwelling where but one of these conditions is fulfilled. Needless to say that water it must be always, this being the more important of the two. Without this life-giving element conveniently near, even the best shelter, in point of structure and with a southern exposure would have been scorned by any Indian intending to camp there for any length of time; whereas, he might have chosen a rock with a northern exposure, dispensing with the sunshine, provided there was water nearby. Furthermore, these rocks were used only temporarily and chiefly during the hunt. Of this we may be quite certain in view of the Indian's nomadic proclivities.

Lastly, all the shelters gave positive proof of a succession of culture-horizons, as based on the absence or presence of pottery in the various strata of the debris.

ROCKLAND COUNTY, NEW YORK.

In entering upon the second part of our treatise, relating to some aboriginal shelters situated in that part of the Ramapo Mountains which is included within the counties of Rockland and Orange, in New York state, a brief description of the region in question will not be amiss. This beautiful range of hills has always been an Eldorado for lovers of Nature. Its southern portion, which is but thirty miles north of New York City, stands out in bold relief to the undulating hills of Northern New Jersey and Rockland County by reason of superior height and the rugged character of its contour. All along the southern base, which extends in a straight line from Pompton to the Hudson River, perpendicular ledges and inaccessible cliffs rise from the lowlands and fertile plains through which the Ramapo River meanders. Beginning at Suffern and extending northward, a natural pass, the Ramapo valley, divides this mountainous tract into an eastern and western section. In places it is so narrow that river, highway and railroad fairly seem to compete for the right of way. Two hills, the Noorde Kop and Hoghe Kop, east and west of Suffern, sentinel the entrance to the valley. The level ground between the Ramapo River and the foot of Hoghe Kop marks the site of an ancient village, once peopled by the Tuscarora Indians. They were strangers to the native inhabitants, having come here from the south, about the year 1718, on their way to join the Five Nations.

At Suffern a number of Indian trails converged, among which we may mention the Pompton trail along the banks of the Ramapo River, and the Haverstraw trail following the course of the Mahwah brook. Probably the most important trail ran from Suffern northward through the Ramapo Valley. Between Hillburn and Ramapo, a mile north of Suffern, the glacial moraines, flanking the river, reveal many traces of erstwhile Indian occupation. This is particularly the case at a point almost opposite the Ramapo station, where the Torne brook empties into the Ramapo River. Here, there is a high bank bordering that picturesque water course, level on top and situated at the entrance to the Torne Brook valley. This valley stretches forth into the very heart of the Ramapo Mountains, for a distance of nearly nine miles, with the Torne Mountain bounding it northward. In the shade of this beautiful mountain, which reaches an altitude of 1220 feet above sea-level and forms a tumbled wilderness with the adjoining hills, seven square miles in extent, we have thus far located three aboriginal rock-shelters. These, in connection with two others farther north, constitute the five Rockland County shelters noted above.

Torne Brook. The first to be discovered is situated northeast of the village of Ramapo, two miles up the Torne Brook valley. It was in the spring of 1907 that I happened to pass along the woodroad which runs from Ramapo through the valley. Scanning the rocky slopes to the north, my attention was drawn to a peculiar structure a hundred meters up the hillside. The character of the locality is just such as might have appealed to any redskin looking for covert. In front of it, a brook rushes down, issuing from one of those little side valleys above that cleave the mountain at short intervals. Its channel is worn deep into the rock and full of natural basins that hold back some of the water, which would otherwise be carried off in its precipitous journey downhill. Thus, even during the dry season, water may be found here, collected in small pools. There is nothing unusual about the shelter itself, excepting that the rocks composing it are piled up in a heap, the one on top jutting out fully six feet, quite high above the floor. The space underneath is greatly reduced owing to the presence of two large boulders, one of them taking up the centre of the floor, the other all the room to the left. As a consequence, the remaining portion of the shelter, available for use, amounts to no more than about one-fourth of what it would be, if the obstructions were removed. In spite of this, there was room for a half dozen savages to sit around the campfire. To compensate its tenants for this slight disadvantage, the place had a southwestern exposure and this meant to them plenty of heat and light, comfort and cheerfulness. With water and sunshine to add to its attractiveness, this place was much resorted to, a fact amply attested by the quantity of objects left there.

The available space underneath the rock is about forty square feet. As usual, it was covered with a layer of vegetable mold which, to all appearances, had never been disturbed by any White man. Having removed the leaves, a careful inspection of the top layer revealed at once the presence of many potsherds scattered all over the surface. They were especially plentiful close to the boulders mentioned above. In all, there were at least six hundred fragments, the largest about three inches square. Less than one-third their number were ornamented, the cord-mark design predominating. Some of the pieces were decorated with dots arranged in a series of parallel lines; others were incised. Further examination showed that much of the pottery was as far as eight inches below the surface. This, then, is seemingly a deviation from former experience, from a rule which obtained uniformly in all the New Jersey shelters. However, it must be borne in mind that the pottery lay deep only in three well-defined spots close to the rocks, and these spots proved to be the sites of fireplaces. Outside of them it occurred only on top or in the upper stratum of debris. These fireplaces were remarkably deep, deeper, in fact, than any of the New Jersey fireplaces. To be sure, in some of the latter, pottery was imbedded, but even then quite superficially and never anywhere near bottom. Yet, after all, the position of the pottery near the base of the hearth cannot be regarded as contravening former experience in the sense that we may infer from it an early introduction of the art. Moreover, there exists some likelihood that the pottery may have been washed down into the holes dug for the fireplaces. Matters would, indeed, assume a different complexion, if pottery occurred in lower layers even outside of fireplaces, but now no special significance attaches to their being imbedded far down in certain spots only, and we may conclude that these fireplaces were dug during the last period of occupancy of the shelter and that those who dug them were acquainted with the art of pottery. Accordingly, the theory of an early introduction of ceramic art, at least as regards this shelter, proves untenable. The salient point, as in all the New Jersey shelters, is that, excepting the fireplaces, all the pottery lay in the upper strata.

Of other relics we found but a limited quantity, viz., six arrow points, made of chert and flint, three broken spear-heads, a scraper, a rubbing stone, some burnt pebbles, hundreds of chips and many bones, for the most part belonging to deer. Doubtless, much cooking was done here as evidenced by the fireplaces, the pottery and bones, and the traces of fire and smoke on the rocks. It was a convenient place for the Red hunter who, having foraged in the mountains, came hither to partake of the spoils of the chase and to recuperate from the fatigues incident thereto.

Torne Mountain. Torne Mountain is, in truth, a complex of many hills, all organically connected, a rocky wilderness, torn and jagged and covering no less than seven square miles. Its summit looms bald and weather-worn high above the valley of the Ramapo River and the wooded slopes beneath. Though rough and broken in all its sections, its ruggedness appears to be most marked at its southern extremity. Here the mountain rises in a succession of terraces, the chief feature of each being a cliff with a gorge in front. These cliffs are from twenty to fifty feet high and scalable in but few places. About half-way up the southern slope of Torne Mountain and on its fifth terrace, if we remember aright, there is an exceptionally picturesque ravine with precipitous rocks flanking it northward. Everything hereabouts is rough and jagged and the face of the crag abounds in rifts and projecting rocks. The upper part of the ravine contains a swamp which is drained by a brook. It is a gloomy-looking locality and well-shaded by large trees. Amid these somber surroundings I discovered a cache, not of the kind, though, hiding ready-made implements, but one filled only with the raw material used in their manufacture. This place is at the foot of the ledge and is simply a deep hole about five feet high with the floor and roof slanting downward and backward at an easy incline.

Owing to its limited height, it was not suited for habitation, unless, indeed, its tenants were willing to assume a stooping posture. Yet, while there is nothing to show that this place was ever inhabited, there are indications that it has been used as a cache. For that purpose it was admirably adapted with its floor hard and smooth, and well-confined within the walls of the ledge. Excavation of the subsoil brought to light hundreds of flint nodules, all showing the well-known conchoidal fractures and ranging in size from a goose egg to a man's fist. To dispel all doubt as to this material having been deposited here by the Indians, we also found along with it an imperfect arrow point or reject. There was not the slightest trace of any other antiquities. The presumption that all these nodules occurred here naturally, is to be utterly discredited, in the first place, because flint does not occur nearby, and elsewhere in this region it is met with only sporadically and certainly not in such quantities, all thrown in a heap; secondly, because they were most obviously split and made up into convenient sizes by some intelligent mind, and deposited there for future use. Most rocks hereabouts are composed of granite and gneiss, with some mica here and there.

Ramapo River. The third and last shelter, within the Torne Mountain range, to engage our attention is situated in its extreme southernmost portion, at the very edge of its terminal ridges and less than ten meters from the banks of the Ramapo River. Sterlington on the other side of the river lies almost opposite, that is, a little to the north of it. It is an overhanging rock, typical of many other in this section. Its roof projects nearly ten feet and inclines towards the rear, thus forming with the floor an acute angle of, say, fifty degrees. Being high above in the forward part and the centre, one may stand erect. Large boulders enclose this place laterally. With the river flowing in front and the sunshine flooding it all day, the locality was sufficiently alluring to attract the attention of the native inhabitants. Potsherds afforded, as usual, the first signs of the red man's whilom presence. To determine their position and relative number, the surface was at first left undisturbed. Having recovered all that lay on top, the soil was dug up, until at a depth varying from six to twelve inches, the rock bottom was reached. In this way it was found that the proportion of fragments on top to those buried was about one to three. During this process it was shown once more that the pottery occurred in upper layers only, a fact hinting again at a succession of culture-horizons and a relatively recent introduction of the ceramic art. While thus it lay at most an inch or two below, there was one narrow circumscribed spot, where it was buried fully five inches. This spot was obviously the site of a fireplace, as indicated by charcoal, heat stones, etc. Its presence at such a depth in this one place does therefore not clash in the least with conclusions previously arrived at. The ornamentation on potsherds was along conventional lines, the cord-mark design prevailing. Aside from the hundred or more pieces of pottery, this shelter yielded three arrow points, the base of a spear-head, two scrapers and a large quantity of chips. Bones were entirely lacking. Certain indications go to prove that an Indian thoroughfare passed by this rock, running from Ramapo to Tuxedo along the eastern bank of the Ramapo River. The lay of the land was, at all events, quite favorable to such a trail. Again, south of this shelter and in the direction of Ramapo, the cliffs stand well back, and on the high and level bank intervening between mountain and river, I found at three different places the signs of erstwhile Indian camping-grounds. Hence, there is good ground for believing that the shelter on the river's bank was often visited.

One of the wildest and most charming regions within this territory lies directly north of the Torne Mountain range. A deep and lovely valley forms the dividing line. Starting at Sloatsburg it runs in a northeasterly direction to St. Johns, a little settlement amid the hills. The highway which connects both places clings close to the Stony brook, one of the eastern tributaries of the Ramapo river. A ramble through this valley with its ever changing scenery is at once enjoyable and inspiring. To the right, one observes the Torne Mountain chain with its many summits, all thickly timbered; to the left, there greets the eye a group of hills and massive crags, rising abruptly hundreds of feet in the air. Most conspicuous among the latter are two hills, locally known as Mine Hill and Pound Hill. Amid their rocky fastnesses we discovered two more spots of archæological moment, the last ones within the county of Rockland that remain to be discussed.

Pound Hill. One of them is not far from the summit of Pound Hill, on its southeastern slope, about three and one-half miles northeast of Sloatsburg and a mile and a half north of the Stony Brook road. The place is well-nigh inaccessible and everything seems to conspire to hide it from sight. A maze of rocks and a jungle of wild laurel and thick underbrush surround it on all sides, and above it all, there loom loose and disjointed crags of fantastic shapes and strange outlines. Here chaos seems to hold full sway. In keeping with these environments there is this singular structure of an overhanging rock, gloomy and dark, deep and spacious, but with a roof so low as to necessitate crouching. This roof is less than five feet high and projects at least fifteen feet. It is perfectly horizontal. The cliff faces southeast, and a short distance from it, there is a swamp drained by a brook. The harvest comprised a score of chips, a few bones and three fragments of arrow-heads. Pottery was wholly lacking. But for the low ceiling, it would have been an ideal covert.

Mine Hill. Mine Hill is situated southwest of Pound Hill and between them there lies a plateau, or, to be more precise, an exceedingly rough tract of elevated land which is crossed by many gorges and steep ridges. About midway between the plateau and the top of Mine Hill a cliff of considerable length extends across its southeastern declivity. There is one spot in particular, not far from the boundary line which separates Rockland and Orange counties, where the formation of the cliff is strikingly grotesque. At this point an overhanging rock of huge dimensions may be noticed. Its lofty roof juts far out, and in front there is a colossal boulder parallel to the ledge and forming with it a passage-way about twenty feet long and five feet wide. To the left of it a rocky mass as high as the cliff, stands out prominently at right angles and far into it there enter two cavities, side by side. This remarkable place has been but partly explored for reasons given below. Examination of the passage-way revealed some slight traces of an ancient fireplace near the centre, as indicated by blackened soil, heat stones, etc. Furthermore, a quantity of chips were found, distributed over the surface and upper strata. It may appear strange that a place of this character should prove so disappointing. However, there was one great disadvantage which could not but be prejudicial to any shelter, no matter how excellent in other respects. This was the absence of water in the immediate vicinity. The nearest supply is afforded by a brook about two hundred meters away, a distance too great to suit the comfort-loving Indian.

Orange County, New York.

The last part of our narrative will be devoted to the study of the three Orange County shelters. We shall attempt to give a synopsis of the character and distinctive features of each and of the objects found there. All three are within the township of Tuxedo, i. e., in that part of it which lies east of the Ramapo River. As regards their distribution, one is in the southernmost portion of the township, the second near the centre, and the last, in the north, close to the Woodbury township line. While the first one is on the very outskirts of the mountains and easily accessible, the last two are high up among the lonely hills, miles away from human habitations. Again, while the first one is least interesting from the archæological view point, the others, notably the second one, proved to be veritable mines of prehistoric relics.

Tuxedo. Being most easily accessible, the former was discovered and investigated long before the others. It is situated on the eastern bank of the Ramapo River, two miles north of Sloatsburg and one mile south of Tuxedo. Between the latter places, the cliffs marking the extreme western bounds of the mountains, run more or less parallel with the river, at a distance averaging about three hundred meters. Toward Tuxedo, they approach the river more closely and their configuration becomes one of greater ruggedness and increasing height. Here we came across our first Orange County shelter. Its roof is smooth and slopes down to the floor, like an inclined plane, at a dip of some fifty degrees. As a consequence, one cannot stand upright under it, except in the fore part. The maximum elevation of the roof along the outermost edge is about seven feet and the dimensions of the floor are twenty feet long and ten feet wide. The rock faces west and the river in front is no more than a hundred meters away. In point of finds, this shelter was far from prolific. The total yield consisted in a few broken arrow-heads or rejects and a quantity of chips. There was no vestige of potsherds or bones, nor did we succeed in finding a fireplace. However, the search has thus far been carried on rather perfunctorily, and pending further investigation it would be rash to make any definite statements.

Horsestable Rock. In the following, we shall treat at some length, of a place which may well be deemed the monarch of aboriginal rock-shelters for many miles around. Structurally, it is the finest type of shelter which it has been our good fortune to discover; but it also excels vastly all the others with respect to number and variety of antiquities left there. This place is locally known as Horsestable Rock. We knew of it from hearsay, years before we had any conception of Indian rock-shelters. Indeed, our first efforts to locate it were not at all prompted by ethnological interest, but rather by purely historical considerations, since Horsestable Rock had played a certain part in the Revolutionary history of the Ramapo Mountains, by having been the headquarters and hiding place of a noted Tory chief and brigand, called Claudius Smith, surnamed the Cowboy of the Ramapo Mountains. To conceive of its having been the haunt of prehistoric people was reserved for a much later period.

Horsestable Rock lies four miles N. N. E. of Sloatsburg and two and a half miles east of Tuxedo. It is a place quite difficult of access, for though there are some rough wood-roads about, none lead close up to it, save one, and this is almost obliterated. As its altitude above tidewater is about one thousand feet, the neighboring hills look rather insignificant, with their tops not exceeding twelve hundred feet. The rock faces west overlooking a comparatively level tract of woodland, and right in front is a swamp, covered with luxuriant vegetation. In order to give a better idea of the topography of this section, be it remarked that the mountain rises in terraces, of which the level space just mentioned forms the second from the summit. The next terrace, some forty feet above, occupies the top of the cliff back of Horsestable Rock, and is bounded eastward by a much higher and more rugged crag known as Claud's Den, the top of which marks the highest elevation of the mountain, i. e., 1150 feet. Tradition points to this crag as having been the chief hiding place of Claudius Smith, already alluded to as a guerilla of Revolutionary fame. At the foot of it there is an overhanging rock, and half way up its face a kind of gallery or covered passage, four feet wide and fifty odd feet long. Although we left no stone unturned in searching this spot, we did not succeed in finding remains, either ancient or modern. As regards Horsestable Rock, it is said to owe its name to the fact that Claudius Smith used it for stabling the horses and cattle which were carried off during the frequent depredations committed by himself and followers against the Dutch patriots. How much of truth there is in the traditions investing this rock, what is idle fancy, what authentic history, is hard to ascertain. However, later investigation furnished certain evidence which really seems to give countenance to some of the stories current in regard to it.

As already stated, Horsestable Rock is by far the largest rock-shelter for a radius of many miles. Its roof inclines backward, showing along its outermost edge an elevation above the floor of from nine to twelve feet. As it does not slant all the way down, but joins the vertical back wall at an average height of four feet above the floor, one can stand upright in nearly all parts of the shelter. The covered space has a frontage of seventy feet and a uniform width of fifteen feet. At the extreme right there is an additional protection in the shape of a protruding rock with adjoining embankment. Near the extreme left, water trickles through a crevice on the inner wall, collecting in a natural basin which is always filled, except during periods of great drouth. The floor slopes in a gentle curve from either side towards the centre, the depression not exceeding three feet. Within this hollow space, which, indeed, appeared almost level, there were found deposited two boulders of about equal size and weighing at least two thousand pounds each. They were placed close together so as to form an acute angle and this position suggested at once the site of a fireplace, a supposition borne out afterwards by the remains there discovered. Apart from its great size, Horsestable Rock is remarkable, in that it can draw on a threefold water supply. First, there is the swamp in front; second, the water oozing through fissures on the inner wall of the shelter; and last, a spring at the head of swamp north of the rock and less than a hundred meters distant. While the first-named sources generally dry up during midsummer, the spring is always filled with an abundance of ice-cold water.

It goes without saying that to explore a place of such magnitude was by no means an easy undertaking, even under favorable circumstances and with the best of tools. In our own case, matters were aggravated because of the inadequacy of the tools at our command and we were therefore prepared for a long and arduous search. Being thus handicapped, the investigation progressed quite slowly and has hitherto been limited to the lower middle portion, comprising about one third of the entire space. This section was selected, because there was good reason for thinking that it would contain a majority of relics. Before we had begun digging, many chips were found scattered over the surface — fore-runners of the antiquities that were soon to follow. Suffice it to say that the area excavated as yet comprises upwards of three hundred cubic feet, and near its centre are the two boulders above described. The débris overlying the rock bottom varied between one and two feet in depth and all this mass was gradually removed together with a number of large rocks imbedded in it. Many of the remains lay close to the boulders, some even underneath them.

A minute search of the débris yielded the following antiquities. In the upper layers, there occurred three large English copper coins of 1729 and 1737. These modern curiosities lay from one to three inches below and on one side of the boulders. Next came four leaden bullets, all cast in a mold, three of them as large as ox-heart cherries, the other, half their size. They occurred far apart and quite near the top. Mingled with them were chips, bones and other objects in great profusion. Primitive culture was represented by a hundred and thirty-eight specimens, in varying conditions of preservation. First, there were two spear-heads. One was of argillite, five inches long, leaf-shaped and with a straight stem; the other, was three inches long, of flint and lanciform. The harvest included furthermore, seventy-nine arrow-heads of which fifty were perfect, besides fifty-six fragments of heads and one scraper. Two of the points were less than one inch long and triangular in shape, sixty-one, between one and two inches, and sixteen, more than two inches. One was barbed, another twisted, some serrated, nine triangular and without notches, and the rest were all notched. A few of these points were corroded and calcinized, as if very old. The material used in their manufacture was flint, quartz, limestone, chert, argillite and slate. In addition, there were thousands of flakes and bones, the latter belonging for the most part to the deer family; but there were also the remains of many other animals, among which we may mention bear, wolf, raccoon, opossum and beaver. Of particular interest were two deer's horns and one beaver tooth, the latter gracefully curved and four inches long, The deer's tines lay at the site of the fireplace; the beaver tooth under one of the boulders at a depth of about five inches. The deposit within the fireplace and close by contained a disproportionately large number of relics and probably fifty per cent of the objects were here crowded into some twenty cubic feet of soil.

The fact that Horsestable Rock did not contain the slightest vestige of earthenware, may appear anomalous at first sight. Still, its absence may be accounted for satisfactorily by taking into consideration the general inaccessibility and remoteness of this rock from the nearest aboriginal settlements. To carry pottery over miles of an exceedingly rough territory would have been not only very cumbersome but useless, bound as these Indians were on a hunting trip.

In this connection we wish to comment on an observation, which if well founded, will tend to vitiate somewhat the testimony heretofore adduced, at least in so far as it pertains to the objects of modern origin. In the course of the investigation we could not help suspecting that the layers had been disturbed. There were, to be sure, no fresh traces of any such disturbance; still, the subsoil appeared to have been dug up in places at some not very recent period. It is indeed conceivable that treasure hunters had searched this shelter, it having always been rumored that Claudius Smith had buried his booty hereabouts. Another point worthy of notice is the fact that more than two-thirds of the relics, i. e., the arrow-heads, were mutilated. In nearly all these cases, the points had been broken off, while the bases were practically intact. By reason of this curious medley of ancient and modern remains, Horsestable Rock must be regarded as the most interesting of all the shelters hitherto explored. It is unique, invested as it is with memories both prehistoric and modern. Moreover, there may be a grain of truth in the traditions relating to this locality, since, irrespective of other evidence, it is not at all impossible that the four bullets, above alluded to, date back to revolutionary times, when it is said, this rock was one of the haunts of Claudius Smith, surnamed the Cowboy of the Ramapo Mountains.

Goshen Mountain. If accident ever played a part, it surely did so in the circumstances attending the discovery of the last aboriginal rock-shelter which remains to be discussed. With a view to reconnoitering a tract of land which was then terra incognita to us, we started from Arden, a station on the Erie Railway, on the 22nd of November, 1908, bound for the wooded hills east of it. On we went, until we reached the Goshen Mountain, five and a half miles east of Arden. Scanning the country to the right and left, we happened to see a rocky eminence, a hundred and fifty meters from the wood road and scarcely visible from it, owing to the heavy timber obstructing our view. Squeezing through the tangled underbrush we approached the cliff, with little thought of finding here a remarkably good Indian shelter.

This place, the farthest north of all the seventeen shelters, is situated in the northernmost portion of Tuxedo township close to the Woodbury township line. It is perched on the western slope of Goshen Mountain, a hundred and thirty feet below its summit, at an altitude of 1160 feet above sea level. It faces south, overlooking a swampy piece of ground nearby. West of it, fifty meters lower down and some three hundred meters distant, there lies a placid sheet of water, called Cedar Pond, three quarters of a mile long and one-third of a mile wide.

Although structurally not differing greatly from other overhanging rocks, it has still some features of its own. Its roof is horizontal and projects five feet at right angles to a vertical inner wall. Westward, it is protected by a protruding mass of rock, also at right angles to the inner wall. The inside dimensions of the shelter are twelve feet long and five feet wide. Prior to excavation the height of the ceiling above the floor was less than five feet. Afterwards, when rock bottom was reached, it was over six feet. This was no doubt the original elevation of the roof, until the gradual accumulation of débris decreased it. The surface was quite even and overlain by vegetable mold, over which numerous bones were scattered. Potsherds in great abundance occurred in upper layers to a depth not exceeding three inches. Mingled with them were other bones and hundreds of flakes. Two inches below the top, the first arrow-head came to sight. Deeper down many more were dug out, some of them lying eighteen inches below on rock bottom.

Two fireplaces could be distinguished, one in the corner formed by the lateral projection and inner wall; the other, four feet east of it close to the wall. Here the soil was almost black through admixture with charcoal, and imbedded in it were charred bones, fire-cracked pebbles, chips, points and nearer the top fragments of pottery.

Examination of the shelter is not yet complete, for while most of the inner portion has been explored, there remain for future search all the outside accumulations. Thus far, the following implements were obtained:— three scrapers, fashioned of bluestone, and triangular in shape. Seventeen perfect arrow-heads made of flint, argillite and chert, of which, ten were notched, seven were without notches, so-called warpoints and also triangular. One was over two inches long, eleven between one and two, and five less than an inch. Besides, there were fourteen fragments of heads. Then there were a piece of a bone, a little over an inch long, perforated at one end and probably used as a pendant; one deer's horn and the upper part of another; the lower jawbone of a deer with some teeth, and numberless other bones, also mostly of deer. In addition to all this there occurred upwards of a thousand chips, distributed from top to bottom in every part of the shelter.

In contradistinction to Horsestable Rock, the Goshen Mountain shelter, if we may so term it, contained potsherds in plenty. Their absence in the former was ascribed to topographical reasons, that is to say, to the ruggedness of the territory surrounding it, which precluded transportation. At all events, this theory seems to be the most plausible of any that may be advanced. Moreover, its correctness is substantiated in the case of the present shelter. Notwithstanding its higher altitude, this place is far more easily accessible, although probably farther removed from the sites of erstwhile Indian villages than Horsestable Rock. The northernmost section of Tuxedo township is not nearly as rough as the former, a few miles farther south. Its slopes are gentler and the character of the land, high up among the hills, is more undulating, alternating with level stretches here and there. Hence, pottery could be conveyed with little difficulty; hence also, its presence at the Goshen Mountain shelter. The quantity it yielded was equivalent to a dozen pots or more. Few of the pieces were ornamented, and these were either cord-marked or incised. The conditions under which they were found were wholly analogous to previous experience, inasmuch as they occurred in upper strata only. Since these strata averaged less than one-fifth of the entire accumulation, this fact admits, as formerly, of but one conclusion. Primarily, it suggests two epochs of material culture; and, more particularly, it points to a relatively recent use of pottery in rock-shelters, this stage being preceded by long periods during which earthenware was not so used.

That the huntsmen who visited this rock found it a convenient spot is quite evident when we consider its natural advantages. It was a sunny nook with plenty of water nearby and therefore well suited for temporary occupation. That they often camped here may be gathered from the abundance of objects deposited in débris. Furthermore, it is certain that the occupants of this, as well as of the other sixteen shelters were of Algonkin stock. While two of the many subdivisions of this race are known to have roamed over this territory, viz., the Lenni Lenapé and the Mohegans, it is not an easy matter to determine with any degree of accuracy the distribution or geographical boundaries of each. As regards the frequenters of the North Jersey rock-dwellings, we may be reasonably sure that they were members of the Wolf clan or Minsi, the most ferocious and warlike of the Lenni Lenapé. In the case of the Ramapo Mountain shelters it is a mooted question whether they belonged to the Minsi or to the Mohegans. As the latter were, however, closely allied to the Lenni Lenapé and, by the way, near kinsmen of the ancient inhabitants of Manhattan, the problem is, after all, of little importance, involving, as it does, some finer distinctions of tribal relation.

ANCIENT SHELL HEAPS NEAR NEW YORK CITY.

BY

M. R. HARRINGTON.

Of all the traces left by the aborigines along the New York seacoast, the most abundant and familiar are the shell heaps — the beds of refuse marking the sites of ancient villages, camps and isolated wigwams. Wherever the fresh water joins the salt and especially where open water for fishing, a creek with its clam beds, and a spring for drinking come together in happy combination, there is generally to be found some such evidence of Indian occupation, unless, as is often the case, settlement and improvement have buried deep the shells or carted them away.

The typical shell heap is not a "heap" at all, for leaf mold, the wash from neighboring high ground and often cultivation have made it level with its surroundings (Fig. 27). Very often, unless the land be plowed, no shells whatever show on the surface, and the only way of finding out the conditions

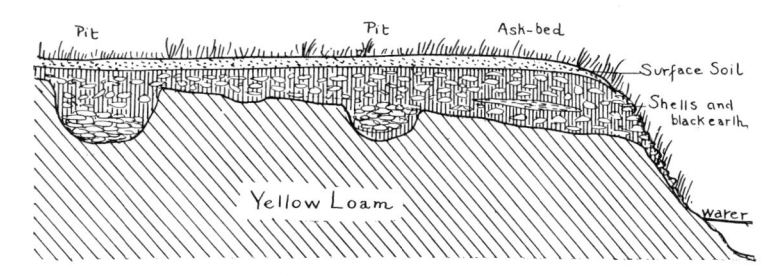

Fig. 27. Diagram of a Typical Shell Deposit.

of things below the sod is to test with a spade or a crowbar. If shells are present, their crunching soon gives notice of the fact. Sometimes shell heaps have been located by shells thrown from mole and woodchuck burrows, or by outcropping in gullies washed by the rain, or banks broken down by the surf. They are generally located near some creek or bay on low but dry ground, preferably with an eastern or southern exposure, and, as before mentioned not far from drinking water. Some have been found fronting on the open Sound, but such cases are rare. These deposits consist of large quantities of decayed oyster, clam, and other marine shells mixed with stained earth, with here and there ashes, charcoal and fire-broken stones to mark the spots where ancient camp fires blazed. Among the shells are usually scattered antler of deer, fish bones, bones of animals and birds split for the marrow, quantities of pottery fragments, and broken implements, in short, the imperishable part of the camp refuse left by the Indians. Now and then, perfect implements and ornaments that had been carelessly lost in the rubbish or hidden for safe-keeping are discovered. Little did the Indian think, as he laid away his little hoard, that his handiwork would never see light again until he and his people had long been gone and forgotten.

Shell heaps vary from a few inches to four feet in depth, and in area from a few square yards to several acres — all depending on the length of time the settlement was occupied and the number of dwellings comprising it. Deep shell heaps are often divided into layers, the deepest of which are, of

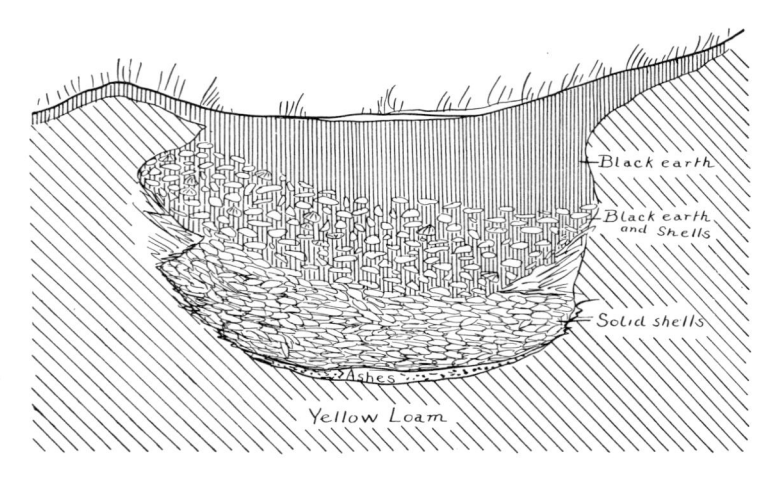

Fig. 28. Cross Section of a Shell Pit.

course, the oldest. Under and near most of these deposits may be found scattered "pits" or fire holes, which are bowl-shaped depressions in the ground filled with layers of stained earth, shells and other refuse, with an occasional layer of ashes. Some pits are as large as ten feet wide by six feet deep, but the average is four feet deep by three feet. It is supposed that they were used as ovens or steaming holes and afterwards filled up with refuse (Fig. 28). Some contain human skeletons, which may have been interred in them during the winter season when grave digging was impossible. Pits as a rule, contain more of interest than the ordinary shell layer. The closely packed regular masses of shells form a covering which tends to preserve bone implements, charred corn, and such perishable articles from decay, in a way that the looser shells of the general layers fail to do.

The implements, utensils and ornaments found in the shell heaps include objects made of stone, copper, bone and antler, shell and baked clay. Arrow points are among the most abundant of stone relics and exist in great variety, while larger points evidently intended for knives or spears are not uncommon. Drills are rare, but some very fine narrow blades of this class have been secured. Implements of stone called scrapers, with chipped beveled edges were probably used for scraping down arrow shafts or for scraping skin and the like, as a piece of glass is used by modern woodworkers. Sometimes mere flakes of stone show signs of use as knives or scrapers. Even more abundant than the arrow-heads themselves may be found rejects — the failures of arrow point making — stones that proved too obdurate to work, that broke, or that flaked improperly. Quartz was the favorite material for chipped implements in Westchester County and Long Island, probably because it might be found on any beach, while chert and jasper were harder to get, and argillite had to be imported from what is now New Jersey. This was frequently done, however, for greatly weathered argillite blades and fragments are often found in the local shell heaps.

Stone axes of two kinds have been found — the celt or grooveless axe which was probably set in a hole in its club-like handle, and the grooved axe, around whose groove was wrapped a handle of withes. Pestles are cylindrical stone implements used for crushing corn and herbs, probably in wooden mortars, though stone mortars, mere slabs with cup-shaped depressions, alone survive in the shell heaps to-day, the wooden ones having long since been destroyed. I do not think the long stone pestles were used in the stone mortars, their place being taken by flat cobbles. These implements, called muller, often show long use and wear, and have been found resting on the mortars. Hammerstones are often found, usually mere natural cobbles battered by use, but sometimes slightly pitted on one or both sides to keep the fingers from slipping. Another style of implement having a shallow pit and slight encircling groove may have been hafted and used as a maul. Stones showing traces of being pounded upon are called anvils, and flat pebbles notched on opposite edges for the cord, were used as net-sinkers. Sometimes net-sinkers were grooved. Large cobbles chipped to an edge probably served as hand-axes or choppers and split stones and large flakes were slightly altered for use as hoes and skin scrapers.

Flat tablets of stone called gorgets, with one or more perforations, were probably used as ornaments. Crescent-shaped flat stones, notched in the middle and usually of red limonite, occur, and are classed with the drilled "banner stones" or "ceremonials" of unknown use. I have never discovered any of the drilled variety in a shell heap, but have heard of their being found. Occasional fragments of cooking vessels made of soapstone are obtained from the shell heaps — vessels that were long and shallow, with a projecting knob on each and beneath which supporting stones could be placed when the pot was on the fire.

I know of but few stone pipes that have been found in perfect condition in or near the shell heaps of this region. One was discovered near Inwood, on Manhattan Island and is now in the possession of Mr. Bolton (Plate XVII); the other came from a child's grave near a shell heap at Tottenville, Staten Island, and was collected by Mr. G. H. Pepper (Plate IX). It is a beautiful specimen of the "monitor" or "platform" type and appears to be made of steatite. Several other pipes of stone, one of the so-called trumpet type have also been found in this cemetery while several fragments were found on the surface. Pieces of red and black soft stones such as limonite and graphite, deeply scratched for paint are numerous in some shell heaps.

The only metallic objects found that date back before the coming of the Whites are bits of copper pounded out flat and rolled into the shape of cylindrical beads. Even these are rare. Bone and deer antler implements were extensively used by the New York seacoast Indians and are often found in the shell heaps. Awls are the most abundant of these and exhibit all degrees of elaboration and finish, from the mere sharpened splinter of bone up to the finely rounded and polished implement showing little of the bone's original surface. They were undoubtedly used in sewing as the shoemaker uses his awl to-day. Often the joint of a bone has been left to serve as a handle for the awl. Bird bones were sometimes used, but deer bone was the favorite material. Occasionally awls show grooving or perforation for suspension, in which case they were probably hung on a string about their owner's neck (Fig. 7).

Broad, flat, bone needles sometimes made of the curved surface of a rib occur in small numbers, but are usually broken across the eye. The Sauk and Fox and other western tribes use such needles for making mats of cat-tail flags.

At the Shinnecock Hills, barbs suitable for tying on fish spears were made of bone, as were sometimes arrow points, the latter fashioned so as to use a part of the marrow canal as a socket for the shaft. A bone implement resembling a draw shave, probably used for removing the hair from skins, was made by cutting away a portion of a deer's leg bone so as to leave a narrow blade in the middle with the joints at both ends to serve as handles. Bird bones were made into beads or tubes and beaver teeth into knives.

The antlers of deer were found useful as material for the implements of the Indian's daily life. Arrow points were made by sharpening an antler prong, cutting it off and drilling out the base of the cone thus formed to receive the shaft. Sometimes a projection was left on the side to serve as a barb. Near the shell heaps at Tottenville, Staten Island, Mr. G. H. Pepper found three human skeletons, among whose bones were twenty-three arrow points, all but three of them, of bone and antler. One barbed antler point had actually penetrated a rib, the point projecting on the inside (Plate III). Antler points in process of manufacture and antlers from which prongs have been cut are frequent in the shell heaps.

The exact use of the cylinders of antler so often found, is not definitely known, but it is thought they may have been used as flaking tools, held between the stone blade and the hammerstone to be worked. Some antler prongs show signs of having been used to remove fine scales of quartz or flint by pressure against the edge of the implement to be finished. A few wedges of antler have been obtained — long, and often showing the natural curve of the horn. The edge has been made from one side only, after the fashion of a chisel. A curious and, as far as I know, unique implement in this region, was found at Dosoris, near Glen Cove, Long Island. A prong had been cut from an antler and squared at the thick end which was divided from the rest by a notch having a flat-topped projection. On this, five parallel lengthwise grooves had been cut. The implement must have been a stamp or marker used to draw parallel lines — perhaps on pottery and showed excellent workmanship.

Cups or bowls were made of turtle shell, with the rim cut straight and the inside scraped smooth. Fragments of these are common, but perfect specimens are seldom seen. At Pelham Bay Park, one of these objects was found, having a double row of small perforations crossing it diagonally — for what purpose it is impossible to say — it may perhaps have been used as a rattle.

Shell, although the chief component of the deposits marking the old village sites does not seem to have figured much as a material for the making of implements. A few shells have been found that show signs of use as scrapers, others have had large, round holes made in them for some unknown reason. Among the shells so perforated are those of the oyster, soft clam, and periwinkle (*Busycon carica*). Shell beads are sometimes discovered merely Olivella or Marginella shells as a rule, with holes rubbed in, to facilitate stringing. Nothing is rarer than a finished wampum bead, although on the Iroquoian sites of western New York these are found by the tens of thousands, unfinished beads occur, however, though not abundantly.

Next to the shells themselves and the split animal bones, in point of quantity, are the pieces of broken pottery — the countless fragments that are scattered throughout most shell heaps — the remains of the cooking and water vessels of the ancient people. Very few pots have survived in perfect condition, but now and then all or most of the pieces of a vessel are discovered in a pit where it has been crushed by the weight of the earth. Then the fragments may be fitted and glued together and a complete jar is the result.

For convenience sake, I divide the ancient vessels found about New York City into two classes — Algonkin and Iroquois. The Algonkin pot is more or less pointed on the bottom, and there is no raised rim or constricted neck. The decoration on this style of ware is often composed of impressions of twigs wrapped with cord, but parallel lines and chevrons drawn with a sharp point are not uncommon. Any attempt at the human face on these vessels is rare, but a few have been found. The ware is usually coarse. The Iroquois pot, on the other hand, has a round bottom, with a much constricted neck and a raised rim, often rising in a series of points. The decoration is usually confined to this raised rim, and the angle or points frequently show elaboration of the design or the rude conventional representation of the human face. Patterns composed of combinations of parallel lines and notches prevail, and thin, well made pottery is the rule. I call this style "Iroquois" because such pottery is abundant on eastern Iroquois sites, and exists in Westchester County, where intercourse with that people was probable; while it is not so common on the neighboring western end of Long Island and becomes more and more rare toward the eastern end, where Iroquoian influence was less strong, as is the case on Staten Island, where it occurs most frequently on the northern end which was most open to Iroquois inroads, in the early days. Among the thousands of potsherds found by the Museum expedition to Shinnecock Hills which is on the eastern end of Long Island, there was not one piece of the Iroquois type. Near Trenton, New Jersey, the Iroquois pottery is almost unknown and the Algonkin type prevails. I do not claim the pottery of the Iroquois style found near New York City was made by that people but that it shows their influence.

Both varieties are usually tempered with sand or pounded shells or mica mixed with the clay. In several instances pots have been found with cracks on both sides of which holes had been bored for the purpose of lacing the fissure together and preventing further spread. Many sherds and vessels bear imprints of rude fabric and cord as if the jar had been modelled in a hole with the cloth as protection against the earth or as if the pot had been patted with a paddle covered with cloth or cord.[1] Bowls and very small pots are rare. One of the latter was found at Pelham Bay Park, split in half, lengthwise. It had been used since the break occurred, for the broken edges were worn smooth.

---

[1] See Holmes, Aboriginal Pottery of Eastern United States, 20th Annual Report of the Bureau of American Ethnology, p. 73.

Pipes were also made of baked clay with short thick stems usually set at an obtuse angle to the bowl — sometimes on the same plane with it. The bowl is often highly decorated in the same fashion as the pottery. Such pipes are more common on Long Island and Staten Island than in Westchester County. Stone pipes of both trumpet and platform, or monitor types, occur.

Among the animal bones found are those of the elk, deer, black bear, lynx, wolf (?), dog, beaver, raccoon, woodchuck, skunk, mink and squirrel. Wild turkey and other birds, several kinds of turtle, the snake, the crab, the shark, sturgeon and other fish were also represented. These were undoubtedly the creatures whose meat and skins were used by the Indians. Shells of almost every species common to these waters have been found, and show another source of food supply. Vegetable substances from the shell heaps include nuts, acorns, calamus roots, and corn, all preserved by charring. Charred wood is frequent.

In the upper or more recent layers of some shell heaps, are occasionally found relics showing contact with the Whites. These consist mainly of gun-flints and broken white clay pipes of the sort traded to the Indians by the early settlers.

The nearest shell heap, readily accessible to New Yorkers, is situated on the northern extremity of Manhattan Island opposite Spuyten Duyvil Station at a place called Cold Spring. This has been badly disturbed by collectors and shows its original form in a few places only. It is thought that the canoes which attacked Hendrick Hudson's ship, the Half-Moon, came from this village. Many of the specimens in the Chenoweth Collection at the Museum were found here.

Ancient encampments were plenty in what is now Pelham Bay Park, and shell heaps attesting the fact are scattered all along the shores. One of these, near "Jack's Rock" was explored for the Museum in 1899. The shell heap itself yielded little, but the pits near by and on the adjoining knolls contained much of interest, including three skeletons and a quantity of pottery, together with many bone and stone implements. These knolls are mentioned by R. P. Bolton in his "History of Westchester County" as a burial place of the Siwanoy Indians — one of the few cases in which "Indian Cemetries" have proven anything but the burial grounds of the early White settlers. The collection found here is now at the Museum.

The street car line from Bartow to City Island passes two large glacial boulders on a knoll just south of the road. Beyond this knoll, running down to the salt meadow, lies another shell heap only partly explored. Here, were found stone and bone implements, part of a pot, and the usual material.

One of the deepest and oldest shell heaps near New York lies within the Greater City, at Weir Creek Point, Throgg's Neck, not far from Westchester. In the lower layers, sometimes thirty-eight inches below the surface, were found a number of archaic-looking arrow points mainly of the "lozenge-shape" type, and some very rude pottery. One jar, as shown by the fragments recovered, must have had a flat bottom — an unusual feature in this vicinity where the ancient vessels generally have rounded or pointed bottoms. Mr. Ernest Volk discovered at Trenton, New Jersey, a portion of a similar pot under circumstances pointing to great antiquity, so it seems probable that this form is an old one. Implements of bone and antler, a native copper bead, and rude hammerstones, anvils and net-sinkers, were found, many of them heavily encrusted with shell-lime. Hearths and ash-beds were frequent, but pits were rare. In fact, no typical pits were found here, the nearest being on the grounds of the Century Golf Club, some distance away, where there were several. One of these had a cyst of stones near its bottom, containing the bones of two young dogs, with many deer bones and sturgeon scales imbedded in coal-black earth.

Almost directly across the Sound from Pelham Bay Park is Port Washington, Long Island. There, a large Indian village once stood, situated near the mouth of a salt creek, one mile north of the town on what is now the property of the Goodwin Sand Company. As might be expected, there is a spring near by, and the village site fronts south, a very good situation for a settlement. The principal shell heap is roughly, 200 feet in diameter, though only about one foot deep. It is overlaid, however, by another foot of soil disturbed by plowing.

Near this deposit on the land side were 101 pits, some of them beneath the shell heap itself. Many of these contained interesting relics and seventeen of them human skeletons. Sometimes three infants, an infant and an adult, or two adults were found in the same grave. The bodies were never laid out straight, as is the custom to-day but were usually buried on the side, with knees drawn up and hands near the face. No trace of any boxes or wrappings were found, but it is probable that the corpses were bundled in mats or skins. The skeletons usually lay within three feet of the surface and seldom were any relics found with them. One child's skeleton had three beads of "Olivella" shells near its neck; another had been buried just above a large dog, whose strained position suggested burial alive. An adult skeleton lay on a bed of shells, below which were found the bones of a young dog with an arrow point among the ribs, as if the animal had been shot to accompany its master on "the long journey." A fire had evidently been kindled on this grave, for there was a small ash-bed near the surface. Similar ash-beds were found on other graves. The upper skeleton of one double burial lay in good order with the bones in their natural position, while the lower was completely disarticulated and the bones mixed, one of the ribs was even within the skull. No feasible explanation of this has been offered and probably never will be. One cannot help wishing that those bones could speak and tell their story. War and violence existed then as now, for one skeleton was found with skull crushed as if by a blow, while another was headless. A smashed skull found in a pit ten feet away probably belonged to the latter. Many pits had ash-beds, some dog skeletons and some charred nuts and calamus roots.

A large number of stone and bone implements of many kinds were obtained, together with a nearly perfect pottery vessel found inverted in a pit, several incomplete pots and a vast number of fragments. Broken stems of terra cotta pipes were not uncommon, but bowls were rare. In one case, a bowl and stem were found which could be fitted together. Among the bowl fragments was one which represented a human head, probably broken from the front of the pipe.

There were pits and shells scattered about the vicinity and on the top of a neighboring knoll, where they had been exposed by digging for sand. Some loose adult bones rolling down the bank and the protruding skeletons of two children attracted my attention to the place.

There are many shell heaps about Oyster Bay, especially in Center Island and along Millneck Creek toward Bayville and Locust Valley. At Matinecock, near the latter town, is the one that was explored for the Museum. This fronted eastward on a little swampy brook flowing into the Peter's Creek branch of Millneck Creek. The deposit was rather large but seldom more than eighteen inches deep; and pits were not numerous, neither did they generally contain much of interest. The only human bone found was a small piece of skull. Many of the usual stone and bone implements and ornaments were secured however, including a grooved axe and a perforated gorget. Pottery was abundant, but no whole vessels were found.

Beneath some grand old trees that must have been standing in Indian days was found another shell heap, on Mr. James G. Price's place at Dosoris Pond, near Glen Cove. This attained the depth of 41 inches, showing that the Indian wigwam had stood in the little hollow beside the brook, many years, probably generations. For many years the Prices had in their possession the Indian deed to their property, signed by the marks of its former aboriginal owners. On the hill behind the main shell heap is located a smaller one, and here many human bones were found — parts of several skeletons. The most important relics discovered in the main shell heap, were the unusual antler implement with parallel grooves probably used by the Indian potter to draw decorations on her vessels, and a series of cores of columellae of the periwinkle shell (*Busycon carica* and *canaliculatum*) showing the different steps in the manufactures of white wampum, from the almost unworked shells to the ground and smoothed cylinders partly cut in lengths suitable for beads. A number of these were found bunched together with a white quartz flake and a small bone awl, as if they had been in a bag. Quantities of the usual relics were found.

Shell heaps, while abundant along the seacoast are seldom found inland except on salt creeks or other streams having access to salt water. They may be seen all along the east shore of the Hudson River at more or less frequent intervals up as far as Peekskill, and on Croton Point and between

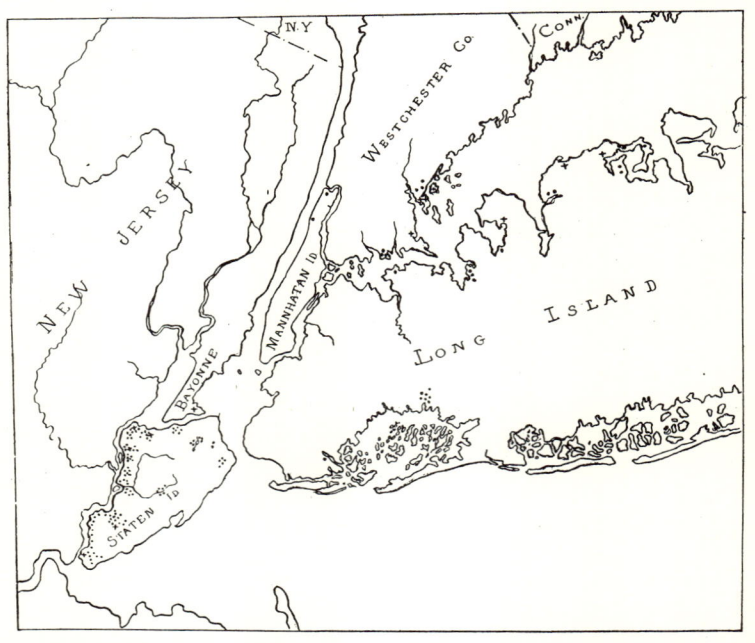

Fig. 29. Map, Giving the Locations of Shell Deposits. Those marked + have been explored by the writer.

Nyack and Hook Mountain on the west shore they attain considerable size. There are a few small deposits, however, composed mainly of brook clams (Unio) situated on fresh water lakes in the interior of Westchester County. One of these, near White Plains, on the north shore of Little Rye Pond was examined for the Museum. The shells were much decayed and averaged about one foot deep. Two pits of the common sort were formed, one containing a raccoon skeleton and the other beaver bones and pottery fragments. In the shell layer were animal bones, broken pottery and bone implements, scattered stone implements and a few marine shells. It looks as if two or three lodges had stood here for a long time in the days when beaver and deer were plenty. Several somewhat similar camping places have been found about this lake and the adjoining Big Rye Pond, but shells were not so plentiful in these — not enough to call them shell heaps.

There are many shell heaps on Staten Island and these are described at length in another part of this volume. Shell heaps occur or did occur on Constable Hook, New Jersey, and at intervals between there and Jersey City along the western shore of New York Bay.

The foregoing discussion is based mainly upon the Museum explorations of the writer in Long Island and Westchester County. The shell deposits actually excavated are indicated on the map, together with the locations of all other deposits so far noted by us (Fig. 29). This map is no doubt far from complete.

NOTES ON THE MOHEGAN AND NIANTIC INDIANS.

F. G. SPECK.

INTRODUCTION.

The following ethnologic notes refer to two tribes of the eastern branch of the Algonkin linguistic stock residing in Connecticut, east of the Hudson River. These tribes with others of the Atlantic coast region were among the first to come into contact with European settlers, almost three hundred years ago. Unfortunately, nothing systematic or thorough regarding native life was recorded by the early colonists, so we have little chance of ever constructing a detailed account of it in Connecticut and Massachusetts. It is also to be expected that, by the present time, the elements of their own culture have been almost entirely forgotten by the modern mixed blood Indians themselves. It will therefore be seen that the whole cultural structure of the southern New England tribes has now been lost, only a few artifacts, practices and folk-beliefs remaining here and there.

An acquaintance with the Indians of New London County, Connecticut, covering about six years, gave the writer the opportunity for questioning nearly every Mohegan. As practically nothing more can be expected to turn up from these sources, most of the older people having died, it seems best to place the material where it will be available. Mrs. Fidelia Fielding, who died in 1908, at about 80 years of age, was the chief source of information at Mohegan. She was also the last to retain knowledge of the Mohegan language.[1] From time to time, quite a little has been published regarding the history of the southern New England tribes, particularly the Mohegan and Pequot, and some ethnological points could perhaps be extracted from the colonial historical documents; but no attempt has been made to do this in preparing the present paper.[2]

---

[1] Information of a general character relating to this tribe can be found in the "Handbook of American Indians," under the tribal name, and a historical sketch is contained in De Forest's "History of the Indians of Connecticut."

[2] The following short papers relating to New England linguistics in which the writer collaborated with Professor J. D. Prince, and some fragments of Mohegan myths have already been published:
- (a) The Modern Pequots and their Language. J. D. Prince and F. G. Speck. American Anthropologist, Volume 5, Number 2 (1903).
- (b) Glossary of the Mohegan-Pequot Language, J. D. Prince and F. G. Speck. American Anthropologist, Volume 6, Number 1 (1904).
- (c) A Modern Mohegan-Pequot Text, F. G. Speck. American Anthropologist, Volume 6, Number 4 (1904).
- (d) Dying American Speech-Echoes from Connecticut, J. D. Prince and F. G. Speck. Proceedings, American Philosophical Society, Volume XLII, Number 174 (1904).
- (e) A Mohegan-Pequot Witchcraft Tale, F. G. Speck. Journal, American Folk-Lore, Volume XVI, Number 61 (1903).
- (f) The Name Chahnameed, J. D. Prince. Ibid.
- (g) Some Mohegan-Pequot Legends, F. G. Speck. Journal, American Folk-Lore, Volume XVII (1904).

THE MOHEGAN INDIANS.

The Indians with whom this paper is chiefly concerned call themselves Mohĭksīnag, from the tribal term Mohī'ks, 'wolf,' compounded with Ī'nag, 'men,' and Mahīganī'ak. The latter term has received various interpretations at different hands.[1] Before presenting the tribe further, the relationship between this people and the neighboring Pequot should be briefly mentioned. The two tribes were linguistically identical, so that, in speaking of their language, the term Mohegan-Pequot has been preferred. It is rather difficult to determine just what the ethnical relations between the two tribes were. Previous to about 1640 the Mohegan had no separate tribal identity; for it was not until Uncas, the son-in-law of a Pequot chief, organized a band of renegades and founded the tribe that the name appeared in local history. It is fairly certain, however, despite the lack of historical proof, that the Mohegan and Pequot, if not a single people, were, before 1640, two very closely related tribes who invaded the territory where we find them, coming from the north. The likelihood, too, is that they were a part of the Mahican of the upper Hudson River. Mrs. Fielding stated that there was a recognized tradition among the old people that the tribe originally came from the north where there were lakes and where their neighbors were the Mohawk.[2] This knowledge of the Mohawk and the ancient fear in which the latter were held, is still a live sentiment at the Mohegan village. After the rupture between the Mohegan and Pequot, the tribal affiliations became entirely separate. They became and remained enemies, the Pequot after their destruction by the English being given as slaves to the Mohegan. The unfriendly feeling is still retained between the latter and the few mixed bloods who represent the last of the Pequot at Ledyard, only a few miles away across the Thames.[3] The Pequot held the shores of Long Island Sound about the mouth of the Thames, while the Mohegan moved up the river to where we find them.

---

[1] Cf. Handbook of American Indians.

[2] If the ideas of the Indians are to be considered as at all correct, it would seem that the Mohegan, when they left their old seats, removed themselves from old influences, adapting themselves to new conditions in their migrations. The line of dialectic demarkation being somewhere between the Housatonic and the Connecticut River, the tribes west of the Mohegan, including the so-called Manhattans and their neighbors, as evidenced by a Scaticook vocabulary, had closer affinities with the Delaware, while those east of the Connecticut should be grouped more properly with the Narragansett and Massachusetts.

[3] In 1903, a visit was made to the Pequot remnants at Groton and Ledyard, Connecticut, where there are two so-called reservations. About twenty-five individuals were seen, all more or less of mixed negro blood, but inquiry in every direction elicited absolutely nothing of ethnologic or linguistic value. The mixed bloods are thinly scattered over the district inland from Stonington, seemingly most numerous near Lantern Hill where they engage in wood-cutting, fishing and small farming. Some Narragansett from Rhode Island, likewise with negro admixture, are intermarried with them.

East of both tribes, their neighbors were the Narragansett and Eastern Niantic, with whom they were intermittently hostile. Their northern neighbors were the Nipmuk, about whom nothing is remembered.[1]

The tribe and village of Mohegan was located on the western shore of the Thames River, in what is now New London County, Connecticut. The tribal hunting territory included this valley and its tributary streams the Yantic and Quinnebaug, but did not extend quite as far south as Long Island Sound. The main settlement of the Mohegan was on the western shore of the Thames, extending from Trading Cove, just south of the city of Norwich, to Massapeag, covering a linear distance of about six or seven miles. This tract is known as Mohegan which was the name of the old Indian settlement, and here the descendants of the tribe still survive.

The Mohegan, from the time of their founding, were never very numerous. The highest estimate, referring to this tribe alone, gives them a population of seven hundred and fifty in 1705. In 1774, they numbered two hundred and six; and by 1804, only eighty-four were left at Mohegan. In the meantime, many had emigrated to the Iroquois, in company with other Connecticut Indians, and formed the nucleus of a new band, the Brotherton Indians. Their descendants are still living in Wisconsin with the Stockbridge. It seems likely that much additional ethnological material could be secured from the western band as the language is still spoken there. In 1832, the enumeration at Mohegan gave a total of three hundred and fifty. At the present day (1908), they number about a hundred. None are of pure Indian blood, and some of the families have imbibed a negro strain. The Indian family names of Hoscutt, Hoscoat, Tantaquidgeon and Skeesucks are still represented.

Local Traditions. A few details of locality and local legends are remembered. The Indian village was a rather scattered settlement with several "forts" or stockades for refuge. Although the details of these stockades have been forgotten, some of their locations can be pointed out.

---

[1] I have used the following characters to represent the sound in writing Mohegan words. Consonants are generally like the English, owing perhaps to the loss of a distinct Indian pronunciation. However, tc is like English ch in church, and c is like sh. The vowels ā, ī, ō, ū have their continental values and are long; a, i, o, u are short; â is like a in the English word fall; ạ is obscure like u in sun. The semi-vowels are h, w, y. Accent is denoted by ' and vowel aspiration by '. Diphthongs are au, oi and ai.

A few brief phonetic comparisons may help to define the position of Mohegan-Pequot among the eastern Algonkin dialects. Professor Prince has given these with examples in a previous paper (Ref. (b), p. 19.). Mohegan shows a strong tendency toward medialization in replacing many surd consonants (p, t, k, s) in neighboring dialects with corresponding sonants. The s, when not sonantized, frequently appears as c in Mohegan. Where, in other dialects l, r, and n appear between vowels, Mohegan-Pequot elides them, and the vowels combine in a diphthong, or replaces them with y. There is, furthermore, evidence of the mingling of several dialects at Mohegan which is a very natural thing considering the heterogeneous elements in the tribe.

One of them was on the summit of a rise known as Fort Hill, just west of the main road between Norwich and New London, opposite the Mohegan church. Another, was on Uncas's Hill on Olin Browning's farm between the river and the main road. Uncas is said to have maintained a sort of garrison of young men here, training them in maneuvers, after the fashion of the English. The third and probably the most important site was at Shantic Point where the present Mohegan burying ground is situated. Shantic Point is a point of vantage commanding an excellent outlook up and down the river and naturally protected by bluffs on the water side; an admirable location for defensive works. This is where the Narragansett attacked the Mohegan in the wars of 1645.[1] A legendary account of this engagement is still related at Mohegan and will be given later. Archaeologically, this site appears to be quite rich. It contains a shell heap, and the usual surface finds are abundant. A rubble monument commemorating the Indian battle has been erected on it. A little further up the river, overlooking it, is a natural chair-like rock, called Uncas's chair. Here, he is said to have sat while directing a canoe battle on the river, between the Mohegan and Narragansett. As the native population was never very large, the settlements of the tribe did not extend far from the vicinity of the main village, but a few of the outlying hamlets should be mentioned.

A short distance south of Shantic Point is Muddy Cove, the Indian name for which was Baságwanantakság (derivative from baság, mud). Southwest from this cove is a rocky ledge on the hillside, at the foot of which in one place there is a reddish discoloration of the rock, having the general outline of a human figure sprawled out. It is called Papoose Rock and the following tale accounts for the peculiarity, according to Mrs. Fielding.

"There was a Mohegan who went across to Long Island and took a wife from one of the tribes there. After some time, he tired of her and came home. Soon after, she had a child. She said to herself, 'My child's father has left me to take care of him. I cannot do it alone.' So she made ready for a journey and set out for the Mohegan country across the Sound to look for her husband. She found him at Mohegan and said to him, 'You must take care of me and the child.' But he paid no attention to her. Then she went down to where there was a steep sloping rock not far from the river. Standing on the top of this slope, she took her child in one hand and grasped its head with the other. Then she twisted the head and it came off, the blood flowing down the rocks. The woman cast the head down, and the body she threw farther out. Where the head fell there remained a splotch of blood, and where the body struck, there was left an imprint stained upon the

---

[1] Cf. De Forest, op. cit., pp. 213, 215.

rock in the shape of the child. That is the story. The blood is there yet, and it tells of her deed when she has gone."

A mile or so, west of the village of Mohegan, near Stony Brook, is an immense glacial boulder, known as Cutchegan Rock. What appears to be a partially excavated room is under the lower side, which is said to have been occupied quite frequently by the Indians. The last man to live there was Caleb Cutchegan, after whom it was named. On the top of this boulder are a few stones said to be the remains of a chair in which the presiding chief sat when councils were being held in the woods.

Near Trading Cove, not far from the river, is a valley about half a mile wide, containing not much else but sand. Here, it was related by Jimmie Rogers that a tribe, whose name has been forgotten, came and camped. "It was not such a place as it is now, but fertile and pleasant. The tribe was on friendly relations with the Mohegan, but before long some disease came among them and killed them off like sheep. Ever since that time this valley, where their settlement was, has never grown any grass. Their bones are often unearthed."

Material Life. The details of the original type of house have been forgotten; but, until several generations ago, a primitive form of habitation was in vogue, which may have had something of an aboriginal character. This type of house (jokwĭ'n) was a partly subterranean affair. The excavation was about four feet deep and fifteen or twenty feet square. The sides were shored up with boards. The portion above ground consisted of logs, and the roof was of the same material. Sods, brush and other protective matter were thrown on top of the roof. A sloping entrance led to the door (ckwa̠nd), and a hole in the back of the roof over the fire (wīyū't) allowed an exit to smoke. No other first hand details are forthcoming, but several of these cellar sites are pointed out to-day at Mohegan. Another temporary camp shelter, which still survives in the "wigwam" of the modern Mohegan church festival, consisted of upright crotched posts, supporting beams for a roof of birch saplings with the leaves left on. Secondary upright poles serve as a base for the weaving in and out of birch saplings to enclose the sides. This makes a very pleasant bower, suitable for summer camping, and it is asserted to have been formerly much used by the Indians, for temporary purposes. The accompanying descriptions are based on specimens in the possession of Indians and private collectors.[1]

---

[1] A collection, made by the writer some years ago, is now in the possession of Mr. George G. Heye of New York, who very kindly furnished me with photographs from which the cuts were made. The Slater Memorial Hall of Norwich, Connecticut has several specimens in its collection from the Mohegan, which are illustrated in an article by Mr. C. C. Willoughby in the American Anthropologist, Volume 10, No. 3.

There were several types of wooden mortars made to be used with a stone pestle. The most characteristic of these is the polished and carved pepperidge-wood mortar (dạkwáñg) about eighteen inches high and twelve across. The pit of the mortar was hollowed out by burning to the depth of at least six inches. The walls are straight some distance from the top, then suddenly taper inward and come out again forming a pedestal at the base. In three places, where the sides converge towards the bottom, straight vertical bars are left by the carver to serve as handles or side grips.

Another kind of mortar is less elaborate, being simply thinned at the waist somewhat after the fashion of an hour-glass. Still another was common, this was of the plainest sort with plain sides and the tree bark left on. The pestle (gwánsnâg, literally, long stone) was always of stone, and needed to be, as they say, as long as an Indian's fore arm.

Wooden spoons of several types have been obtained. The native soup ladel (gīyámmạn) was often made of apple wood, the handle and bowl together being about twelve inches long. The bowls of these ladles are round, straight-sided and flat-bottomed, while the handle is almost straight, with a "roll" carved at the end (Fig. 4, Plate XXI). A smaller spoon of similar form, used for eating johnny-cake, is six inches long with a round shallow bowl. A carved spoon was seen, about eight inches long, with a leaf-shaped shallow bowl and some animals, carved on the end of the handle, facing outward. Modern spoons are made for commercial purposes, with bowls probably patterned after metal spoons. Some fairly old and much-used specimens, similar to these, however, have been seen and possibly something similar to this type may also have been native.

Wooden bowls (bīyótī) made of pepperidge knots were formerly used as food trenchers. They were frequently inlaid with bits of mother-of-pearl, from fresh-water mussels, and wampum, in fantastic designs representing, as is remembered, the human face. The rims of these bowls were also elevated on the ends and carved with animals' heads, one on each opposite side looking toward the bottom of the bowl.[1]

Several varieties of knife (bạnnī'dwañg) employed in the manufacture of these wooden objects, deserve mention. In one, the blade is in the same plane as the wooden handle and curves in almost a half circle. This knife (Plate XXI, Fig. 3) is used in carving spoons and bowls, and is drawn toward the operator. In another type of knife, from the Scaticook Indians of Litchfield County, the blade curves around through several inches and its cutting edge is in a plane perpendicular to that of the wooden handle (Plate XXI,

---

[1] In a recent article, American Anthropologist, Volume 10, No. 3, pp. 423–434, Mr. C. C. Willoughby figures and describes five Mohegan wooden bowls.

Fig. 2). This knife was used in hollowing out bowls and canoes. In both specimens, the blade is simply set in the end of a wooden handle. The canoes used by the Mohegan were dug-outs, but no details of construction are remembered.

A smoking pipe (támmaṇk) is made from the knotty excrescences which grow on chestnut trees. These bowls are barrel-shaped with a hole near the bottom for a hollow reed stem. Fanciful relief carvings of the human face usually adorn the front of the bowl, in other parts of which realistic figures, probably modern in origin, are scratched.

Brooms and smaller scrubbing brushes were made of birch sticks. They varied much in size, according to their intended use. In making them, the end of the stick was frayed and strips of the fibre split down, then turned backwards, gathered in a bunch, and bound together with cord.

The manufacture of several types of baskets (manū'dac, inanimate plural of manū'da), is still carried on at Mohegan. The material used is hickory splints. Swamp maple was formerly much used. Four foot logs are hammered until the grain separates, then strips are pulled off. These are shaved with a spoke shave until they are smooth. For making smaller splints, a gauge of wood set with knife blades for teeth was and still is used. A specimen from the Scaticook Indians of Litchfield County, Connecticut, is figured (Plate XXI, Fig. 1). In working with the knives and shaves, a piece of leather is tied over the knee as a protection. The modern splint baskets for commerce are of various shapes and sizes. They are started at the bottom with the checker-work pattern, the bottom splints are then turned up to form the standards for the woof filling. A thin splint runs around the edge of the bottom and is the binder, called (bambáig). The walls of the basket are then filled in with thinner strips. The rim is bound around with an inner and an outer hoop, every alternate upright end being bent down over the highest strand of the woof. Most of the baskets are given handles. This type of basket is very common everywhere, nearly all the mixed blood Indians in New England putting them out wherever there is a demand.

Another kind of basket, called the melon basket, is made occasionally. Several very old specimens of this type have been collected (Plate XXI, Fig. 5). In this, the handle runs right around through the bottom of the basket and another hoop is fastened at right angles to it. The lower section is then filled in with short horizontal warp strips and fine splints are woven over and under them, until the lower half is enclosed. These baskets are said to be rather difficult to make.

Bows consisted of a simple stave of hickory, sassafras or tulip. Some specimens show a double curve. This is given by steaming the stave until it bends easily, and fastening it, with the desired curves, on a board by means of nails. The bows range from three to four feet in length with about an inch of breadth and half an inch of thickness in the middle. In section, the stave is rounded on the outer side and flat on the inner (Fig. 31). The ends are usually notched at both sides, to afford a purchase to the bow-string. The only arrows known, are the blunt-headed bolts, and they exhibit considerable variety in shape and weight. The feathering on these arrows is rather peculiar. Two holes are drilled through the shaft near the nock and the ends of two feathers, shaved on one side, are inserted in the holes and held fast by wooden plugs (Fig. 32). Sometimes a single feather, shaved as usual, is pushed through one of the holes, bent into the other hole and plugged there. Ownership or identification marks on the arrows consist of series of notches on one or both sides of the shaft near the notch. Anywhere from two to six notches are common. The common arrow release is that known as the primary, where the nock is grasped between the thumb and the forefinger joint.

The cultivation of corn and beans was an important activity in the life of these Indians, and these vegetables played quite an important part in their dietary. The following are the native ways of preparing them. Corn (wīwátcạmạn), to be boiled was left on the ear and placed in a vessel of cold water over the fire until it began to boil. The moment boiling commenced, it was taken off and eaten. This kept it very tender.

Fig. 30. Mohegan Bow.

Beans (máckạzīts) of a brownish variety, were boiled in water with lumps of fat. An excellent dish (sū'ktac, succotash) was concocted of corn and beans. The beans were first put on to boil for two hours with a lump of fat, nowadays pork. The green corn was then scraped from the cob and added to the beans, the cobs being put in, too, to add their milk to the whole. It was then allowed to boil only twenty minutes. With the addition of a little seasoning, this succotash is delicious. It is still made in quantities by the Indians.

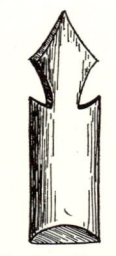

Fig. 31. Cross Section of a Bow.

A kind of dough was made of corn flour and baked in round biscuits (tákạnig, literally, rounded). The chief use for the corn crop, however, was to dry it on the cob and store it away to be used later. When occasion required, the dried kernels were scraped from the cob and browned in a pan over the fire. When they are browned enough, they are placed in the mortar and pounded to powder. This corn flour (yókeg) was a Mohegan staple. It could be eaten clear, mixed with water or made into bread. For journeys it was stowed away in a pouch and the traveler either ate it dry or mixed with water. Quantities of the stuff are prepared nowadays for use and for sale to the Whites who think it goes well with ice cream.

Meat (wī'ūs) was commonly roasted. A kind of stew (wī'ūsiboig) was, and is, made of boiled meat. Fish (pī'âmag) were commonly fried or roasted on a scaffold of green saplings over the coals of a fire.

Skunk hunting was a much favored and profitable amusement at Mohegan. The men, armed with clubs, were accompanied by dogs who drove the skunk (ckáñks) to stand at bay in some nook or other. Then the band ran in and clubbed the skunk to death. The meat was, and is, considered very palatable after it has been hung for four or five days in some damp place. In regard to the skunk hunting, Jimmie Rogers remembers, when a boy, how he went with the men on his first hunt. The dogs drove the animal into a clump of brush. Rogers was then told to go in and find the skunk. He crawled in on his hands and knees, and received the full discharge of the animal in his eyes. The effect, he states, lasted for days. They thought it a great joke on the boy.

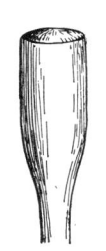

Fig. 32. Heads and Feathering of Mohegan Arrows.

Clothing and Ornaments. The only articles of clothing and ornament of which the Indians preserve any knowledge, are women's leggings; men's leggings (gū'ngū, inanimate plural, gū'ngạwantc); the woman's dress (bī'tkạz); the hunting, or shot pouch, and carrying bag, (bágenūd); the moccasin (mákạs, plural, mákạsạntc); and silver brooches which were used to ornament clothing.

An old pair of women's leggings of cloth were long enough to reach half way up to the knee. They were of black cloth and had open beadwork on the border. At the corners, were flower designs in bead embroidery. The flaps were several inches wide, and occurred either at the front or side.

An old pair of Mohegan moccasins were of dark tanned buckskin with the seam running up the instep covered with porcupine quill embroidery showing the interlocked zigzag technique with straight and curved line border. The lapels are of cloth heavily beaded.

All that is remembered of the other articles of clothing is that they were of buckskin, that the men's leggings covered their thighs, and that women had shell fringes and ornaments on their dresses.

A specimen of hunting pouch with a woven bead front and homespun cloth back is represented in Plate xxi. This object is of an old type. The colors employed are dark green, white, black and yellow arranged in a geometrical design, for which, unfortunately, no interpretation was remembered.

Lester Skeesucks, a Narragansett-Mohegan from Brotherton, Wisconsin, returned to Mohegan, and died there some years ago. He spoke the language and owned a complete costume, which, although of comparatively modern make, undoubtedly represented, to a certain extent, an early New England Indian get-up. He is represented in Plate xxii, standing before a brush wigwam of the sort already described. His headdress consisted of long, upright plumes, mounted on a head band decorated with beads. On this and on all other articles of his costume, the beadwork embroidery represented leaves, flowers, birds, stars, circles and flags. Over a colored shirt, he wore a heavily decorated, halter-like collar, beaded arm-bands and wrist-bands. A similarly ornamented belt and carrying pouch suspended on a broad shoulder strap completed his upper articles. An elaborately decorated kilt, reaching half way to the knees, was a characteristic piece. Leggings with beaded garters, bead necklaces, medals and a sheath knife completed his costume. Other individuals at Mohegan had portions of dress similar to those described.

Several silver brooches were seen. Some were wheel-shaped with a pivot pin in the center. The wheel-disk was said to represent unbroken friendship. The outer edge of the disk brooch was scalloped and a series of small circles was inside this. The circles were said to be suns, the endless period of time through which the friendship should last. The brooches were chiefly used as ornaments, and badges of friendship between men, and were highly prized. The brooches were evidently made with chisels and hammers from silver which was pounded out in the cold state. Several brooches of the intersecting heart type so common among the Iroquois were seen. Skeesucks had modified one of these somewhat to enable him to use it as a nose pendant. Little lumps of solder had been fastened to opposite points which grasped the septum of the nose.

On the whole, there appears a significant similarity between the Mohegan silverwork preserved by Lester Skeesucks, who, it should be remembered, was born at Brotherton, Wisconsin, and that of the Iroquois.[1] It is not at all unlikely, that still closer affinities may be found between Brotherton Mohegan and Oneida silverwork, which may show the former to have been borrowed from the latter. The Mohegan who went west were at one time adopted by the Oneida.

A string of six beads of the old type of wampum were seen in the possession of an Indian woman. They were slightly over one-eighth inch long and one-eighth inch thick, and cut, so that the purple was grained with gray and brown. The former function of these beads was not known by anyone.

Customs and Miscellaneous Notes. The knowledge of their native customs possessed by these Indians is lamentably meager. At best, only a few miscellaneous fragmentary facts are forthcoming which for convenience will be given under this heading.

The tribe formerly had a regular head chief (sánjąm). After the advent of Europeans, the power of this office was much increased. For many years, the descendants of Uncas held the chieftancy, applicants for the office claiming the right, some through maternal some through paternal descent, but according to all accounts, the paternal claim was the stronger. This form of tribal leadership was replaced in later times by an elective chieftancy and council of three, which represented the tribe in public matters. The chief council were elected by the people for a term.

The list of Mohegan clans given by Morgan [2] are grouped under three phratries as follows: The Wolf, Bear, Dog and Opossum clans form the Wolf phratry; the Little Turtle, Mud Turtle and Great Turtle clans form the Turtle phratry; and the Turkey, Crane and Chicken clans form the Turkey phratry. The clans were exogamous and maternal, with a hereditary chief in each. He also states, on the authority of a Narragansett woman, that the Pequot and Narragansett reckoned clan descent on the mother's side. Judging from the Indian names of the above clans, I am inclined to believe that Morgan derived his information from a Hudson River Mahican, and that the list applies to that tribe, now bearing the name of Stockbridge, rather than to the Connecticut Mohegan.

The only Mohegan terms of relationship remembered by Mrs. Fielding, which are available for comparison were: —

nūc, my father
nânnáñg, my mother
nū'jąnâs, my grandfather

---

[1] Cf. Iroquois Silverwork, M. R. Harrington. Volume I, part 6 of this series.
[2] Ancient Society, L. H. Morgan. New York (1878), p. 174.

nânna', my grandmother
nątánīs, my daughter
nąmákkīs, my son
nīdámb, my friend
ktcais, husband, old man
wīnai's, wife, old woman.

The dead were disposed of by burial, the body of a man being carried to the grave suspended from a pole by thongs at the neck, waist and heels, and carried by two friends. Food was placed in the grave and a fence was then made to surround the spot. To provide further for the soul, a horse, dog and usually some useful articles were interred with the body. At the old Shantup burying ground at Mohegan village, sunken graves may still be seen. The Indians also had the custom of putting a stone or some other remembrance on graves as they passed by them.

The old Indian dance was called mątága, and the singing that accompanied it, gątū'ma. No one living in the last eighty years has witnessed these performances and nothing whatever is remembered of them. Judging, however, from the cognate Delaware matagen, machtagen (ch as in German), to fight, the Mohegan dance meant by the above term was a war dance.

There is no doubt though, that the Mohegan, like most of the Atlantic coast sedentary tribes, had a ceremony to signalize the season of the corn harvest. This ceremony, known widely among other tribes as the Green Corn Dance, has a degraded survival in a modern September festival. The festival is now simply a sort of fair for the benefit of the Indian church. A suitable time is appointed by the church women, and the men proceed to erect a large wigwam as a shelter. An area adjoining the church at least sixty feet square, is covered by this arbor. Crotched chestnut posts are erected in the ground about ten feet apart, and, from one to the other of these, cross pieces are laid, a construction previously described (p. 188). Quantities of green white birch saplings have been cut and are then strewn over the roof quite thickly. The sides are filled and woven in with these also, in such a manner as to make a fairly weather-tight enclosure. A portion of the wigwam's side is visible in the background of Plate XXII. For some days before the festival, several men are kept busy pounding up quantities of corn for yókeg which the women and children have roasted. Several large mortars are kept exclusively for this purpose, and are the common property of the tribe. The days of the festival are merely the occasion for a general informal gathering of the Indians from far and near, and the sale, for the benefit of the church treasury, of such things as they are able to make. Many articles of Indian manufacture already described are displayed on benches in this wigwam, for sale as souvenirs and articles of utility; while various dishes of food, ancient and modern, are made and sold on the grounds. Some other sort of amusement is usually introduced from outside for the three days, and an admission price is charged. They also have someone appear in full Indian costume as an added attraction. The Mohegan make this annual gathering a sort of tribal holiday. The fact that it takes place at the height of the corn season, and that corn products, particularly yókeg and sū'ktac, play such an important part in it, are clear indications of the early nature of this festival.

One other, the custom of making friendship between two men, is remembered. In such a case, the contracting persons symbolized their compact by the giving of the silver brooches which have already been mentioned.

According to Lester Skeesucks, Mohegan men had a death-song which every one would try to sing at the last moment before death. It served to announce to inhabitants of the spirit-land that another spirit was about to start thither. The words of the song, as he remembered it, were, "Yū nī nē nē andai; jībai oke; nī kī pī ai; nī mạs sētcū," which Professor Prince translated, "Here I am. To the spirit-land I am going. I shall pass away." The music and analysis were given in a previous article.[1] The Mohegan war-cry consisted of three short rapid yells, pronouncing the syllable, ai, ai ai. While the Mohegan were evidently a warlike tribe, the only memories of their activities are a few traditional exploits of their chief Uncas. Some references to his career have been given. Another tale in which a Mohegan conjuror figures will be given under the subject of personal magic. A few other memories of Uncas; his murder of Miantonomoh and the eating of some of his victim's flesh; his escape from the latter at Uncas's Leap rock, near Norwich; his defeat of the latter by strategy at Uncas's Plains above Norwich; and other tales in fragment, are recounted.[2] It is likely that local historical essays have refreshed and added to these accounts, if they are not entirely responsible for them.

Shamanism. By putting together the fragments of knowledge which the Indians possess, it is possible to form at least some idea of Mohegan shamanism and personal magic. The shaman, or witch, as he or she is commonly called, is termed moigū' (animate plural, moígūwạg). Any person who is believed to have communication with supernatural powers is referred to by this word. Such persons, being inclined to malicious actions, were generally feared and avoided in the later days, owing to their supposed relations with the Devil. How witchcraft is acquired is not known, but a wizard is not long in being found out by his magic. Witches are remem-

---

[1] Ref. (a), pp. 210–211.
[2] Cf. De Forest, History of the Indians of Connecticut, for historical accounts of these events.

bered chiefly for having been able to transport themselves instantaneously from place to place, to achieve various desires by special individual magic, to concoct charms for various purposes to cast spells over persons, animals and things, and correspondingly to remove them at will, and also to effect the cure of disease by the use of herb medicines which they knew. Also any peculiar occurrences and uncanny noises not thoroughly understood, were attributed to them, when not ascribed to a ghost (jībai'). It is commonly asserted at Mohegan that the times of the witches or shamans, is past; that, since the Indians have taken up Christianity, the witches have gone off to the heathen where they still flourish and cause evil. Several witches, however, seem to have developed, within the last two or three generations, and died mysteriously.

About the last one at Mohegan was Israel Freeman. He claimed to have cured many complaints and, on the other hand, was thought to be responsible for much affliction. He had two good-looking wives, but became jealous of them and rendered them hideous as a punishment by turning up their eyelids so that they remained permanently disfigured. This may have been a survival of the custom of mutilation for adultery. A remedy of Freeman's for warts was to rub the warts with bean leaves, and throw them away without looking to see where they went. Dogs always growled and snarled at Freeman, but he could quiet them by pointing at them with a handful of weeds.

The following few narrative accounts told by Mrs. Fielding, Jimmie Rogers and others, show how the shaman and his witchcraft were looked upon.

"When the Narragansett had landed on Shantic Point and taken up their position of siege, it looked to the Mohegan as though they were to lose; for the enemy outnumbered them. Now, there was one Narragansett who had climbed a certain tree not far off, where, by means of his elevation he could command an advantageous view of the Mohegan behind their palisades. From his perch he directed a destructive fire into them, adding insult and raillery to his attacks. 'Are you hungry?' he would ask in taunting tones. In order to remove such an obnoxious element from their view, the best of the Mohegan marksmen engaged in trying to bring him down, but without result. His abusiveness increased as their shots failed to touch him. Then they concluded that he was a moigū'. At length, a Mohegan, who possessed power equal to that of the Narragansett, appeared and ordered the others to desist. Taking a bullet from his pouch he swallowed it. Straightway it came out of his navel. He swallowed it again and it came out of his navel. Again he did it with the same result. Now he loaded his rifle with the charmed ball and taking aim, fired at the man in the tree. The Narragansett dropped out of the branches, dead."

A few days later Col. Leffingwell from Saybrook Fort, effected an entrance by night, bringing the carcass of a steer to the starving Mohegan. The following morning, they stuck the quarters up on poles and waved them in derision where the enemy could see them and know that succor had arrived. Then the relief party on the heels of Leffingwell appeared on the river and the Narragansett were dispersed.

"A hunter returned to camp one day, with a deer that he had killed. His sweetheart during his absence, had grown very jealous of him on account of rumors that had come to her. When he stepped before her, he was disappointed to find her in a jealous mood. His anger was aroused, he stepped up to her, placing the antlers of the deer upon her forehead where they immediately took root. The antlers grew larger and larger until they threatened to reach the roof of the house. It was only possible to remove them with the help of a powerful shaman who possessed a magic oil."

"In the olden times no one could keep anything. The witches stole nearly everything, even money. Then, when they had taken the things, they had to divide them in shares for each. On one occasion, they entered a schoolhouse. A black man got in there before them and hid himself in the place where the ashes from the grate are put. Then along came the witches. They did not know that the man was in the building. So they started to divide the money, and handing each one his share, they said, 'This is yours. This is yours.' And so on. Now the black man jumped up from the ashes. 'Where is mine!' he shouted. The witches, seeing such a sight as the black man all besmeared with ashes before them ran away in confusion. So the black man had all the money.'

"They say that the old time Mohegans used to go down the Thames River and across Long Island Sound in dug out canoes. They were fond of visiting the Indians over there. So, one time Martha Uncas, who at that time knew no English and was unacquainted with Christianity, being in need of a little rest and recreation, was carried over to Long Island on a visit.

When they arrived, they found the Islanders, probably Montauks, gathered at a meeting in a large shelter. The Mohegans went in and mingled with them, but did not understand the words of the speaker. He was a Christian and was preaching. Soon he began to pray, and Martha instead of bowing her head with the rest, gazed around in curiosity. All at once, a long shrill whistle sounded above the trees. Upon looking up she beheld a figure which she recognized as moigu, standing in the doorway, beckoning the worshippers with his hand to come out. They all arose without a word and left the meeting, following after the moigū'."

"A long time ago a woman had a grudge against a man who owned some fine cattle. Soon after, the man noticed that something was bothering the herd. At night, they would not sleep and so became greatly run down. He sat up one night to watch. He saw a goose come into the yard and bewitch the cattle. Having a gun loaded, he fired, but the goose flew away unharmed. This was repeated several nights, until at last he loaded the piece with a silver bullet and wounded the goose in the wing. The next day the old woman who had the grudge against him was found to have a badly wounded arm. By that they knew that she was a witch who took the form of a goose."

"Two men lived together in a house and had a black man to work for them. They were very strange people. Once the black man overheard some strange things going on in their room, and being curious to know about them, peeked in through the keyhole. There he saw his mistresses standing near a big tub of water in the center of the room. In the bottom of the tub was an animal's jawbone. Now one of the women got into the tub and repeated the following words 'in the keyhole, through the keyhole.' Immediately she disappeared. Then the other woman got into the tub and said the same, and she vanished too. Now the man thought they must be witches, so being a curious man, he went in and got into the tub. He repeated the words he had heard them say, and the next thing he knew, he was over in England. He found himself in a crowded street. People were going in and out of the shops. It was London. Thinking that he had better have something bracing, he bought a bottle of rum. He soon saw his mistresses in the street, but was afraid to meet them. They would be angry with him. Pretty soon he thought that he had better be going home. So he tried to recollect the words he had heard. But he could not recall them, try as he would. He never could think of them again. He must be there now."

"There was another woman around here who had a black man to work for her. Every morning when he woke up he found that he was as tired as though he had been working hard all night. He tried every way to get rest, but in spite of it all, he couldn't. Nobody knew what to make of it until one night some person saw that woman riding as though on horseback, at breakneck speed through the country. When the person looked closer he saw that she was riding on the back of the black man, and he was bridled and saddled like a saddle horse. That was how they found out that she was a witch."

Some witch tales from the Scaticook Indians of Litchfield County, Connecticut, who were made up largely of Mohegans and Pequots joined to the Mahican of western Massachusetts and Connecticut, were obtained from James Harris, and are given here.

"Two men were travelling together. One of them had witchcraft power. When they came to a swamp he would go over it through the air, and when they came to a steep hill he would go right through it as though it were level. Now all this made the other man very miserable, because he had to wade through all the muck and mire whenever they passed a swamp, and climb all the way up and down when they came to steep hillsides. So, after a while, he asked the first man how he could do such things. 'Well,' said the man, 'You just have to say, Under thick and over thin, then you will get along all right.'

Now they went on and soon came to a swamp. So the fellow got ready to repeat what he had been told. He said, 'Over thick and under thin.' And he expected to find himself starting over the swamp, but instead of that, he found himself going down into the mud. He went through the swamp over his head in all the water and mire. The first man floated over without touching. And when they came to a hill the fellow had to go right over it the longest and highest way. It was because he had forgotten how to say the charm as it should have been said. Then he found out that he was n't equal to the witch man."

"There was a little boy who lived all alone with his father in the woods. One dark night, there came some strange Indians to visit them. As the evening went on, the boy's father sent him to a neighbor's house to borrow some tcâ′hīg (cider) for his guests. The boy took a torch of pine and started out through the woods to the neighbor's house. Before he had gone very far, he heard strange noises overhead but he thought that it was only the wind. He went on and did not mind the noises much. When he got the 'tcâ′hīg' he turned towards home, but all the way he heard the same noises, and now he became so frightened that he broke into a run and reached the house in terror. He told his father about the noises. Then the strange Indians when they heard about it, went outside and listened. There were voices, the same ones that the little boy had heard. But these Indians could talk with them and understand them, although the little boy and his father could do neither. Those Indians must have been witches too."

"In the old days, there was a woman here whose name was Viney Carter. She could do a great many things that no one else could. Some evenings she would be here, and in the morning she would be gone, nobody knew where. But by night she would be back here again. Then soon after, we would hear that she had been up to Stockbridge, on the day that she was n't here. She used to visit the Indians up there, and everybody said that she was a witch."

While the shamans were supposed to be especially skillful in concocting herb medicines and healing maladies, knowledge of herb medicines was not exclusively theirs. The women of nearly every family were more or less capable of fixing medicines, which they administered to the sick without any attempt at conjuration. While all remembrance of the conjuration has been lost, a few of the simple herb remedies (ámbạsk) are as follows:

Indian turnip root steeped is for sore throat.

Tea, as a beverage, is made of the cockle burr plant.

Blood-root scraped and brewed is for croup, and is also an emetic.

The marrow of a hog's jawbone is known as a 'drawer' for removing splinters and inflammation.

A spring tea is made of sassafras, pipsissewa, princes pine, and a number of other ingredients.

Sassafras tea is used in very hot weather. It is said to cool the blood.

Cuts are treated with mashed plantain, or the inner bark of the willow.

Skunk oil is applied to all parts of the body to allay pain.

Yarrow tea is given for fevers.

Puff balls and spider webs are used to stop bleeding.

Sounds, the white gristle lying along the backbone of a fish, are used for glue. When dried they are also used to settle coffee.

An old and much feared wonder worker used to have a root which he called 'whistling root.' When it was put on a rock it would disappear with a whistling sound. He is said to have kept it in a bottle.

Barberry is chewed for toothache.[1]

Tea is made from sumach blossoms.

Wild rhubarb tea is said to benefit the nerves. Another remedy for the same trouble is burdock, ginseng and chickweed.

While the Mohegan witch idea has undoubtedly been affected by European lore, it is possible to find Indian cognates for some of its elements. The idea expressed by the word moigū′, shaman, is evidently cognate with Narragansett mannêtu, Natic, manitto, Abenaki m' daúlinu and Delaware meteu and central Algonkin, tcīsa'ka and waubīnu.[2]

Beliefs and Folk-Lore. All the surviving ideas of native deities are embodied in the one term múndu, God; cognate with Algonkin manito. The term, in later years, came to refer only to the Christian God, in which case it was Gántcī Múndu. The archdemon corresponding to the Devil was mátcī múndu. Another name for the same being is dī'bī. While native ideas in regard to these terms have been completely replaced by Christian ones, still the natural inference, based on the similarity of terms, is that the common Algonkin manito concepts were shared to some extent by the Mohegan.

---

[1] The remnants of the Uncachogue or Poosepatuck Indians of Long Island also employ this for the same purpose.

[2] Cf. reference (b), pp. 19 and 32, where Professor Prince shows the similarity between Mohegan moi and Narragansett manni. Mohegan shows an elision of l, r, n, in cognates from neighboring Algonkin dialects. Delaware has malliku, witchcraft.

It seems characteristic of the Algonkin tribes, in particular, to believe in numerous varieties of fairies, forest elves and river elves of all kinds. The Mohegan claim to have believed in the existence of many of these in former times, but only one kind is now remembered. These are the makiáwīsag, little people (singular makkī′s). The following short narrative of Mrs. Fielding explains all that is known about them.

"The makiáwīsag were dwarfs who lived in the woods. They were the ones who made the pictures and scratchings on the rock which stood on Fort Hill.[1] The old glass bottles which are plowed out of the ground here and there were left by them, as were also the brass kettles found in graves.

The last of them to be seen around here were some whom Martha Uncas told about. It must have been before 1800. She was then a child coming down the Yantic River in a canoe with her parents. They saw some makiáwīsag running along the shore. A pine forest grew near the water and they could be seen through the trees. Her mother saw them and said, 'Don't look at the dwarfs. They will point their fingers at you, and then you cannot see them.' She turned her head away. There did not seem to be many of them.

The dwarfs came to people's houses, asking for something to eat. According to the old Indians, one must always give the dwarfs what was wanted; for, if they refused, they would point their fingers at one, so that one could not see them, and the dwarfs would take whatever they chose.

There was an Indian and his wife who lived near here long ago. They saw some makiáwīsag. It was in this way. One stormy night there was a rap on their door. When the woman opened the door, the wind blew very hard. Someone was standing outside, but she did not know who it was. When she found out what the person wanted, she told her husband that someone wanted her to go and take care of a sick woman a long way off. She decided to go, and packed up her things to leave. The person was a dwarf, but she thought he was a boy. He led her far away through the storm. After a while they reached a small underground house. The dwarf led the Indian woman inside and there lay a dwarf woman ill on a bed of skins. The Indian woman then recognized them as makiáwīsag. She stayed with them some time and cared for the sick one until she got well. When she was ready to return home, the dwarf gave the Indian woman a lot of presents, blindfolded her and led her back to her home. She was very well treated. The Indians often tried to find these dwarfs, but they never succeeded. They were never heard of afterward. I believe these were the last. They generally kept away from the Indians, but never molested them. People

---

[1] Since blasted out by road makers.

used to think that the mounds in this part of the Thames Valley were made by the dwarfs."

Ghosts or wandering spirits, (jībai'), are believed to be round about. Besides indulging in many mystifying capers, such as appearing suddenly before people at night and making peculiar and terrifying noises, they are thought to take vengeance on their enemies and help their friends on earth in various ways. It is hard to separate the Indian from the European elements in such tales.

The will-o'-the-wisp is called gáckaṭcaṅg. The Indians believe it to be caused by spirits who are travelling about with lights. They are greatly feared, and are thought to be more numerous at certain places and at particular times of the year. Here are given some short anecdotes.

"One dark, stormy night a woman was coming down the long hill toward Two Bridges, having been up to New London. Looking across the swamp to the opposite slope she beheld a light approaching in her direction. When they drew near to one another the woman saw that the light was suspended in the center of a person's stomach as though in a frame. There was no shadow cast, and yet the outline of the person could be distinguished as it surrounded the light. The woman was badly frightened and ran all the way home.

Another time Tantaquidgeon was riding home, and when he was passing the same swamp two dogs dashed from the bushes, and from their mouths they breathed fire. They ran along side, blowing flames at the horse's flanks until he had passed the swamp. A white horse's head has been seen lying there too, but when the person approached it, it moved further along just keeping ahead of him. Women who have gone through the bars near the swamp at night have felt hands holding on to their skirts, and even herds of pigs have dashed out to terrify belated travellers at night. Some Indians claim to have felt hands grasping their feet as they went by."

Mrs. Fielding was aroused one night by a light that shone from the hill above her house, and while she stood watching it from her window, she saw it ascend the hill to a small heap of rocks, where it blazed up high and subsided. Then it moved to another rock and blazed high again, subsiding as before in a few moments. She had reason to be certain that no one was in the pasture, and the next morning she found no evidence of burning about the rocks. The thing was repeated a number of times and she considered herself to have been visited by spirits.

Some children have a rhyme, the meaning of which is not all clear. It is said to be part of an old song. "Pétīkạdâ's nū'djạnâ's káṅgạyai' n'tūlipâs'," approximately, "My grandfather brings it, my turtle carries it."

A children's puzzle is, "Injun cut me out. Injun tear my shirt and leave me in the dirt." Answer, a broom. The puzzle refers descriptively to the process of making brooms from birch wood by splitting the end of the stick and shaving, bending back and tying the strips.

A certain kind of cry in the woods at night is made, it is said, by the devil's bird. The bird makes its cry in one place and then goes on to another for a while. The sounds are said to resemble those made by owls, but need not be confused with them. The same bird is thought to have something to do with thunder.

The following are a few miscellaneous scraps of folk-lore:

"Just back of the Mohegan chapel there is a rock having a distinct impression of some animal's foot, much like a cow's, extending to the depth of about ten inches. This footprint is said to belong to the devil, made when he left Mohegan. He is believed to have gone east, some say to England."

"Several years ago a woodcutter in felling a chestnut tree near the river, picked up a roundish knot that dropped from it. He noticed that its outline and marking resembled a human face. Bringing it to Mrs. Fielding he was told it was the head of a woman who had been slain by her husband a hundred years ago. The couple lived in the grove where the man was cutting, and the head of the woman was believed to have transmigrated to the tree, to warn people of the evil of murder."

"When the moon is like a hook in the sky with the ends turned up, it is to hang your powder horn on. That means that it's going to be too wet to go hunting. When it hangs so that you cannot hang your horn on it, then take down your pouch and go hunting, for the weather will be good. That is the dry moon."

"When the tree frog croaks, he is calling for rain."

Myths. Several myths referring to the exploits of a being called Tcā'namīd were obtained at Mohegan from Mrs. Fielding. They were published in the Journal of American Folk-Lore as they were told, but will be given below in abstract for the sake of completeness. As far as could be ascertained, Tcā'namīd figured in many tales as a trickster generally outwitting his opponents by his magic tricks. If these few tales be accepted as typical of the original mythology of the tribe, it would seem safe to assume that in the person of Tcā'namīd we have the Mohegan trickster, corresponding in position to Eastern Algonkin (Passamaquoddy and Micmac) Gluscap,[1] and central Algonkin (Otchipwe, Menominee) Nanabozho, Mänäbush. Tcā'namīd is said to mean "glutton." Professor Prince supports this translation by his analysis.[2]

---

[1] Cf. Gluscap the Master, C. G. Leland and J. D. Prince. New York, 1902.
[2] Reference (f), p. 107.

Employing the newly invented catch-words for mythological motives, we recognize in these few tales the widespread American themes of the unsuccessful imitation, the magic flight, the vivifying forces and the trickster tricked. The themes of some of the tales given, undoubtedly show European influence.

Tcā'namīd Wins the Eating Match.[1]

Tcā'namīd disputes with another over his eating capacity. They agree to hold a contest. Tcā'namīd fastens a bag under his shirt. A barrel of soup is brought. When they begin, Tcā'namīd secretes the food in the bag instead of eating it. When his opponent gives up, Tcā'namīd challenges him to stab his stomach and dies.

Tcā'namīd Squeezes the Stone.[2]

Tcā'namīd challenges an opponent to a contest of strength. He boasts that he can squeeze water out of a stone. He takes a lump of dough instead of a stone, climbs a tree and squeezes water out of it. The people are deceived. His opponent takes a stone, climbs a tree and squeezes the stone so hard that it cuts his hands and he has to come down.

Tcā'namīd Killed by a Woman.[3]

Tcā'namīd abducts a girl and makes her his wife. She plans to desert him. She makes dolls and puts them about the house in corners with a little dried dung near each. A larger one she places in her bed and defecates near it. She puts a mortar, pestle and some eggs in a canoe and escapes when Tcā'namīd is absent. After she has gone, he returns and discovers her absence and the dolls in the house. Every time he turns his back one of the dolls screams. When he searches, he finds the large doll in the bed and strikes it with a club, thinking it is his wife. This doll screams louder than the others. Tcā'namīd sets out in pursuit of the woman. He follows her in a canoe and gains on her. When she sees this, she throws out the mortar and a bar of mortars obstructs his way. He crosses this and gains again. She throws out the pestle and a bar of pestles hinders him. He crosses this and gains on her again. She throws out the eggs and a bar of eggs is formed. He crosses this; and for the last time she takes a hair from her head, which becomes a spear, and kills Tcā'namīd with it.

---

[1] Cf. Journal of American Folk-Lore, Volume XVII (1904), pp. 183–184.
[2] Cf. Journal of American Folk-Lore, Volume XVII (1904), pp. 183–184.
[3] Journal of American Folk-Lore, Volume XVI (1903), p. 104.

THE SCATICOOK INDIANS.

Mention should be made here of a small band of fourteen Indians known as Scaticook (also Skaghticoke) in Litchfield County, Connecticut, on the Housatonic River, who are closely related to the Mohegan. This band I visited in 1903 and 1904. The only results obtained were a small vocabulary, some ethnographic specimens and a few items of ethnology.[1] A brief account of the tribe and the list of Indian words with commentaries of Professor Prince, have already been published.[2] The nucleus of this tribe was made up of Hudson River Mohican, as was evidenced by the vocabulary, and recruited from neighboring Connecticut tribes among whom Mohegan and Pequot figured largely. The dialectic affinities of this composite tribe, however, are evidently with the Delaware to the west, rather than to the Mohegan to the east.

Several references to the Scaticook have been made before in this paper and some of their tools described. The description of a few other specimens and a few additional ethnologic facts will be given. What I was able to secure appeared to exhaust the store of knowledge of the fourteen individuals then on the reservation.

The Indians made an annual emigration from their inland home on the Housatonic some forty miles down the river to Long Island Sound near Bridgeport, for the purpose of obtaining stores of shell fish. The old trail is remembered to have followed the eastern shore of the Housatonic down to the Cat's Paw Rocks, near New Milford, where it crossed to the west shore and thence led to salt water. Quantities of shell fish were brought back by the Indians on their return trip each fall. The journey took two days and one night.

A bow and arrows, some baskets and a mortar and pestle formerly in the possession of James Harris, who claimed to be a full blood, afford the basis for description. The bow was a simple stave, rudely rectangular in section and about three and a half feet in length. The string is attached to a short notched stub at the ends of the stave. The arrows were of the unfeathered blunt-headed type. A basket resembling in shape, the bark buckets or pails of the northern tribes is commonly made and sold by the Scaticook. The bottom is slightly wider than the top. The weave of the bottom is of the simple checkerwork pattern, the side being filled in, in

---

[1] Averages of measurements made on two Scaticook individuals in 1903, give the following: Value Kilson (part white, 88 years), cephalic index 81.2, facial index 85; Jim Harris (full blood (?), 54 years) cephalic index 81.2, facial index 86.

[2] Cf. reference (d)

simple alternate twill with fine maple splints.[1] The mortar was made of a plain log and stood about one and a half feet high, with plain sides. The pestle was of wood with the hand grip in the middle, for both ends, as Harris stated, were employed in pounding. Dug-out canoes were made until several generations ago.

Nothing in the way of custom or belief was remembered by any Scaticook except that, more than fifty years ago, they elected a "queen" and that upon that occasion she was crowned with a silver headband and wore an Indian costume. Harris also stated that the Indians formerly believed in the magic power possessed by individuals to transport themselves at will, to effect their designs by wishes, and to practice other things, included under witchcraft in general. There were localities, he stated, where the Indians, in passing by, made offerings of food or property for the purpose of appeasing the demon believed to reside there.

The former hostility of the Iroquois toward these Indians still lingers in their memory. Rather strangely, the salutation in vogue at Scaticook was given as sē'go which is ostensibly borrowed from the Iroquois.

THE WESTERN NIANTIC.

The location of this tribe was southeast of the Mohegan on Long Island Sound. At an early time, the Niantic (Nayàntikuk, Point of Land People) probably occupied the shores of this body of water from the Connecticut River eastward to the Pawcatuck which divides Connecticut from Rhode Island. If historical evidences are correct, the tribe was cut in two by a southerly invasion of the Pequot. The eastern section naturally coalesced with the neighboring Narragansett and became separated from the western section which fell under Pequot control. The eastern Niantic thenceforth remained identified with the Narragansett and were lost sight of. The accompanying notes refer solely to the western Niantic who retained an independent existence until about fifty years ago. The territory of the latter extended from the Connecticut River eastward along the Sound to the Niantic River. Their principal village was at Black Point, south of the present town of Lyme. The village extended along what is now known as Crescent Beach and the Indian burying ground was a short distance back from this.

There was another village near the present town of Niantic where the

---

[1] Cf. Southern Workman, Volume XXXIII, Number 7, pp. 383–390, (1904) where W. C. Curtis has an interesting article in which shapes, weaves, and designs of western Connecticut Indian baskets are figured and discussed.

Niantic River joins the Sound.[1] The western Niantic did not extend far inland. They were apparently a small and unimportant tribe numbering only one hundred in 1638, and eighty-five in 1761.[2] Until recently they occupied a reservation at Black Point but, since the last claimants have died, nothing now remains of it. Some Niantic emigrated with other Connecticut Indians to Brotherton, New York, and thence to Wisconsin. The last three men surviving at Black Point were Sam Sobuck, Wawkeet and Zach Nunsuch; all presumably of unmixed blood. One woman, Mrs. Henry Mathews (Mercy Nunsuch) who was bound out to service among the Whites when a child, married a Mohegan and still lives with her husband's people among whom she has children and grandchildren. She is a full blood Niantic and the last of her tribe. The few historical and ethnologic facts presented here were obtained from Mrs. Mathews and her nephew Albert Nunsuch, while the other scattered bits of information came up from time to time at the Mohegan village. Hitherto, nothing has been recorded of Niantic ethnology, and the original sources, outside of possible ones among the Brotherton Indians of Wisconsin, may be considered as practically exhausted.

Owing to the fact that Mrs. Mathews left her people at the age of seven, she recalls nothing of her native language save one term: buskacâzạn, to fall down. The cognate Mohegan term is buckạⁿzitiásạn. Both the living Niantic and the Mohegan assert that the two languages were mutually intelligible in part when spoken slowly, but that the Niantic were characterized by having weak, high-pitched voices and a high intonation.

The Niantic spent the spring and summer seasons near the sea shore at Black Point where they fished and cultivated a little ground, chiefly raising corn and beans. In winter, they moved back into the woods where they could keep warmer and where firewood was easier to get. The permanent house or wigwam was made of logs and planks. Logs formed the sides. Inside and out, between the logs, the spaces were smeared with a kind of plaster consisting of clay thoroughly mixed with pounded clam and oyster shells. Wawkeet was the last Niantic to have occupied one of these houses, and A. S. Nunsuch, now living, remembers helping him renew the chinking of his house in the manner described. The roof was of planks, over which quantities of brush were thrown. The enclosure formed one room without windows. The floor was laid with boards. At one end of the roof an opening was left as an exit for smoke. Directly beneath this opening was the

---

[1] On the eastern bank of the Niantic River, a short distance north of the Railroad bridge, an unexplored shell heap is to be found. The wagon road cuts through a portion of it.

[2] For historical and statistical data, cf. Handbook of American Indians, part 2, Bureau of American Ethnology and De Forest, History of the Indians of Connecticut.

fireplace. At the end opposite the fireplace was the door. When the family was away from home, it is said, a cross-stick and support were laid across the door opening, as a sign to forbid entrance. On one side of the house were two beds which consisted of scaffolds made of slats supported on crotched uprights and covered with bedding. Personal effects were kept in large covered baskets which will be mentioned later. The mortar and pestle were used in pounding up corn. The mortar was a log hollowed at one end, and the pestle a long stone, both being similar to those of the Mohegan. The pestles were usually elongated water-worn pebbles which were found along the beaches. The Niantic are said to have carried on some trade with their neighbors by means of these pestles. They would obtain suitable stones and leave them on the beach to be rolled together and ground smooth by the waves.

Mr. Nunsuch who was born at Niantic and who later removed to Mohegan offers the following information which applies to the Niantic and the Mohegan as well. Bowstrings were made of strips of twisted rawhide or strips of deer sinew. Arrows were often tipped with an iron nail, in later days, the end of the nail being inserted into the end of the shaft where the pith had been removed. Archery was kept up by boys and men until lately for purposes of amusement, small game hunting, and betting on marksmanship. The Niantic boys were taught to hold the bow vertically in the left hand with the forefinger resting on the poised arrow. The nock of the arrow was held between the first and second fingers of the right hand with the thumb over the arrow nock, the tips of the first two fingers catching on the bow string. This release is similar to that recorded of the Eskimo except that the thumb is employed. For a quiver the men made a rather long narrow basket of splints which was carried suspended from the shoulder.

There are a few objects of Niantic manufacture, whether exclusively of Niantic origin or not, which ought at least to be described here.

A type of storage or trunk basket was fairly common in their wigwams, being used in a general way for the reception of personal property and provisions. Some of these baskets are still to be seen around Niantic and several were formerly at Mohegan. In size, they averaged about two feet in length, eighteen inches in width and a foot or so in height, the sides all being straight. The warp and woof are composed of thin-shaven maple (?) splints about an inch and a half wide, interwoven in the simple checkerwork pattern. A telescope cover, almost as large as the body of the basket, fits down over the top, allowing a considerable extension of its holding capacity. In the center of each of the four sides, on all of these baskets seen, is a conventional design painted in black and red or pink (Fig. 33).

Beaded bags are remembered by Mrs. Mathews who at times, manufactures a few, after an old model. They are about six inches wide and six inches long, and rounded at the lower ends. Over the opening is a drop flap decorated with beads. A simple string of beads serves as a handle or carrier. They are intended for women's use. The modern material is, of course, of European make and the beads are the ordinary trade beads, The surface decoration of these bags usually consists of flowers and leaves, some of them more or less conventional. Daisies, black-eyed Susans, leaves, hearts, and forget-me-nots, are the most commonly seen. The beaded border is also general.

In how far the eastern flower designs are entirely of European derivation is a question about which there seems to be little actual knowledge. As Indian products, however, generally found throughout the Algonkin tribes, they deserve a comparative and analytic investigation. As will be seen, the Niantic and Mohegan flower figures resemble those of the other eastern and northern tribes, with a few characteristic minor variations.

As regards social organization and customs in general, nothing could be obtained. A short account of burial is all that Mrs. Mathews recalls. The dead were buried in the ground in a sitting posture. Objects, weapons, clothing or utensils, which the deceased was fond of in life were buried with him. Besides these, a mess of corn and beans, succotash, was placed at the grave and left to be consumed by the ghost. Mrs. Mathews remembers that an old white man used to come, after Indian burials, and make a meal on the succotash left at the grave. When the Indians would return and find this food gone, they were greatly pleased at the thought that the ghost had accepted and eaten it. The living are said to have feared the possible evil which ghosts could bring upon them.

Fig. 33. Basketry Design.

Another custom which Mrs. Mathews mentions was the prohibition of marriage out of the tribe, applying to the females. Should a woman marry a stranger, she had to leave the place and forfeit her inheritance. However, when her husband died, she was at liberty to return. Owing to this practice, all the surviving Niantic were of pure blood. Whether this regulation had any bearing on the tribal sociology or whether it was merely a development due to colonial pressure, it is hard to conclude.

The only fragment of lore which could be obtained is a short historical account of an attack on the Niantic village at the mouth of the Niantic

River. A short distance from the river there is a ridge of rock in which is a small cavern known locally as the Devil's Den. In this, a band of Niantic retreated on one occasion when hard pressed by an enemy, some say Mohawks. Fortunately, expecting a siege, the Niantic carried some mortars and pestles with them, but they had no corn. The enemy, unable to dislodge them, settled down outside to starve them out. Soon, however, they heard the sounds of corn pounding and merriment from the cave and thinking the Niantic were provided with grain they gave up the siege and left. Local traditions attributes mysterious noises in the cave to the Devil.

ARCHAEOLOGY OF THE NEW YORK COASTAL ALGONKIN.

BY

ALANSON SKINNER.

Introduction.

In the term New York Coastal Algonkin, the writer includes the tribes along the coast from Tottenville, Staten Island, the extreme southern point of the state, to the Connecticut boundary on Long Island Sound, including to a certain extent the shores of New Jersey immediately adjacent to Staten and Manhattan Islands, the east bank of the Hudson River as far north as Yonkers, and exclusive of Long Island except the western end. From the examination of the remains of the New York Coastal Algonkin area preserved in many collections, both public and private, it becomes obvious that the objects found may be roughly divided into three groups: articles of stone, articles of bone and antler, and articles of clay, shell and metal. The first group is, from the imperishable nature of its exponents, naturally the largest and comprises a number of sub-groups to be briefly described and commented upon in this paper.

Chipped Articles.

Arrow Points. Two general types may be recognized, and these are the stemmed or notched, and the triangular forms. The former are by far the most abundant, and while these are usually made of the nearest local rock possessing the necessary conchoidal fracture, in some cases, they occur of material brought from a long distance. Specimens made of pink flint resembling stone from the Flint Ridge of Ohio, and of jasper found to the south of this region have been recorded. Blunt arrow points are rare, the Indians probably preferring wooden arrows for this purpose. Many of the so-called "blunt-points" found in collections, appear to be scrapers made over from broken arrow points of a large size.

The triangular type has long been regarded by the local collectors of this vicinity as being the type used in war, the argument being that as it has no stem, it was necessarily but loosely fastened in its shaft and, if shot into the body, would be very liable to become detached and remain in the flesh if any attempt were made to withdraw it by tugging at the shaft. While it was no doubt perfectly possible to fasten a point of triangular shape to the shaft as firmly as a notched point, the discoveries of Mr. George H. Pepper at Tottenville, Staten Island, where twenty-three arrow points were found in and among the bones of three Indian skeletons, tend to strengthen this theory. While the majority were of bone or antler, all those made of stone were of this type, and indeed most of the bone points were also triangular in shape. However, it is well to bear in mind that arrow points of triangular type have been used for every purpose by all the early Iroquois tribes of New York.

Spear Points and Knives. None of the early accounts of contemporary European writers seem to mention the use of spears (other than bone or antler-headed harpoons) by the Indians hereabouts, and it is probable that the larger arrow-point-like forms found, were used as knives or cutting tools. They are usually notched or stemmed, rarely triangular, and occasionally round or oval. They vary in size; but it must be remembered that one tool may have had various uses, and that drills, knives, and scrapers may often have been combined in one implement.

Scrapers. Scrapers were probably used in dressing skins, and in sharpening bone implements, woodworking and for various other purposes. These are usually mere flint flakes chipped to an edge on one side. Nevertheless, notched and stemmed forms, requiring some care in their making do occur. Broken arrow points were occasionally chipped down to serve this purpose. A single serrated scraper has been found. These are very rare in both the Algonkian and Iroquoian areas of New England and the Middle Atlantic States. One very large stemmed scraper, of a type more common in the far west, also comes from this locality.

Drills. These are usually chipped tools presenting an elongated narrow blade and a considerably swollen or expanded base, suitable for grasping in the hand. In some cases the base was absent and those were probably hafted in wood. Specimens whose blades have a square or rectangular cross section are very rare. The finding of cores left in half-drilled objects shows the use of a hollow drill, and it has been suggested that a hard hollow reed used with sand and water on a soft stone would produce this effect. To bear out this assertion, it has been reported that a half-drilled implement has been found (outside this area on the upper Hudson) in which the remains of the reed drill were found in the cavity left by its action.

ROUGH STONE ARTICLES.

Hammerstones. These vary from simple pebbles picked up and used in the rough, showing merely a battered edge or edges acquired by use, to the pitted forms. They are generally mere pebbles with a pit pecked on two opposite sides, perhaps to aid in grasping with the thumb and forefinger. Some have battered edges, but many have not, suggesting, when round and regular, a use as gaming or "Chunké" stones, or as implements used only in pounding some soft substance. Hammerstones, pitted on one side only, and others with many pits on all sides, occur. These latter may have had some special use, and are not to be confounded with the large flat, slab-like stones having pits only on one side, found in other regions, and perhaps used as receptacles for holding nuts while cracking them. While these are common in the Iroquoian area, they are unknown here.

Large stones, single or double pitted, resembling oversized hammerstones occur, and these may have been used as anvils in chipping flint, etc.

Grooved clubs or mauls, also showing use as hammers are found. These are rare and are usually either rough pebbles, grooved for hafting, as in the case of the grooved axe, or grooved axes, the blades of which have become so battered, broken, and rounded by wear as to preclude their further use for chopping.

Net-sinkers. On all sites near the water, either salt, or fresh, net-sinkers show the prevalence of fishing. These are of two types. In one case a pebble is notched on opposite sides of either the long or broad axis; in the other a groove is pecked around the entire pebble in the same manner. The latter type is comparatively scarce, as the former, being more easily and quickly made, was just as useful to the savage. The modern Cree and Ojibway, residing in the forests north of the Great Lakes, still use pebbles for this purpose, but those observed by the writer were not notched or worked in any way. Occasionally, sinkers notched on both axes are found in this region.

Hoes. These are usually ovoid implements, chipped from trap and sometimes notched to facilitate hafting, and sometimes not. They usually show a slight polish on the blade, caused by friction with the ground. This type of hoe is the form mentioned by early writers; but perhaps hoes of shell, bone, or tortoise shell, and wood were used also. None of these, however, are still in existence.

Hand Choppers. Pebbles chipped to an edge on one side, for use as hand choppers, occur. These are occasionally pitted on both sides.

Grooved Axes. For the purposes of this paper, the writer, while aware that many grooved axes are well made and polished, has decided to include them under the head of "Rough Stone Articles," as by far the greater majority of the grooved axes and celts from this region lack the polish and finish belonging to other articles later to be described. Grooved axes are of two sorts: *a*, those made of simple pebbles, merely modified by grooving and chipping or pecking an edge; and *b*, axes which have been pecked and worked all over and sometimes polished. The latter (*b*) may be said to include:

1. Groove encircling three sides of blade, one side flat.
2. Ridged groove encircling three sides of blade, one side flat.
3. Groove encircling three sides of blade, longitudinal groove on flat side.
4. Groove encircling three sides of blade, longitudinal groove on flat side and opposite.
5. Groove encircling blade.
6. Ridged groove encircling blade.

A seventh type, having a double groove encircling the blade, may occur in this territory, but has never been reported. A specimen from the Hudson River region, just north of the area here dwelt upon, is in the Henry Booth Collection in this Museum. While most worked stone axes have been pecked into shape, a few have been fashioned by chipping, but these seem to be rare.

Grooved axes were hafted in various ways. During the summer of 1908, the eastern Cree dwelling in the vicinity of southern Hudson's Bay told the writer that their ancestors, who made and used such axes, hafted them by splitting a stick, and setting the blade in it, then binding the handle together with deer-skin (probably rawhide) above and below the split. No specimens of the grooved axe in the original haft, seem now to be extant from any locality in the east. From the battered appearance of the butts of these axes, it may have been that they were sometimes used in lieu of mauls or hammers. It is possible that they may have been used in war. It is generally supposed that in cutting down trees, making dug-out canoes and other kinds of wood-working, fire was used as an adjunct to the stone axe, the former being the active agent. The process of burning and charring having gone on sufficiently, the stone axe was used to remove the burned portion. However, some stone axes seem sharp enough to cut quite well without the aid of fire.

Celts. Ungrooved axes or hatchets, usually called celts, are frequent throughout this area; but are nowhere as abundant as the grooved axe, especially near the southern border of the region. The grooved axe seems to have been the typical cutting and chopping tool of the local Algonkin. The widespread idea that the celt was sometimes used unhafted as a skinning tool, has no historic proof; but may possibly have some foundation. The Cree of the southern Hudson's Bay region use an edged tool of bone for this purpose, a fact which is somewhat suggestive although it differs in shape from the celt. Celts with one side flat and the other beveled to an edge may have been used as adzes. From the worn and hammered appearance of the polls of some celts, it is possible that many of these implements were used as wedges in splitting wood after constant manipulation in their chopping capacity had permanently dulled their edges.

The celts of this region are, as a general thing, poorly made, a pebble of suitable shape having an edge ground on it with little or no preliminary shaping. However, more rarely, they were carefully worked all over by pecking and polishing as in the case of the grooved axe.

In type, aside from the general division of rough and worked celts, we may add that most celts in this region have slightly rounded polls, the bit broader than the butt, although some exceptions have been found. The forms are as follows: *a*, rough stone celts, pebbles with one end ground to an edge, but otherwise scarcely worked: and *b*, worked stone celts, which include the following:

1. Wedge-shaped, poll narrower than bit, and angles rounded; common.
2. Like number one, but with bit much broader than poll. Very rare. Cross-section oval.
3. Like number one, but one side flat, other beveled at one end to make a cutting edge.
4. Like number two, but with cutting edge flaring, broader than body. "Bell-mouthed type." Very rare.

North and west of this region, we find the Iroquois territory where most worked celts are angular, having almost invariably a rectangular cross section and squared butt. Types 1 and 3 also occur, but the celt with the rectangular cross section seems most typical of the Iroquoian region. Many small celts, made of flat fragments or chips of stone, are also found in this area, and these could scarcely have had a use as chopping tools.

In the Niagara watershed and extending eastward as far as the Genesee valley, an angular adze like form having a trapezoidal cross section occurs. It is found principally in what was the territory of the Attiwandaronk, Kah-Kwah, or Neutral Nation (an Iroquoian tribe, early annihilated by the Five Nations). It also occurs, as has been stated, on the sites of villages of the Iroquois proper, but is not abundant. South of the Iroquois in central Pennsylvania, another form which does not occur in this region is the chipped celt, usually of flint or other hard stone. This form is, however, frequent in the country about the headwaters of the Delaware.

In the "American Anthropologist," Vol. 9, No. 2, p. 296 *et seq.*, Mr. C. C. Willoughby has figured and described the celts of the New England region with remarks on the methods of hafting employed. These seem to be two in number, and consist, in the case of the larger forms, of setting the blade through a hole in the end of a club-like handle, the butt or poll projecting on one side and the blade on the other as in Fig. 34, found in the muck of a pond bottom at Thorndale, Dutchess County, New York, a region once in the Mahican territory. Smaller celts were set into a club-like handle, the butt resting in a hole or socket.

Adzes. These seem to be of two kinds, the first and most simple being celt-like, but flat on one side, the other side being beveled to an edge on one side. The second form is like the latter, save that it is grooved and the groove is not infrequently ridged. Occasionally, adzes with two parallel grooves occur. It was probably hafted by taking a stick at one end of which projected a short arm at right angles with the shaft, laying the flat side of the blade against this arm and binding it on with sinew, thongs or withes. The groove, of course, being of aid in securing the blade to the handle. Adzes of stone, hafted in this manner, have been obtained on the

Fig. 34 (1–1865). A hafted Celt from a Pond at Thorndale, Dutchess Co., N. Y. Length of celt 16.6 cm.

North Pacific coast. The celt adze seems not uncommon, but the grooved adze is rare, neither form being nearly so abundant as in the New England region.

Gouges. The stone gouge is rare, and seems always to be a plain, single-bladed affair without the transverse grooves so frequently seen in New England specimens, and hereabouts is always easily distinguished from the adze. Less than half a dozen specimens have been seen by the writer from this entire area, although probably quite as much work in wood was done by the New York coastal Algonkin as by the New England Indians.

Pestles. The long pestle occurs throughout the region of the Coastal Algonkin of New York, but is nowhere as abundant as in New England. They seem always to have been used with the wooden block mortar hereabouts, and are mentioned by the early writers as part of the household equipment of the natives. They do not seem to have been used by the Iroquois to the north and west of this area either in early or later times. The wooden pestle of dumb bell shape seems to have been preferred by them. The latter is used by the Canadian Delaware and may have taken the place of the long stone pestle to a great extent in this region.

Mullers, Grinders, and Polishing Stones. These are frequent, and consist merely of rounded pebbles, shaped and worn by use, probably most often in crushing corn. They are mentioned by De Vries as being used by the Indians with a flat stone slab for grinding corn when travelling. Some seem to have been used for polishing stone implements, but it seems hard to draw the line as the appearance gained from friction would be quite similar. Such mullers and their attendant slabs, used for preparing corn meal have been collected within a few years in use among the Oneida Iroquois of New York, one specimen being in the Museum's collection.

Sinew Stones. These are pebbles showing grooves along the edges, popularly supposed to have been worn there by rubbing thongs and sinews across the edges to shape them. They occur generally, but are not common.

Stone Mortars. These are common, and rather local, some sites having none at all, and others a good many. One locality on Staten Island is notable for the numbers found there, whereas they are rare elsewhere in that vicinity. They may be divided into the following types:

1. Portable mortar, hole on one side.
2. Portable mortar, hole on both sides (New Jersey type).
3. Portable slab mortar or metate, used on one or both sides.
4. Boulder mortar, one or more holes, immovable.

The first two types are the most abundant, the third is not uncommon; but the fourth is very rare, only one or two being reported. As above stated, De Vries claims that the portable mortars were used in bread-making, while the Indians were traveling; but certainly the majority of those found are far too heavy for this purpose.

Pigments, Paint-cups, etc. Fragments of pigments such as graphite and limonite, showing the marks of scratching with scrapers, are found, which have apparently supplied the material for painting. Worked geodes are common on many sites. These show traces of chipping in some instances and may have been paint cups. There is a tiny pestle-shaped pebble in the Museum Collection from Westchester County, which is said to have been found with a geode of this type. The popular theory is that such geodes were used as "paint cups" and this seems probable.

Stone Plummets. These are very rare, in contrast to their abundance in the New England region. ..They consist usually of small worked egg-shaped stones, grooved at one end, probably for suspension. The writer has seen but one, from this area. Their use is problematic.

Stone Masks. While a number of these interesting human masks, or heads, have been recorded from New Jersey by Mr. C. C. Abbott and others, and in spite of the fact that Mr. Arthur C. Parker reports that several have been found in Mahican territory along the Hudson, only one has been listed within the scope of our paper. This was found near Grasmere, Staten Island, and is described on page 21 (Plate ix). It is one of the best examples of Indian stone art from this region, and in point of excellence and skill of workmanship is quite unique, especially for New England and the Middle Atlantic States. It, no doubt, had some importance to its makers, judging from contemporary accounts and modern Lenapé ethnology where carvings of the human face are highly significant.

Semilunar Knives. Knives of rubbed slate, similar in appearance to the Ulu or woman's knife of the Eskimo are found, though rarely, in this region. While sometimes ascribed to Eskimo influence or contact, it is possible that this form (which occurs throughout New England) judging by its distribution, may have been native to the eastern Algonkin also. The eastern Cree still use knives of this type as scrapers. Like most other forms common in New England, it is less abundant in the southern part of this area.

Stone Beads. Various pebbles generally perforated naturally are to be found on some sites, and may or may not have been used as beads or pendants. On Staten Island, at Watchogue, Mr. Isaiah Merrill once owned a number of square beads of pinkish steatite (?), all but one of which have been lost, and which he claims were found on his farm.

POLISHED STONE ARTICLES.

Gorgets. Two types of the gorget occur. These are the single-holed pendant form, which is the least abundant of the two, and the double-holed type. The latter is flat, rectangular in shape and generally well polished. It usually has two perforations a short distance from the middle. The modern Lenapé of Canada claim to have used these as hair ornaments. Probably the two holed variety is typical of the Algonkin peoples of this region, the single-holed form being on the other hand, the most abundant on old Iroquoian sites. Specimens of the latter have been obtained in use among the Canadian Iroquois, and some of them are in the Museum collections.

Amulets. Certain problematic articles of the "bar" and even "bird amulet" type have been found; but these are probably exotic in origin and are not characteristic of the archaeology of the region in question.

Banner Stones. These beautiful polished stone implements of unknown use may be divided into three great classes, with several sub-types as follows:
1. Notched banner stones.
2. Grooved banner stones.
    a. Groove on both sides.
    b. Groove on one side.
3. Perforated banner stones.
    a. Plain.
    b. Butterfly.

All three types seem equally abundant, but the notched banner stones appear to be the oldest form and occur under circumstances pointing to great relative antiquity. They are found, however, on the more recent sites as well. Both notched and grooved banner stones are usually more rough in appearance than the perforated type, and the writer has never seen a polished specimen of the first class. On the other hand, the grooved variety is not infrequently as well finished, as the perforated forms are invariably. Banner stones grooved only on one side are less common than the other forms. While the latter class is generally made of slate, steatite, or some similar soft and easily worked material the notched and grooved forms, especially the former, are often formed either from naturally-shaped pebbles or chipped roughly into shape. Implements, usually naturally-shaped stones with little working, without notches, grooves or perforations, but greatly resembling the notched and grooved banner stones in shape, are not infrequently found on aboriginal sites hereabouts and may have served as banner stones. There seem to be neither records nor plausible theories as to their use.

Pipes. Stone pipes, invariably made of steatite, are very rare. Four types have been noted as follows:
1. Monitor or platform pipe, platform not projecting before the bowl.
2. Monitor or platform pipe, platform projecting before bowl, with or without tiny carved stem or mouthpiece. Of the latter, one specimen is known.
3. Trumpet-shaped stone pipe.
4. Rectangular stone pipe, human face carved on front of bowl.

It may be remarked that more stone pipes have been reported from the Indian cemetery at Burial Ridge, Tottenville, Staten Island, than from all the rest of the area put together. The second and third types are represented by one specimen each from Burial Ridge, and from nowhere else in this region. Four or five pipes of the first class have been found there as well. The last class is represented by a single specimen obtained by Mr.

W. L. Calver at Inwood, Manhattan Island. Undoubtedly the clay pipe was the most common form used in this locality.

Steatite Vessels. These are not at all abundant, though occurring almost everywhere. They were doubtless all imported from New England as there are no steatite quarries within the range of the New York Coastal Algonkin. The single form found is that common in the east, an oblong, fairly deep vessel with a lug, ear or handle at each end (Fig. 35 j). Occasionally, such vessels are ornamented by rude incisions along the rim.

ARTICLES OF CLAY.

Pottery Pipes are common everywhere. They are usually manufactured of a better quality of clay than that used for the vessels, and bear fairly similar designs. They are susceptible of division into the following classes:
1. Straight pipe, bowl expanding slightly.
2. Bowl much larger than stem, leaving it at an angle of forty-five degrees. Stem round.
3. Same as number 2, but stem angular and much flattened.
4. Effigy pipes, (represented by a pottery human head apparently broken from a pipe bowl, obtained by Mr. M. R. Harrington at Port Washington, Long Island).

The straight pipe seems to have been obtained only on Staten Island on the north shore in the region occupied by the Hackensack. While nowhere as abundant as upon the Iroquoian sites of central and western New York, the clay pipe is quite common, and is a prominent feature in the coast culture of New York (Fig. 36a). It is more abundant perhaps in the southern part of the area, but this may well be due to the fact that data from this region is more easily accessible. The triangular stemmed "trumpet" pipe so common on the Iroquoian sites, is unknown in this region.

POTTERY VESSELS.

The pottery of this region may all be considered as being either the native Algonkian in type or showing Iroquoian influence with a third and intermediate variety. Algonkian vessels may be divided into the following groups according to shape:

1. Conical, pointed bottom, slightly swollen sides, circumference largest at the mouth. The typical Algonkin pot of this area, Fig. 35a.
2. Like number 1, but much rounder and broader, Fig. 35b.
3. Bottom pointed, sides slightly swollen, neck slightly constricted, Fig. 35c.
4. Identical with number 2, except that just below the beginning of the

neck, occur small raised lugs, ears or handles. This is rare from this area, Fig. 35d.

5. Rounded bottom, somewhat constricted neck, lip sometimes flaring, or even turning down and back, Fig. 35e.

The intermediate types are as follows:

6. Rounded bottom, constricted neck, narrow raised rim or collar, Fig. 35f.

7. Like number 6, but with sides more elongated and bottom more oval

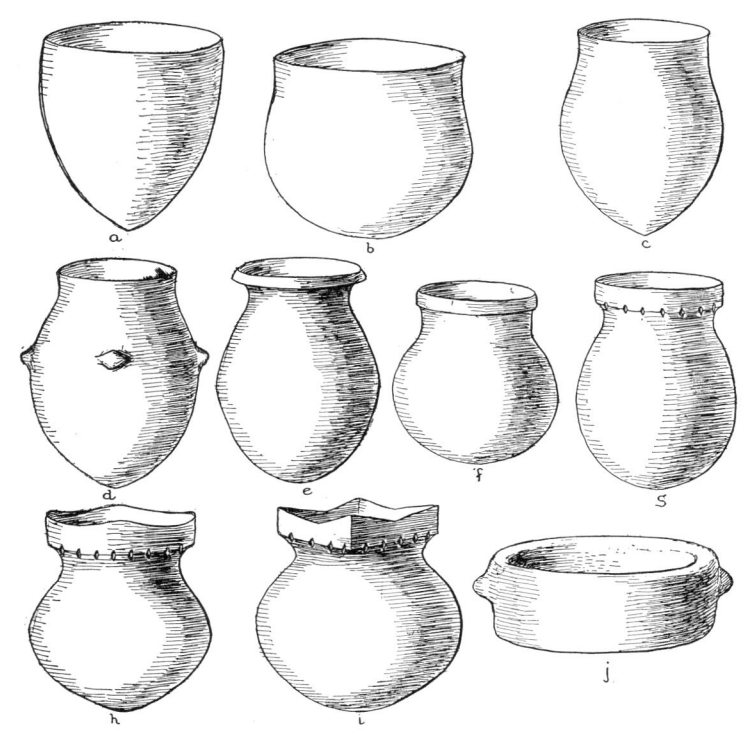

Fig. 35. Pottery Forms of the Coastal Algonkin.

than round, heavier collar, generally notched angle, with or without a series of small humps or projections at intervals, Fig. 35g.

The Iroquoian types are as follows:

8. Mouth rounded, collar or rim heavy, with humps or peaks at intervals, angle notched, neck constricted and bottom rounded; can stand by itself, an unknown feature in local Algonkian vessels, Fig. 35h.

9. Same as number 7, but with mouth square, and humps at every angle. Much less common than the preceding, Fig. 35i.

In size, the vessels range from small toy-like pots to jars of very large capacity. In general they appear to have been made by the coil process, and are tempered with pounded stone or fine gravel, mica, or burned or pounded shell. Sherds showing tempering by fibre or some other substance that disappeared in firing are rarely found. When vessels were cracked or broken, a series of holes was bored opposite each other on either side of the break and the fracture laced together, rendering the vessel capable of storing dry objects, at least.

Life forms are exceedingly rare in local ceramic art. From Manhattan Island and Van Cortlandt Park, there come a number of specimens showing incised human (?) faces. This is not an uncommon form on Iroquoian sites in central and western New York (Fig. 14b and 15). On the Bowman's Brook site at Mariner's Harbor, Staten Island fragments of a typically Algonkian pot were obtained which bore at intervals, rude raised faces (Fig. 3e). With the sole exception of a rather well-modelled clay face, apparently broken from the bowl of a pipe (Fig. 36b) found at Port Washing-

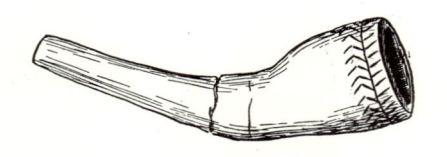

Fig. 36. *a* (20–4642), *b* (20–4526). Typical Algonkin Pottery Pipes from Port Washington, L. I., and fragment of an effigy Pipe from the same Locality.

ton, Long Island, by Mr. M. R. Harrington, this brief statement concludes the list of pottery life forms reported from this area, although others may yet be found here, since some interesting objects have been collected in immediately adjacent territory.

The forms of decoration consist of stamping with a stamp, roulette or paddle, and incision. (Figs. 37 and 38.) Occasionally, but very rarely, stucco work occurs. Under stamping we can enumerate the following processes:

1. Impression with the rounded end of a stick (rare).
2. Impression with the end of a quill, or hollow reed, leaving a circular depression with a tiny lump or nipple (rare) in the center.
3. Impression with a section of a hollow reed, making a stamped circle (rare).
4. Impression with finger nail (doubtful, but perhaps used on some sherds from Manhattan Island).

Fig. 37. *a* (20–4419), *b* (20–2810), *c* (20–2913), (20–3007), Incised Designs from Pottery Vessels: *a*, *b*, and *d*, designs from Iroquoian vessels; *c*, design from an Algonkian vessel; *e*, design from a vessel of the Iroquoian type from a Connecticut rock-shelter, introduced here for comparison.

5. Impression of the edge of a scallop shell.
6. Impression with a carved bone, antler, or wooden stamp.
7. Impression of a cord-wrapped stick.
8. Impression with roulette.

Under the head of decoration by incision we can enumerate the following:

9. Incised decoration, probably made with a stick.
10. Incised decoration, possibly made with a flint object (only one specimen at hand).

The paddle was frequently used to finish the sides and bottom of the pot by imparting an appearance of pressure with fabric when the clay was wet.

11. Stucco. Occasionally, ridges of clay placed on the rim for ornament appear to have been added after the shaping of the vessel.

Ornamentation is usually external, and vessels, either Algonkian or

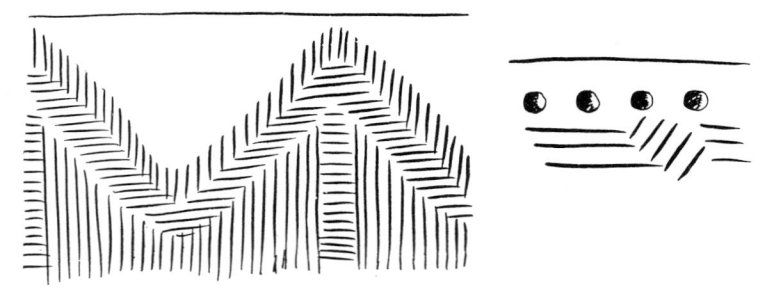

Fig. 38. a (20–4568), b (20–4655). Incised Designs from Algonkin Vessels.

Iroquoian, are rarely ornamented below the rim, although occasionally the designs run part way down the side in the case of the Algonkian forms. Where decoration has been applied by one of the stamping processes, and more rarely by incision, it is sometimes continued over the lip or rim for an inch or less on the inside. This only occurs in the typical Algonkian forms, and is never seen when incised ornamentation is used. The rims of Iroquoian vessels are never ornamented on the interior, nor is stamping so frequently practised on vessels of this class. The intermediate forms, at least the first of the two mentioned, are frequently ornamented on the interior of the lip. This internal decoration is much more common in the southern portion of this area than elsewhere in the vicinity.

In design, we must of course, give up all thought of trying to obtain symbolism, if such there were, for there are no sources now left upon which to base our assumptions. Certain conventional types of decoration seem to have been in vogue, usually consisting in rows of stamped or incised parallel lines and much more rarely of dots regularly arranged in the same manner. Zigzag, chevron and "herring bone" patterns are the most common, but other angular forms occur, and rows of parallel lines encircling the vessel are sometimes to be found. Stamping and incision as decorative processes never seem to occur on the same vessel. Curvilinear decoration is exceedingly rare, and not enough material is at hand to show that patterns were used; possibly these were scrolls of some form. On account of the lack of material, it cannot be determined whether the designs on the Algonkian vessels differ from those on the Iroquoian, except in a very general and unsatisfactory way.

The angle caused where the heavy rim or collar leaves the constricted neck of the Iroquoian vessel is almost invariably notched, and as such collars and angles do not occur on vessels of the true Algonkian type, this feature is necessarily absent from them. It is noticeable that Iroquoian vessels are usually decorated with incised designs, rather than stamped patterns.

Pottery is found abundantly on the majority of the sites in this district; but, while very much more common than in the New England area, it does not equal in abundance that from the Iroquois country. It is rarely found buried in graves with skeletons as in the Iroquoian area; when sometimes found in graves, however, it is usually at some distance from the human remains and apparently not connected with them. Whole or nearly whole vessels are exceedingly rare and the number of those found up to date may easily be counted upon the fingers. Potsherds taken from pits or shell heaps, where they have not been exposed to the action of the weather are often as thickly covered with grease as when they were broken and cast aside.

Articles of Metal.

Beads. Beads of native metal, consisting simply of a piece of hammered sheet copper rolled into a small tube, have been found, but they are very rare. Copper salts but no objects, were found upon the bones, especially on those of the head and neck, of a child's skeleton at Burial Ridge, Tottenville, Staten Island, which seemed to predicate the use of copper beads. A great many beads of *olivella* shell, some of them discolored by copper salts were found about the neck of the skeleton. A single celt of copper is said to have been found in Westchester County, probably on Croton Neck, slightly above the limit of the territory treated by this paper. No native copper occurs in this region, and any of this material must have been brought from a distance.

Articles of Shell.

Wampum. Objects of shell are not at all common, and notwithstanding the coast region of New York was one of the best known localities for wampum manufacture on the continent, wampum beads are almost unknown from local sites. With the exception of completed beads, most of which may have been shipped into the interior, wampum may be found in all stages of manufacture. We refer to the white wampum, for traces of the blue "black" wampum made from the hard clam or quahog, are so far not reported. The process may be shown by shells with the outer whorls broken away in steps until the innermost solid column is reached, ground and polished at the end, and needing only cutting off into sections and perforations to make the finished white wampum bead. These do not occur on all sites, though they have been found here and there throughout the region. Ninety-six conch shells with the outer whorls broken entirely away were found in a grave at Burial Ridge, Tottenville, Staten Island, about the head and neck of a skeleton.

Pendants. Occasionally oyster and clam shells, found unworked save for perforations in them, may have been pendants or ornaments, but certainly have little aesthetic value.

Scrapers. Clam shells seem to have been used as scrapers and some are occasionally found with one edge showing the effect of rubbing and wearing. These are rare, however. Some may have been pottery smoothers; clam shells have been reported which contained central perforations and were identical in appearance with some shell pottery scrapers and smoothers collected by Mr. M. R. Harrington among the Catawba. Contemporary writers mention the use of knives made of shell.

Pottery Tempering. This was sometimes done with calcined and pounded shells, but was uncommon considering the abundance of the material at hand. Pounded stone or gravel seems to have been more favored.

Pottery Stamps. The corrugated edge of a scallop shell was frequently used as a stamp for pottery, as may be seen by examining the potsherds from this region (Fig. 17).

Fossils.

Fossil shark's teeth usually of some species of Charcharodon, and probably from the Ashley River district of South Carolina, are occasionally found on village sites where they may have been brought by the Indians. They are unworked, and, if used by the Indians, their purpose is problematic, although the size and appearance of some suggest a function as arrow points.

Articles of Bone and Antler.

Objects of bone and antler, while perhaps more abundant here than in New England, are far less plentiful in form and number than in the Iroquoian area. Cut bones are frequent in most shell pits and heaps. They were cut by grooving the bone partially through on all sides, probably with a flint knife, and breaking.

Bone Awls. These utensils are the most common of all bone articles in this region, and are found in almost every part of the area. Some are merely sharpened slivers; but others show a considerable degree of work, and are well finished and polished. They are usually made of deer or other mammal bone, but sometimes from the leg bones of birds.

In some instances, the joint of the bone is left for a handle, but these are often cut off. Grooved, perforated, or decorated bone awls are extremely rare in this region. While it is generally considered that these bone tools were used as awls in sewing leather, as by modern shoemakers, nevertheless, they may have served as forks in removing hot morsels from the pot or for a number of other purposes. The latter supposition is supported by the abundance of bone awls found in some shell pits. The Northern Cree of the Hudson's Bay region use a similar bone implement as the catching or striking pin in the "cup and ball" game.

Bone Needles. These are rare, but found in most localities. They are generally made of the curved ribs of mammals, and are six or eight inches long, and even longer. They are generally broken across the eye which is usually midway between the ends. A few with the perforations at one end have been reported.

Bone Arrow Points, usually hollow and conical in shape, have been found, especially at Tottenville, Staten Island, in the Burial Ridge (p. 15). They are rather rare, but this may be due to the fact that conditions are not suitable for their preservation in most localities. Others are flat and triangular in shape.

Harpoons. No actual barbed bone harpoons, such as occur in the Iroquois country have been reported from this region; although the writer has seen what appeared to be part of one from Shinnecock Hills, Long Island, from whence comes a harpoon barb of bone, found by the writer, now in the Museum collection, which was apparently made to tie to a wooden shaft. While neither of these forms seem to occur within this region, several naturally barbed spines from the tail of the sting-ray, found on the Bowman's Brook site, at Mariner's Harbor, Staten Island, may have been used as harpoons or fish spears, for which purpose they were admirably suited by nature. Long, narrow, chipped stone arrow-heads are generally called "fish points" but they do not seem peculiarly adapted for this purpose and the name is probably a misnomer. No bone fish hooks are reported from hereabouts, though suggested by early writers.

Bone Beads and Tubes. While so abundant on Iroquoian sites, tubes and beads made of hollow bird or other animal bones, polished, and cut in sections, are very rare here.

Draw Shaves, or Beaming Tools, made of bone, and probably used for removing the hair from skins, were made by splitting the bone of a deer's leg, leaving a sharp blade in the middle with the joints on either end as handles. The writer has seen none from this immediate region, but they are reported by Mr. M. R. Harrington. A number were obtained for the Museum by Mr. Ernst Volk in the Lenapé sites near Trenton, New Jersey. An implement, evidently made of the scapula of a deer, and perhaps used as a scraper, was found in a grave at Burial Ridge, Tottenville, Staten Island, by Mr. George H. Pepper (p. 23).

Worked Teeth. Perforated teeth of the bear, wolf, and other animals, so abundant on Iroquoian sites never seem to be found here. Beavers' teeth, cut and ground to an edge occur, and may have been used as chisels, or primitive crooked knives, or both, as they were till recently by some of the eastern Canadian Algonkin. Other cut beaver teeth may have served as dice or counters in gaming.

Turtle Shell Cups. These are common, and consist merely of the bony carapace of the box turtle (*Tranene caroline*), scraped and cleaned inside, the ribs being cut away from the covering to finish the utensil for use.

Turtle Shell Rattles. A single box turtle carapace, collected at Pelham Bay Park, by Mr. M. R. Harrington, which is now in the Museum's collection shows a series of perforations on the top, not unlike those found on the turtle knee rattles still to be seen further south among the Muskhogean peoples. This object may have had a similar use.

Antler Implements. Deer antlers and fragments of antler, worked and unworked, occur in all shell heaps and pits. When whole antlers are found, they usually show at the base the marks of the axe or other implement used to detach them from the skull. Cut antler prongs, prongs broken from the main shaft and others partially hollowed and sharpened show the process of manufacture of antler arrow points. These are characteristic of this area and are usually conical in shape, hollowed to receive the shaft, and with one or more barbs; not infrequently, however, they are diamond-shaped in cross section. The shaft fitted into the hollow socket as in the case of the conical bone arrow points. A large number were found in and among the bones of human skeletons in a grave at the Burial Ridge, Tottenville, Staten Island.

Cylinders, neatly cut and worked all over, or cylindrical tines made of deer antler only cut and rounded at the ends, are not infrequent, and were probably used as flaking tools in making and finishing arrow points by pressure. One broken cylinder or pin, found on the Bowman's Brook site, Mariner's Harbor, Staten Island, had a rounded neatly carved head. This specimen, however, seems to be unique.

Pottery stamps, perhaps of antler or bone, but which may be of wood, seem to have been used, judging by the decorations of many pottery sherds. A pottery stamp, carved from antler, was found slightly east of this region, at Dosoris, Glen Cove, Long Island, by Mr. M. R. Harrington, and is now in the Museum's collections.

Trade Articles.

In spite of the frequent mention by old writers of barter of European for Indian goods, the amount of trade material found is small indeed. While it is abundant in the Iroquoian area, all that has ever been found here consists of a few round-socketed iron tomahawks, iron hoes, brass or copper arrow-points of various styles, a little porcelain, a few glass beads, Venetian and plain, and some old pipes, notably those stamped "R. Tippet" on the bowl. All these articles are very rare here, and for this no adequate explanation can be given.

Conclusion.

This area was inhabited during historic times by the following tribes:[1]

A. The Lenni Lenapé, or Delaware, ranging from the Raritan River, including Staten Island, to Saugerties on the west bank of the Hudson.

    Raritan or Assanhican.
    Hackensack.
    Tappan.
    Aquakanonk.
    Haverstraw.
    Waranawankong.

B. The Wappinger Confederacy ranging along the east bank of the Hudson, eastward to Connecticut, from Manhattan Island.

    Rechgawawank or Manhattan.
    Siwanoy.
    Weckquaskeck.

---

[1] On the map shown in Fig. 36, these tribes are shown together with the Long Island and other neighboring tribes as indicated by Beauchamp in the map accompanying his "Aboriginal Occupation of New York," New York State Museum, Bulletin 32, Albany, 1900.

Wappinger.
C. Montauk or Matouwack Confederacy.
Canarsie.

These tribes were surrounded on all sides by neighbors of the same stock, who differed somewhat in their language and culture. On the south

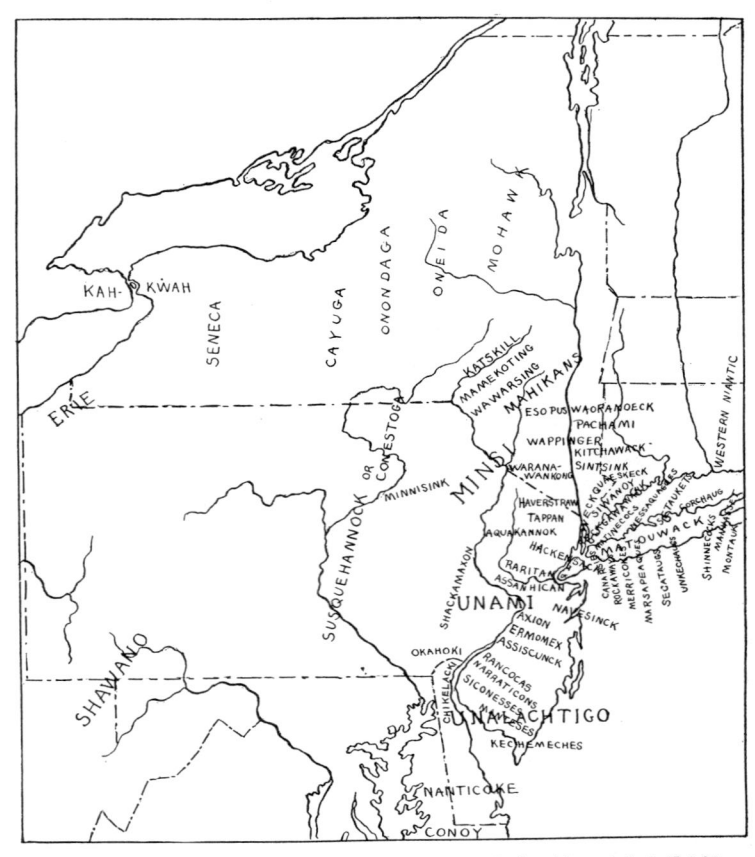

Fig. 39. Map showing the Location of the New York Coastal Algonkin and their Neighbors.

and west, lay the Lenni Lenapé, or Delaware proper; on the north, the Manhattan, and on the east the New England tribes. Almost without exception, these natives were displaced early in the history of this country, and have been long since expatriated or exterminated. A very few mixed bloods may yet be found on Staten Island, Long Island, and Westchester County, but their percentage of Indian blood is extremely low.

The remains of aboriginal life now to be found, consist of shell heaps, occurring at every convenient point along the coast, on the rivers, and, more rarely, inland. Shell, refuse, and fire pits, camp, village, and burial sites, and rock, and cave shelters, most of which have been so fully described in the preceding papers as to render further comment unnecessary. With one prominent exception [1] few or no relics have been found in graves. The typical interment was of the flexed variety, but bone burials are not infrequent.

Dog skeletons complete and intact, bearing the appearance of having been laid out, are sometimes found buried in separate graves. Some writers have supposed that these individual dog burials are the remains of "white dog feasts," or kindred practices because the Iroquois even up to the present day hold such ceremonies. The white dog is entirely cremated by the Iroquois, and so far as we have been able to find out, there is no record of such occurrences among the coastal Algonkin; hence, there seems no reason to attribute this custom to them since other Iroquois traits were so infrequent. It seems more probable that such burials are simply those of pet animals, interred as we to-day honor a faithful dog.

Occasionally, the skeletons of dogs and rarely of other animals have been found in graves associated with human bones. The finding of arrow points among the ribs of some of these and other circumstances seem to point to a practice of killing a favorite animal on the death of its owner to accompany or protect the spirit of its master on the journey to the hereafter.

From their appearance and position, many graves seem to indicate that the dead may sometimes have been buried under the lodge, especially in time of winter, when the ground outside was frozen too hard to permit grave digging. Others, under the same circumstances seem to have been buried in refuse pits. The remains also indicate that "feasts of the dead," were also held at the time of the interment, judging by the quantity of oyster shells and animal bones, in and near the graves. Some graves have rows or layers of oyster shells with the sharp cutting edge upward, placed above the bodies as if to prevent wild animals from disinterring and devouring the dead.

An interesting fact, brought to light by the rock-shelter work of Messrs. Schrabisch and Harrington in their explorations in New Jersey and Westchester County, New York, is that in the lowest and oldest refuse layers of these shelters pottery does not occur. It would be ill advised to infer from this that the earliest occupants were peoples of another culture from the surrounding village dwellers, as the other artifacts found are quite similar

---

[1] Burial Ridge, Tottenville, Staten Island.

to the implements of the latter. Many reasons for this lack of pottery, such as the more easy transportation of vessels of bark or wood, through the mountains and hills suggest themselves, though more or less nullified by the presence of pottery in the upper layers. However, the upper layer may have been made during the period when the natives were being displaced by Europeans and at the same time subjected to Iroquoian raids, when the villages would naturally be abandoned from time to time, for refuge among the cliffs and caves of the mountain fastnesses.

It has been suggested that the rock and cave shelters are remains of an older occupation by people with or without the same culture as the later known savages. The nature of the finds does not support this view, for the specimens obtained are often of as good workmanship as the best to be found in the villages and cemeteries of the latter, while pottery, on the other hand, occurs on the oldest known Algonkin sites. It seems most probable to the writer that, like the shell heaps, the rock and cave shelters form but a component part, or phase, of the local culture, perhaps a little specialized from usage and environment but contemporary with the villages, shell heaps, and cemeteries of the lowlands.

Mounds and earthworks do not occur in the region under consideration, nor does it appear that most of the Indian villages here were fortified, unless they were slightly stockaded. A number of instances of this are known historically, however, and a few earthworks occur just beyond this area.[1]

The remains found, do not bear any appearance of very great geological antiquity. In a few instances, rock-shelters, shell heaps and village sites seem to possess a relative antiquity; but the oldest known remains, in every case, may be placed as Algonkian with considerable certainty. No paleoliths have been reported, and it would seem from the comparative lack of antiquity of the remains that the natives could not have lived in this region for many centuries before the advent of the whites. The accounts of contemporary writers prove conclusively that these archæological remains, if not those left by Indians found here by the early Dutch and English settlers, must have been from people of very similar culture. In culture, the local Indians were not so high as the Iroquois, nor perhaps the Lenapé or Delaware proper from whom they sprang; but they compare very favorably with the New England tribes. Absence and scarcity of certain artifacts such as steatite vessels, the long stone pestle, the gouge, adze and plummet, and the abundance and character of bone and pottery articles show them to have been intermediate in character between the Lenapé on the south and west,

---

[1] An earthwork at Croton Point on the Hudson has been excavated by Mr. M. R. Harrington for this institution.

and the New England tribes on the east and north; and, consultations of the old European contemporaries, show that this was the case linguistically as well as culturally. Examination of the remains also shows that the influence of the Lenapé on the west, and of the New England peoples on the east, was most strongly felt near their respective borders. Iroquoian influence was strong, as evinced by the pottery, and there is also documentary evidence to this effect. Finally, as is frequent throughout most of eastern North America, the archæological remains may be definitely placed as belonging to the native Indian tribes or their immediate ancestors who held the country at the time of its discovery.

INDEX.

Abbott, C. C., 21, 60, 140, 220.
Abenaki, 22, 200.
Adzes, 18, 60, 217–218.
Agriculture, 190.
Agricultural Implements, 114.
Ahakinsack, 53.
Ah-qua-hung, 73, 78.
Algonkin Indians, 7, 11, 21, 26, 29, 44, 54, 61, 183, 214, 219, 220, 230, 231; type of pottery, 55, 56, 57, 84, 174, 222, 226.
Amulets, 220.
Andros, Sir Edmund, 105, 106.
Animal bones, 87, 91, 126, 150, 152, 162, 172, 175.
Antler, arrows, 22; implements, 7, 230; pin, 22; points, 44, 113; prongs, 22, 119, 173; tips, 14; tools, 21.
Anvils, 19, 171, 215.
Appamanskoch, 32.
Aquakanonk, 231.
Archaeological remains, 60, 234; sites, 66–67.
Archaeology of Manhattan Island, 113–121.
Archery, 208.
Armonk, 125, 134.
Arrochar, 16, 21.
Arrow-heads, 67, 90, 146, 149, 162.
Arrow points, 15, 58, 65, 68, 69, 113, 119, 126, 127, 129, 144, 146, 171, 172, 173, 176, 213, 229, 233; bone, 22, 214; brass, 28; stone 43, 44.
Arrows, 190, 205, 208.
Art, on pottery, 53.
Articles, of clay, 222; metal, 227; shell, 228.
Ash beds, 126, 176.
Attiwandaronk, 217.
Awls, of bone, 23, 118, 172, 229.
Axes, 18, 58, 65, 67, 85, 90, 114, 171, 215.

Báganūd, 191.
Bags, 208.

Bambáig, 189.
Banner stones, 20, 88, 116–117, 171, 221.
Banni'dwañg, 188.
Baságwanạⁿtạkság, 186.
Baskets, 189, 205, 208.
Beads, of bone, 230; glass, 28; metal, 227; shell, 28, 227; stone, 9, 27, 220.
Beaming tools, 230.
Bear Rock, 145, 149–150.
Bestavaar's Kill, 67.
Bibliography, 62.
Bī'tka, 191.
Bīyótī, 188.
Bloomfield (Watchogue), 9.
Bloomingdale, 65.
Blue Bell Tavern, 132.
Blunt-points, 213.
Blueskye, William, 22.
Bogardus Corners, 37.
Bone and antler, 229–231.
Bones of animals, 69, 70.
Bone poin s, 44.
Booth, Henry, collection, 216.
Bowling Green, 35.
Bowls, 188.
Bows, 44, 189–190, 205.
Bowstrings, 208.
Brinton, D. G., 30, 32.
Brooches, 192.
Brooms, 189.
Brotherton Indians, 185.
Buckạⁿzitiásạn, 207.
Burial Ridge, 11, 20, 21, 27, 29, 41, 42, 44, 51, 113, 221, 227, 228, 229, 230, 231.
Burials, bone, 50, 51; bunched, 51; of dogs, 70, 79, 89; methods of, 49–50.
Burial Site, 4.
Buskacâzạn, 207.
Byram, 132, 134, 136.

"Cache blades," 20.
Caches, 20, 156–157.
Calver, W. L., 65, 68, 69, 70, 85, 87, 91, 114, 119, 132, 221.

Camp site, 16, 79.
Canarsie, 47, 48.
Canoes, 48–49.
Catawba, 25, 228.
Celts, 6, 18, 60, 115, 216–217, 227.
"Century House," 88.
Ceremonial pits, 84.
Ceremonies, 194.
Charter, 104, 108.
Chenoweth, Alexander C., 66, 68, 69, 70, 81, 88, 92.
Cherokee, 29.
Chipped articles, 213.
Chipped points, 127.
Christopher, Richard, 11.
"Chunké" stones, 215.
Ckáñks, 191.
Ckwand, 187.
"Clam-drying," 17.
Clans, 193.
Clothing, 191.
Clubs, 215; grooved, 19.
Coastal Algonkin, 213–235.
Cold Spring, 66, 68, 69, 85, 88, 195.
Collections of specimens, 17–18.
Copper, 28, 172, 227.
Corlear's Hook, 34, 35.
Costume, 39, 40, 41, 83.
Cooking, 47; utensils for, 47, 171.
Cree, 215, 216, 220.
Crystal eye, 141.
Cultural reconstruction, 38.
Culture-horizons, 153.
Cup and ball game, 23, 118, 229.
Cups, 14, 23, 119, 173, 230.
Curtis, W. C., 206.
Customs, 193–195, 206.
Cutchegan Rock, 187.
Cylinders, 231.

Dances, 194.
Dankers and Sluyter, 33, 39, 42, 48, 53, 61.
Dakwáñg, 188.
Davis, William T., 4, 20, 45, 46, 62.
Decker, Almer, 27, 62.
Decorations, on bags, 209; drumsticks, 21; masks, 21; pipes, 26–27, 189; pottery, 7, 24–25, 57–58, 120, 142, 147, 155, 158, 224–226.
Deed, 99–100.

Defeat of King Philip, 107.
Deharts Brook, 6.
Designs on pottery, 55, 59, 120.
Devil's Den, 210.
DeVries, 33, 34, 40, 42, 48, 51, 219.
Dĭ'bī, 200.
"Dog burials," 70, 93.
Dongan, Governor, 107, 108.
Dosoris, 173, 177.
Draw shaves, 230.
Drills, 115, 171; of stone, 20, 214.
Drying Heaps, 4.
Dutch West India Company, 33.

Earthworks, 234.
Eastern Niantic, 185.
Edhaquaons, 33.
Ethnography of Staten Island, 29.

"Fairy boats," 46.
"Feast of the Dead," 50, 233.
Federal Hill, 143–144.
Fielding, Mrs. Fidelia, 183, 186.
Finch's Rock House, 125–132, 134, 136.
Fireplaces, 133, 142, 146, 148, 151, 159, 164, 208.
Fish hooks, 45; points, 45, 230.
Fishing, 44.
Flexed burials, 50.
Folk-lore, 200–203, 209.
Fort Amsterdam, 65, 97.
Fort Hamilton, 53.
Fort Wadsworth, 34.
Fort Washington, 65, 68, 82.
Food materials, 43, 45, 83, 130; methods of preparing, 190–191.
Fossils, 23, 228.
Fox, 39.
Franklin Lake, 141.

Gá-nos-ho, 22.
Gansevoort Market, 67.
Gántcī Múndu, 200.
Geodes, 219.
Gīyámman, 188.
Gorget, 21, 41–42, 115, 152, 171, 220.
Goshen Mountain, 163–165.
Grants of land, 94–95, 98, 99, 107.
Gouges, 6, 19, 60, 218.
Graves, 50–51, 68, 71, 233.
Green Ridge, 10.

Index.

Grinders, 219.
Grooved axes, 215–216.
Groups of stone articles, 213.
Great Maize Land, 79.
Gū'ngū, 191.
Gwánsnâg, 188.
Habitation, 46, 187, 207.
Hackensack, 34, 35, 36, 43, 54, 60, 61, 222, 231.
Hair ornaments, 220.
Hall, Edward Hagaman, 87.
Halve Maen, 82.
Hammers, 142.
Hand choppers, 19, 215.
Hand hammers, 146.
Harlem Ship Canal, 70.
Harpoons, 214, 229.
Harrington, M. R., 22, 49, 222, 228, 230, 237.
Haverstraw, 231.
Headdress, 192.
Hearths, 126, 147, 176.
Heckewelder, 61.
Helicker's Cave, 132.
Heye, George G., 187.
Historical References, 72.
Hoe, 42, 114, 215.
Holmes, W. H., 25.
Hook Mountains, 150.
Horsestable Rock, 160–163.
Housatonic, 205.
Hrdlička, A., 30, 32.
Hudson, Hendrick, 175.
"Hummocks," 3.
Huguenot, 16.
Hunting, 43–44.
Hussakof, Louis, 23.

"Idol images," 21.
Implements, 221; of antler, 60, 118; bone, 22, 60, 118, 170; cache of, 14; chipped, 114; flaked, 14; stone, 18.
Inag, 184.
Indian attack, 103.
Indian claims, 105.
"Indian fields," 10, 79.
Indian languages, classification of, 72.
Indian tribes, 231–232.
Inwood, 66, 68, 69, 77, 82, 89, 96, 100, 104, 107, 221.

Iroquois, 7, 44, 185, 193, 214, 217, 220, 222, 233; Silverwork, 193; type of pottery, 55–56, 88, 130, 174, 223, 226.
Isham's Garden, 70.

Jar, 88–89.
Jībai', 196.
Jokiwī'n, 187.
Juet, Robert, 82.

Kah-Kwah, 217.
Kalch-Hook, 67.
Kanarekante, 37.
Kanienga, 24.
Kensico, 132.
Kes-kes-kick, 78.
Ketchum's Mill Pond, 16.
Kieft, Director, 95, 97, 98, 99.
Kill Van Kull, 3, 6.
Kingsbridge, 77, 85, 98, 101, 104.
Kittatinny Mountains, 37.
Knives, 20, 115, 188, 214; material for, 20, semilunar, 19, 115.
Knoll, The, 66, 68, 95.
Kreischerville, 37.
Ktcais, 194.
Kuyter, Joachim Pietersen, 35, 95, 96, 97, 99.

Lakes Island, 10, 58.
Leather Man's Shelter, 134.
Ledyard, 184.
Leggings, 191.
Leiden Museum, 120.
Lenapé, 29, 30, 32, 38, 46, 47, 220, 230, 234.
Lenni Lenapé, 153, 165, 231.
Lita-pum-bla-wan, 41.
"Little Ape," 97.
Little Helicker's, 134.
Livingston, 4.
Lodges, 47; sweating lodges, 48.
"Long House," 47, 53.
Long Neck (Linoleumville), 9.
Lovelace, Governor Francis, 28, 33, 36.
Lovelace, Thomas, 36, 105.

Máckazīts, 190.
Mahican, 34, 217.
Mahīgani'ak, 184.
Mahoney Shelter, 134.

Mahquadus, 37.
Maize, 42.
Mai-kan-e-tuk, 78, 81.
Mänäbush, 203.
Mạnnü'dạc, 189.
Mákạs, 191.
Mạkīáwīsag, 201.
Mannetoe, 45.
Mannêtu, 200.
Manitto, 200.
Mariners' Harbor, 19, 20, 22, 23, 43, 58, Arlington, 5; Bowman's Brook, 6, 22, 23, 43, 45, 54, 58, 68, 229, 231; Old Place, 8; Sites at, 6.
Marriage customs, 52, 53, 209.
Mask, of stone, 21, 220; of wood, 21.
Mátci Múndu, 200.
Material culture, 165, 187–191.
Mattano, 32.
Maquas, 33.
Maul, 19, 215.
McGuey, James, 65, 68, 69, 85.
M'daulinu, 200.
Medicines, 200.
Menominee, 203.
Merrill, Isaiah, 9, 220.
Meteu, 200.
Micmac, 203.
Mine Hill, 159.
Minsi, 153, 165.
Minuit Director Peter, 94, 95.
Moccasins, 192.
Mohawk, 7, 24, 36, 55, 96, 100, 184; Iroquois, 38.
Mohegan, 165, 183–210.
Mohīksinạg, 184.
Moigūwạg, 195.
Montagne, Doctor de la, 35, 94, 96, 98, 105.
Montauk, 232.
Mooney, James, 25.
Mortars, stone, 43, 114, 128, 219; wooden, 37, 42, 114, 188, 208.
Mortuary customs, 49.
Mullers, 219.
Muncey, 30, 31.
Múndu, 200.
Muscoota, 78.
Muskhogean Indians, 49, 230.
Mythology, 53.

Myths, 203.

Naig-ia-nac, 67.
Najack, 47.
Nạmákkīs, 194.
Nanabozho, 203.
Nânná, 194.
Nânnáñg, 193.
Napsia, 81.
Narragansett, 185, 186, 206.
Nạtánīs, 194.
Nayạ̀ntīkuk, 206.
Nebo Rocks, 132.
Neagle Burying Ground, 71
Needles, 88, 118, 172, 229.
Neolithic weapons, 84.
Net-sinkers, 114, 215.
New Brighton, 16.
New Haerlem, 102, 104.
New Springville, 10.
Newton's Creek, 6.
Niagara, 217.
Niantic River, 206.
Nīdámb, 194.
Nipmunk, 185.
Nip-nich-sen, 78.
Notassen, 43.
Nūc, 193.
Nū, jạnâs, 193.

Oakland, 41.
Oakwood, 17.
Ojibway, 215.
Oliffe, William, 57.
Oneida, 37; Iroquois, 219.
Onondagas, 71.
Orange County, New York, 159.
Ornaments, 191.
Osage, 39.
Otchipwe, 203.
Oude Dorp, 16.
Outbreak of warfare, 102.
Ownership of Washington Heights, 108–109.

Paint-cups, 219.
Painting, 83.
Paint receptacle, 14, 88.
Paint stones, 172.
Papirinimen, 73, 77, 78, 98, 104.
Parker, Arthur C., 220.

Passaic County, New Jersey, 141, 145.
Passamaquoddy, 203.
Pavonia, 34, 35, 36, 97.
Pawcatuck, 206.
Pawnee, 39.
"Peach War." 36.
Pen-atn-ik, 77, 78.
Pendants, 14, 42, 228.
Pepper, George H., 12, 13, 20, 21, 23, 41, 42, 50, 60, 62, 172, 173, 213, 230.
Pequannock River, 143, 145.
Pequot, 35, 183, 184.
Personal appearance, 39, 40, 41.
Pestles, 37, 42, 60, 114, 171, 188, 208, 218.
Pewowahone, 37.
Phonetics, 185.
Pigments, 42, 83, 117, 219.
Pipes, 26–28, 87, 114, 126, 127, 132, 172, 175, 189, 221; used as a bead, 27; of copper, 28, 83; pottery, 222; stone, 60, 83.
Pitching tool, 22.
Plummets, 20–21.
Pokoques, 37.
Polished stone articles, 220–222.
Polishing stones, 219.
Pomp on Junction, 143–145, 147.
Pompton Plains, 145–148.
Portable Mortars, 219.
Port Washington, Long Island, 222.
Potsherds, 7, 66, 70, 126, 144, 146, 164.
Pottery, 8, 10, 17, 23–26, 53, 58, 68, 69, 70, 71, 79, 85, 120, 130, 133, 141–142, 147, 148, 150, 151, 152, 155, 173–174, 176, 177, 222–227, 233; pipes, 222; stamps, 228, 231, tempering, 228.
Pound Hill, 158–159.
Price's Meadow Island, 10.
Prince, Prof. J. D., 183.

Quartz Quarry Rock-shelter, 135–136.
Quinnebaug, 185.
Quivers, 208.

Ramapo River, 157–158.
Raritan, 32, 35, 37, 43, 61, 95, 231.
Rattles, 230.
Reckgawawancs, 72, 73, 231.
Refuse heaps, 69.
Reed drills, 214.
Relations with the first settlers, 94–102.

Religion, 52.
Revolutionary relics, 65, 70, 89, 91, 132.
Richmond, 16, 119.
Richmond Plank Road, 10.
Riverville, 134.
Riverville Shelter, 136–138.
Rockland County, New York, 154.
Rock-dwellings, 147, 151, 153, 165.
Rock-shelters, 69, 81, 125–138, 141–165.
Rossville, 3, 11, 26, 28, 37.
Rough stone articles, 214–220.

Sabattis, Charlie, 22.
Sánjam, 193.
Sappokanican, 67, 83.
"Sapsis," 84.
Sauk and Fox, 172.
Sau-wen-a-rack, 103.
Scaticook Indians, 188, 205.
"Schorrakin," 95.
Scrapers, 20, 23, 127, 133, 171, 173, 214, 228.
Sĕ′go, 206.
Semilunar knives, 220.
Settlement of New Haerlem, 103–109.
Shamanism, 195.
Shantic Point, 186.
Shell fish, 45, 130.
Shell heaps, 4, 16, 17, 66, 68, 69, 169–179, 233.
Shell-pits, 5, 7, 88, 170, 176.
Shell pockets, 71, 89.
Shinnecock Hills, 47, 172, 229; Indians, 14, 39, 46.
Shirjuirneho, 37.
Sho-ra-kap-kok, 77, 81.
Silverwork, 193.
Sinew stones, 219.
Sinkers, 21, 44–45, 70, 113.
Siwanoy, 175, 231.
Size of pottery vessels, 56, 224.
Skeesucks, Lester, 192.
Skeletons, 5, 11, 12, 13, 15, 85, 87, 91–92, 170, 173, 176; of a child, 14; of a dog, 7, 71, 88, 176, 233.
Smith, Claudius, 160–161.
Social Organization, 52, 209.
Songs, 195.
Sources of food supply, 129.
Spear-head, 144, 162.

Spear point, 148, 214.
Specimens, coll ctions of, 17; description of, 18; first found in New York City, 65.
Spoons, 188.
Spuyten Duyvil, 69, 72, 73, 77, 78, 82, 96, 104.
Stamps, 228, 231.
Staten Island Association of Arts and Sciences, 8, 11, 27, 62.
Steatite, 60; pipes, 27, 114; vessels, 24, 58, 222.
Stockbridge, 37, 185.
Stone, beads, 220; of exotic origin, 113; hoe, 42; material, 113; objects, 126; plummets, 220; pipes, 27, 60, 172; polishing or rubbing, 19.
Stuyvesant, Gov. Peter, 36, 99, 101, 102.
Sū'ktac, 190.
Susquehanna, 32.
Susquehannock, 29.
Swannekins, 96.

Tákạnig, 191.
Tankiteke, 130.
Tantaquidgeon, 202.
Tappan, 36, 61, 231.
Tcā'namīd, 203–204.
Tcisa'ka, 200.
Tompkinsville, 17.
Tools, antler, 21.
Torne Brook, 154–156.
Torne Mountain, 156–157.
Tottenville, 3, 19, 20, 42, 44, 46, 50, 51, 173, 213.
Towakhow, 145, 150–153.
Trade articles, 9, 28–29, 231.
Trade ring, 28.
Traditions, 185.
Transportation, 48–49.
Travisville, 9.
Treaties, 103–104.
Tubes, 230.
Tuckahoe Marble, 125.
Tuinessen, Tobias, 8, 88, 96, 101, 107.
Tuxedo, 159–160.
Types of axes, 215–216; of net-sinkers, 215.

Ulu, 220.

Unalachtigo, 31, 153.
Unami, 31, 153.
Uncas, 184, 186, 193, 195.
Underhill, Capt. John, 35.
Upper Preakness, 141–143.
Utensils, 47, 84.

Van der Capellen, 36.
Van der Donck, Adriaen, 61, 72, 83, 98, 101.
Van Dyck, Henry, 35, 36, 96.
Van der Grist, Paulus Linderstien, 36.
Van Keulen, Matthys Jansen, 98.
Van Tienhoven, Secretary, 33, 97.
Village site, 3.
Vedrendal, 94.
Vegetables resources, 42.
Volk, Ernest, 54, 60, 176, 230.

Wainwright, Capt. R. D., 11, 29, 12.
"Walum Olum," 29.
Wampum, 42, 178, 228.
Wappinger, 72, 73, 231.
Waranawankong, 231.
War club, 120.
"War point," 16, 17.
Watchogue, 20, 21, 28, 62, 220.
Waubīnu, 200.
Weir Creek Point, 176.
West New Brighton, 3.
Western Niantic, 206.
"White Dog Feast," 71, 79, 87, 233.
"Wickers Creek," 83.
"Wickom," 47.
Wickquaskeek, 72, 73, 78, 81, 83, 93, 95, 96, 97, 103, 104, 105, 108, 109, 231.
Willoughby, C. C., 22, 217.
Wīnai's, 194.
Witchcraft tales, 196–199.
Witches, 195–196.
Wī'ūs, 191.
Wīwátcạmạn, 190.
Wūyū't, 187.
Woodrow, 3, 10, 50, 60.
Worked teeth, 230.

Yantic, 185.
Yókeg, 191, 194.

Zeewan, 51, 52.
Zegendal, 95, 97, 99.

BOWMAN'S BROOK SITE.

(Page 7)

GRAVE OF A CHILD — TOTTENVILLE.

GRAVE OF ADULTS — TOTTENVILLE.

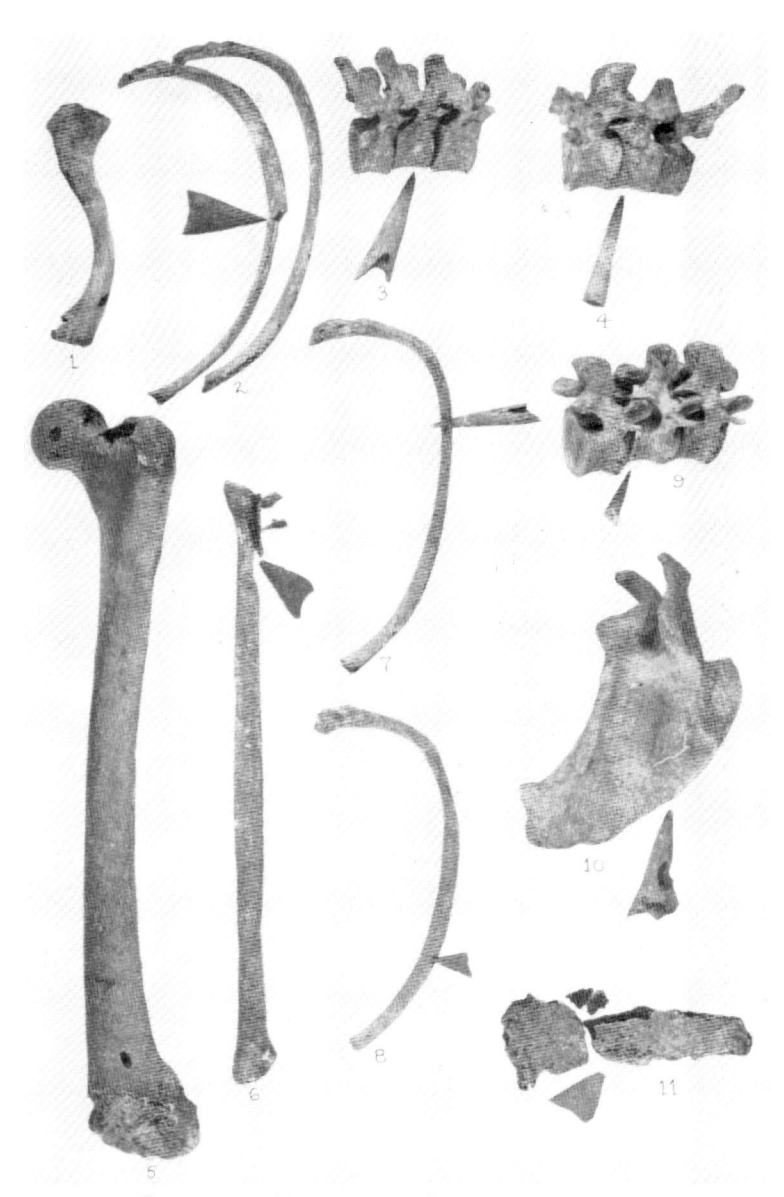

POSITION OF POINTS AMONG BONES — TOTTENVILLE.

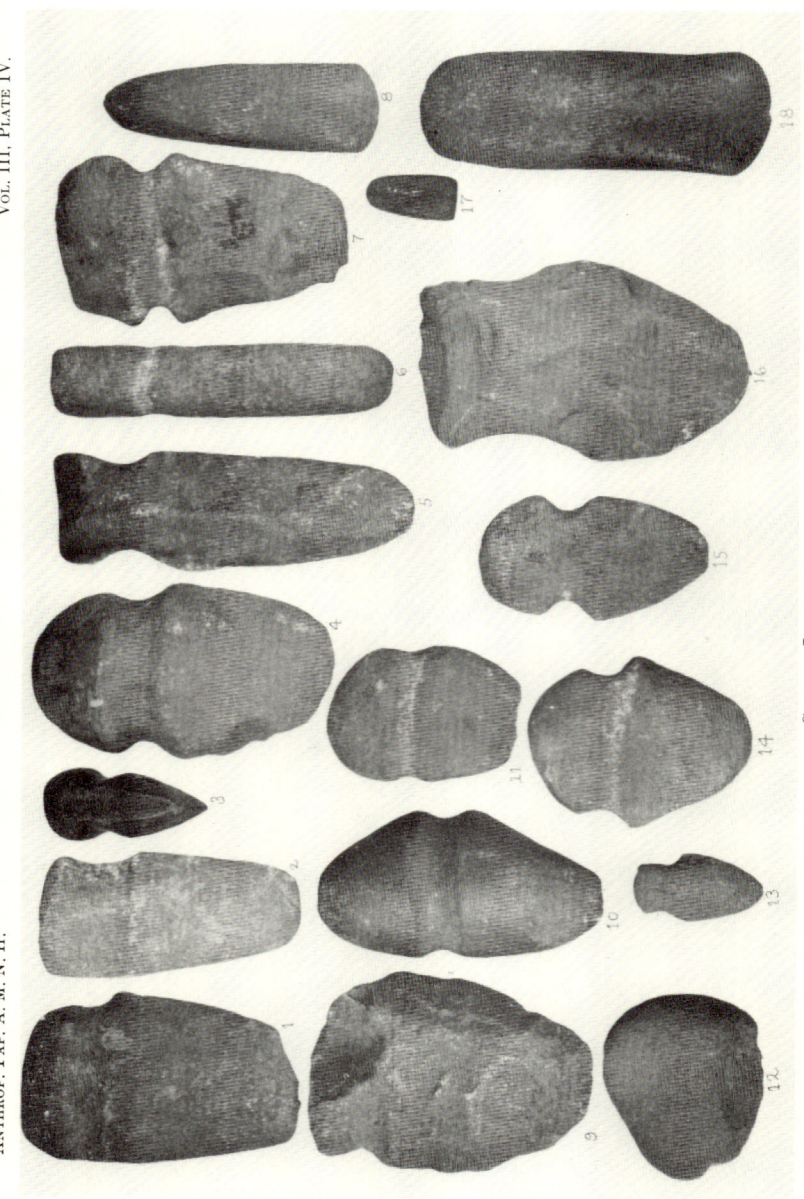

STONE IMPLEMENTS.

STONE IMPLEMENTS.
(Page 19)

DRILLS, SCRAPERS AND OTHER OBJECTS.

(Page 19)

KNIVES AND SCRAPERS.

(Page 20)

BANNER STONES.

(Page 20)

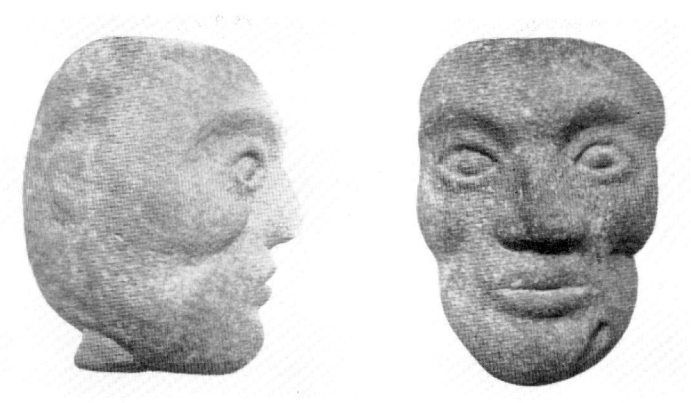

A STONE HEAD — GRASMERE.

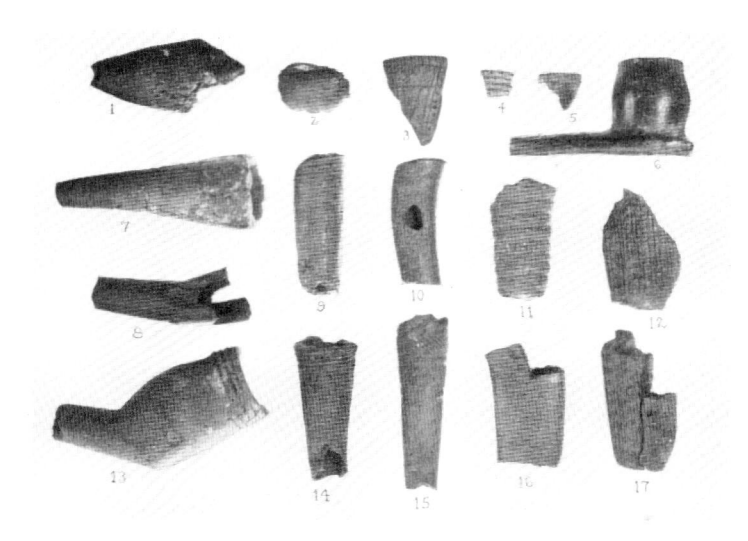

TOBACCO PIPES.

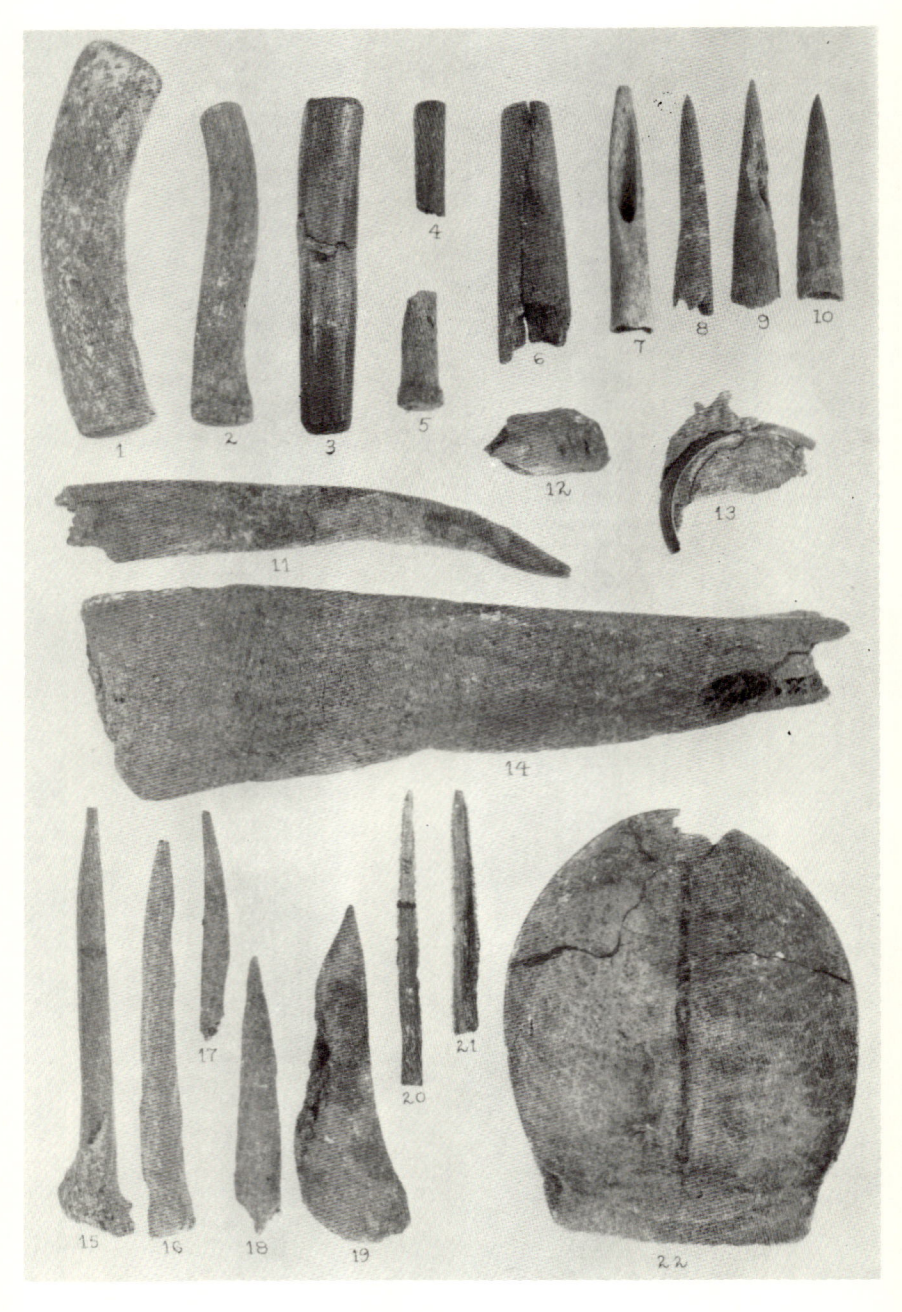

BONE AND ANTLER TOOLS.

(Page 22)

SHELL OBJECTS.

(Page 42)

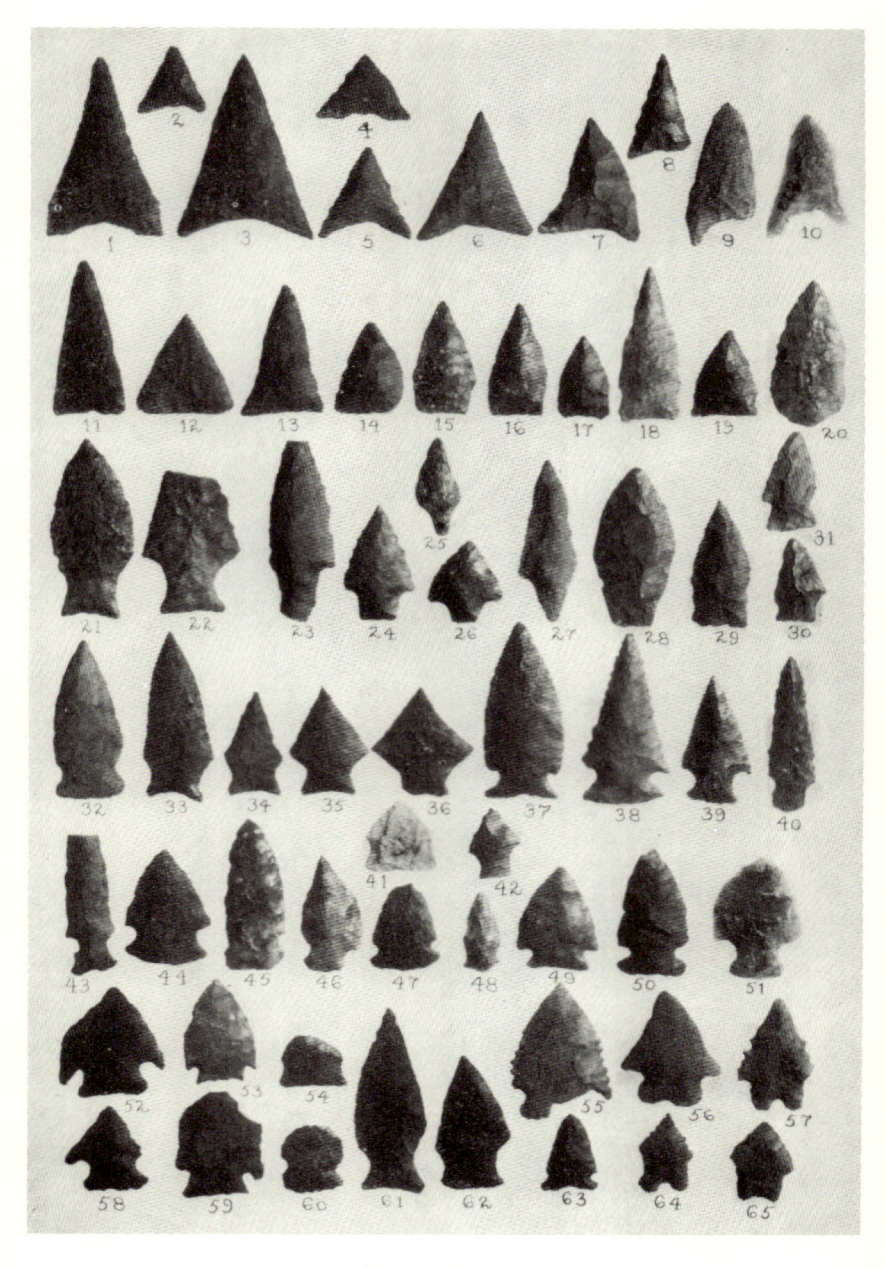

ARROW POINTS.

A Shell Pit on Seaman Avenue.

(Page 86)

The Core of a Shell Pit.

(Page 90).

A Cut on Seaman Avenue Showing relic-bearing Strata.

(Page 86)

Uncovering an Indian Pot at 214th Street and Tenth Avenue.

(Page 88)

A Pottery Vessel found at 214th Street and Tenth Avenue.

(Page 89)

INWOOD ROCK-SHELTER, MANHATTAN.

(Page 84)

AN INDIAN BURIAL ON SEAMAN AVENUE.

(Page 89)

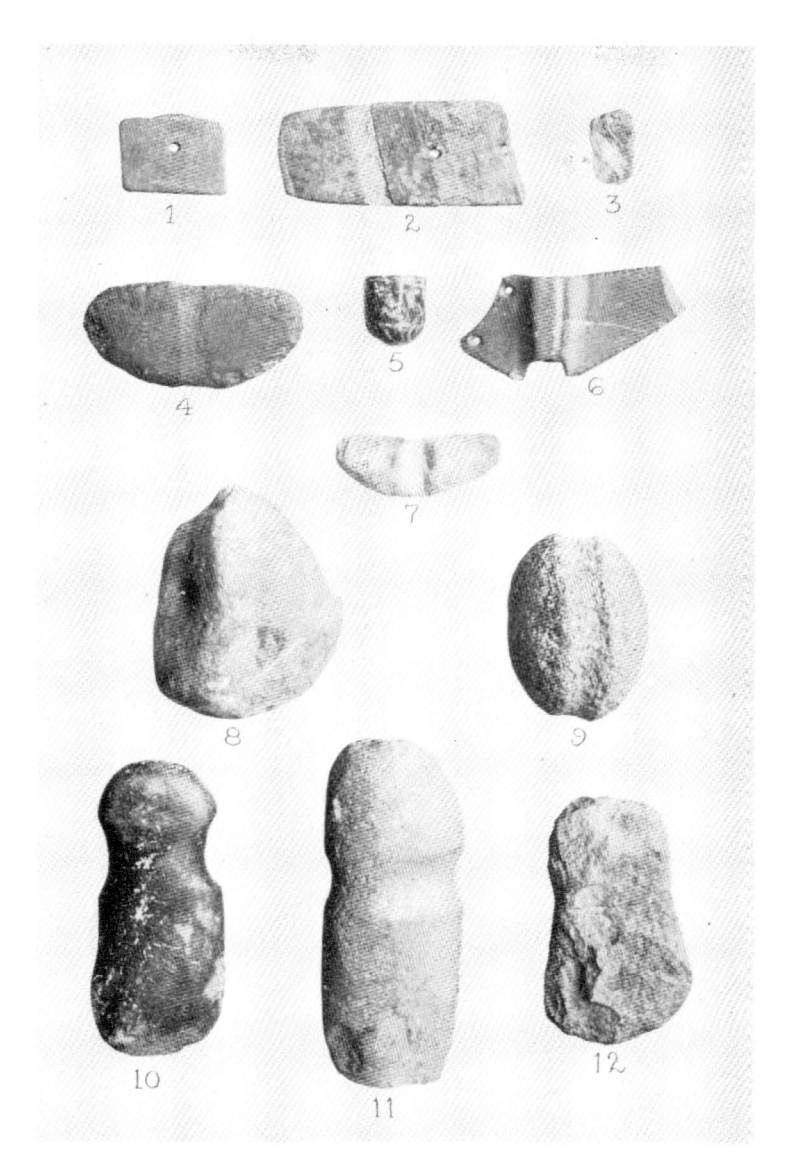

RELICS FROM MANHATTAN ISLAND.

(Page 88)

FINCH'S ROCK HOUSE.

(Page 125)

HELICKER'S CAVE.

(Page 132)

LEATHER MAN'S ROCK-SHELTER.

(Page 134)

RIVERVILLE SHELTER.

(Page 136)

MAHONEY ROCK-SHELTER.
(Page 134)

QUARTZ QUARRY ROCK-SHELTER.
(Page 135)

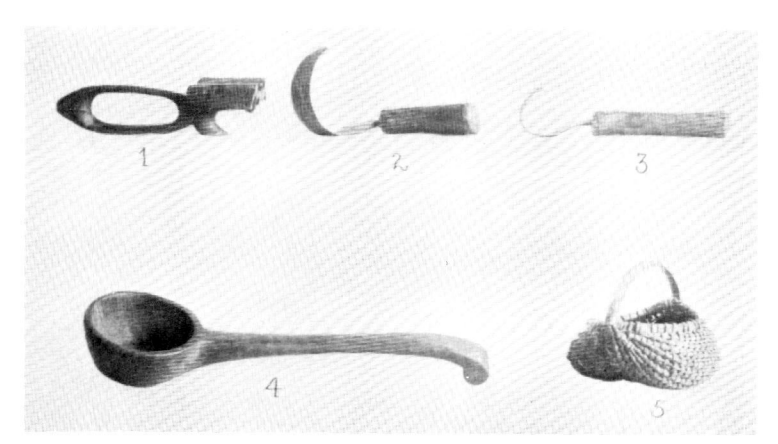

MOHEGAN SPECIMENS.

(Page 188)

BROTHERTON-MOHEGAN IN COSTUME.

GROUP OF MOHEGAN-INDIANS.

(Page 192)

NIANTIC WOMAN.

MOHEGAN WOMAN.

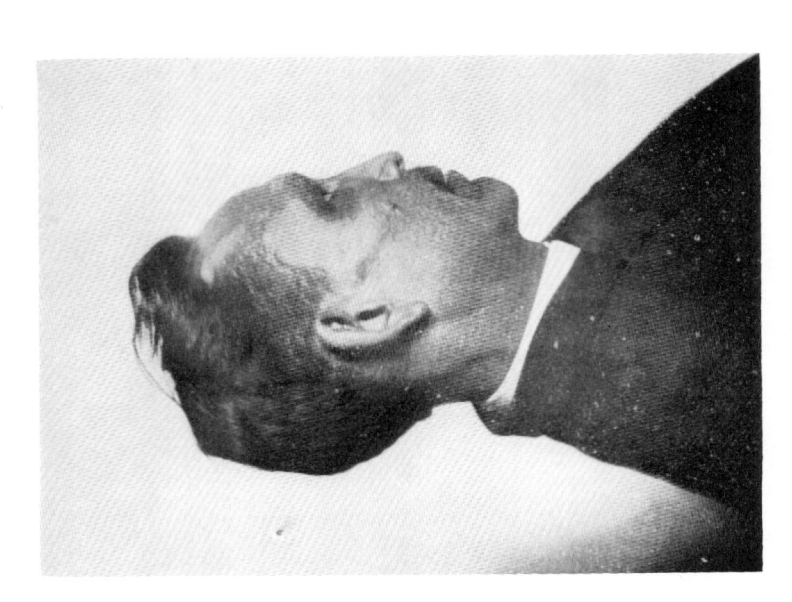

A. S. NUNSUCH, A NIANTIC.
(Page 207)